America's Collectible Cookbooks

America's Collectible Cookbooks

OHIO UNIVERSITY PRESS

The History,
the Politics,
the Recipes

Mary Anna DuSablon

Ohio University Press, Athens, Ohio 45701

© 1994 by Mary Anna DuSablon

99 98 97 96 95 94   5 4 3 2 1

BOOK AND JACKET DESIGNER: *Sharon L. Sklar*

Ohio University Press books are printed on acid-free paper ∞

Library of Congress Cataloging-in-Publication Data

DuSablon, Mary Anna, 1939-
    America's collectible cookbooks : the history, the politics, the
recipes / Mary Anna DuSablon.
        p.   cm.
    Includes bibliographical references and index.
    ISBN 0-8214-1057-1. — ISBN 0-8214-1077-6 (pbk.)
    1. Cookery—Collectibles—United States.   2. Cookery, American—
History.   3. Cookery, American. I. Title.
TX642.D87   1994
641.5973'075—dc20
                                                        93-49602
                                                        CIP

To each and every artist,
A synonym for cook,
Who gave her choicest recipe
And helped to make this book.

—*The School of Housekeeping Cookbook* (1900)

AND

To my mother,
Bernadette Marcella Maxwell Martin

Contents

List of Illustrations   ix

Preface   xi

Acknowledgments   xiv

1   A Genuine American Cookbook   1

2   Manuscript Cookbooks   9

3   Early New England Classics   15

4   The Great Western Expansion   38

5   Teaching the American Tradition   59

6   Little Cookbooks with Motives, Ulterior and Avowed   93

7   The Joy and the Myth   106

8   Imported Influences: Great Chefs   120

9   How to Compile a Best-Selling Homemade Cookbook   139

10   Celebrity Cooks   162

11 The Big, Beautiful Cookbook   170

12 Guru versus Gourmet: A Media
Battleground   176

Glossary of Old and Unusual North American Cooking Terms   186

Selected Bibliography   197

Index   203

List of Photographs

Eliza Leslie, engraving after a painting by Thomas Sully, in *Godey's Magazine and Lady's Book* (Philadelphia: Louis A. Godey, Jan 1846)   18

Sarah Josepha Hale, from an engraving at The Library Company of Philadelphia (ca. 1835)   20

Lydia Maria Child   21

Catharine Beecher, from The Schlesinger Library, Radcliffe College   39

Mrs. Mary Virginia Terhune, in *The Ladies' Home Journal* (Aug 1887)   49

Fannie Merritt Farmer, from The Schlesinger Library, Radcliffe College   62

Mrs. Simon Kander, frontis, *The Settlement Cook Book* (Milwaukee: The Settlement Cook Book Company, 1938)   65

Mrs. Lida A. Seely, from the Darien, Connecticut Historical Society   67

Mrs. Sarah Tyson Rorer, frontis, *Philadelphia Cook Book* (Philadelphia: Arnold and Company, 1886)   70

Mrs. Ida C. Bailey Allen, frontis, *Mrs. Allen on Cooking, Menus, Service* (Garden City: Doubleday, Doran & Company, Inc., 1929)   87

Mr. and Mrs. Eugene Christian, frontis, *Uncooked Foods & How to Use Them* (New York: The Health-Culture Company, 1904)   102

Irma Louise Rombauer and Marion Rombauer Becker through the generosity of Ethan Becker   107

Betty Crocker, Marjorie Child Husted, and Janette Kelley, through the generosity of General Mills   100-11

Oscar Tschirky, frontis, *Oscar of the Waldorf* by Karl Scheiftgiesser (New York: E. P. Dutton, 1943)   122

Henri Charpentier, frontis, *Life á la Henri*, photo by Margaret Bourke-White (New York: Simon and Schuster, 1934)   123

Alessandro Filippini, frontis, *The Table* (New York: Doubleday, Page and Company, 1889)   124

Charles Ranhofer, frontis, *The Epicurean* (New York: Ranhofer, 1908)   124

Preface

Compiling this first cohesive study of North American cookbooks was a heartbreaking task in one way, but only one way,—that is, deciding what not to include. Limited time and finances provide some excuse when one fails in the pursuit of comprehensiveness, but instead of concentrating on exacting the publishing history of old cookbooks, addressing trendy cookbook critiques, or inventing my own reviews, my aim was to encourage collectors and help librarians decide which cookbooks were keepers. More importantly, I wanted to write a compelling but concise true-life drama about the evolution of the American basic cookbook and honor its rightful place in history. I wanted to breathe new life into the women and men who excelled at their craft and had the extra talent to express their expertise to inspire others. I wanted to bring them together to strut their stuff, not just as recipe peddlers but as shapers of the American life-style. I also desired that this be an entertaining and practical everyday cookbook, so I selected culinary rather than home-maintenance receipts to illustrate what the text can only hint at, always with a bias toward the constantly changing and improving national palate.

Thousands of books were handled as my interest transmigrated from casual pastime to intense study during the past thirty years. Judging which books, authors, and publishers would be called upon to furnish the dialog and set the scene for this performance finally boiled down to one word: significant. But what is a significant cookbook? This definition was crystallized in a letter from John J. Vander Velde, curator of the Special Collections Department of the Kansas State University Library, as "a good compilation of basically reliable recipes . . . widely held in households throughout the region and, therefore significant in its time." To verify the significance of the books then chosen, I consulted cookbook collectors (that body of specialists whose often-ridiculed efforts have resulted in the existence of a history in the first place), librarians who cherish these artifacts, and booksellers. Finally, I considered my personal preferences, however risky this decision may have been. I took note of multiple printings and facsimiles. Occasionally I included an outstanding book that seemed to have escaped notoriety but was now significant. In other words, not every significant book or author is mentioned here because of space limitations, but if a book is mentioned, it is because I deemed it or its writer significant.

Locating these treasures was another matter altogether. A massive correspondence was initiated, and soon my rural route mailbox was welcoming envelopes containing beautiful letterheads from our country's most prestigious libraries and historical societies. Guided by the bibliographies itemized at the back of this book and by Lee Ash's *Subject Collections*, my husband, Sean Thomas Bailey, and I drove to many of the repositories suggested and became as adept at thumb-and-index-fingering our way through a card-file drawer as our illustrious town librarian Joann Tudor. We hand-wrote hundreds of recipe selections because machine-copying was out of the question for the fragile old volumes. We dropped off our cockapoo, Big Ben, at kennels at 8 o'clock in the morning and picked him up at 4 o'clock in the afternoon. Then we all exercised together to prevent our bodies from solidifying into a sedentary position. We had wonderful adventures, indoors and out.

My goal when finally compiling the text was to embrace our country's overriding historical and political influences and the impact that these events had on the dinner table and therefore cookbook publication. I added further criteria to the selection of the recipes themselves: They should reflect historical preferences, using regional foodstuffs; and be concise and interesting, producing delicious morsels that any cook might find tempting even today. Humor was intended but not flaunted. I sincerely hope the result will satisfy both historians and discerning cooks.

Because some readers may yearn for more information on the complete works of specific authors, I have compiled a selected list of collections and bibliographies that I believe will be of great benefit. Biographical materials are included; historical material was gleaned primarily from reference materials available in most city libraries. My aim was not necessarily to turn up new information, but to bring together and to light what already existed as a popular—in the purest sense of the word—amusement.

I hope this history will stimulate local cookbook lovers to be aggressive in protecting and promoting regional treasures in private collections as well as in libraries, because this anthology is only representative of the heritage that remains to be discovered. All too often, books turned up missing in our search, and in one Chicago North Shore library hundreds of recipes had been slashed from the pages of several cookbooks. Other conservation measures might include referencing materials currently circulating; publishing fine, limited-edition facsimile-histories that do justice to original author, text, and publisher; compiling library bibliographies and recipe catalogs; organizing regional expositions; restoring cooking school sites as active tourist attractions; documenting the entry and propagation of ethnic foods in America; and such personal challenges as writing vivid, scholarly biographies of these authors—all for the enlightenment of generations to come. I would also urge readers to buy some of the quality cookbooks mentioned herein, because I am convinced (as were our foremothers) that a happy kitchen means a happy home.

In conjunction with the back-to-earth movement of the 1960s and in preparation for the celebration of the National Bicentennial, many old cookbooks were reproduced during the 1970s, particularly by Dover Publications (on acid-free paper) and Arno Press. Unfortunately, many are out of print and can only be obtained at used book stores, where the good ones disappear quickly. University presses got on the bandwagon in the 1980s by reissuing local favorites, usually including historical data—and in the case of *The Carolina Housewife* (South), with memoirs by a descendant of the author. These books are currently available in most cases.

Finally, some recipes have been edited, punctuation changed, or otherwise rearranged to make them easier to follow—but only minimally and where I thought it absolutely necessary to compile a modern cookery book. There is some overlapping of chapter contents but, again, nothing to render my premises defunct. Cooks must call upon their own expertise to adjust the old recipes to fit modern culinary life-styles and nutritional needs, but I have strategically planned—and fervently hope—that doing so won't take too much effort. Besides, most good cooks don't follow a recipe to the letter anyway. Apologies to our dear Fannie Merritt Farmer; we never have, and we never will.

Mary Anna DuSablon

Acknowledgments

Every effort has been made to trace the ownership of copyrighted material contained herein and to make full acknowledgment of its use. If errors or omissions have occurred, they will be corrected in subsequent editions upon notifying me or the publishers in writing. I wish to thank the following for their expert assistance and impulsiveness:

Loveland Branch of the Public Library of Cincinnati and Hamilton County: Bobbie Books, Rose Dugan, Joyce Thalheimer, and Tanya Nelson

Goshen Branch of the Clermont County (Ohio) Public Library: Joann Tudor, Pat Guthrie, Jennifer Smith, Karen Hartman, Annette Cook, Pamela Pauley, Dianna Sissel, Angela Ramsey, and Cristy Malott

Clermont County Technical Services: Melanie Buckner and Catherine Welscher

Public Library of Cincinnati and Hamilton County: Doug Macgee, history; Loren Curtis, Joann Hoelk, Renita Lewis, science and technology; Alfred Kleine-Kreutzmann, Claire Pancero, M'Lissa Kesterman, rare books; the OCLC information staff; and the directory assistance staff

Ohio University Press: Duane Schneider, Holly Panich, Sharon Arnold, Nancy Basmajian, and Helen Gawthrop

General Mills, Inc.: Jean Toll

Texas Woman's University at Denton: Dawn Letson and Kim Grover-Haskin

Mollie Katzen

Ethan Becker

American Antiquarian Society: Joanne D. Chaison

Library of Congress, Rare Books and Special Collections: Joan F. Higbee and Clark Evans

Radcliffe College, The Arthur and Elizabeth Schlesinger Library on the History of Women in America: Wendy Thomas

The Library Company of Philadelphia: Mary Anne Hines

Old Sturbridge Village: Caroline Sloat

El Paso Public Library: Wayne Daniel

Time-Life Books: John C. Weiser, Lyn Stallworth, and Gerry Schremp

The Cleveland Public Library

The New York Public Library

Buffalo & Erie County Public Library

The Connecticut Historical Society: Doreen D. McCabe

St. Augustine Historical Society: Corinne Richardson

The Historical Society of Pennsylvania: Lori E. Scherr

The University of Texas at Austin: William H. Richter

The Bostonian Society: Bridget Knightly

University of Wisconsin at Milwaukee: Stanley Mallach

Milwaukee Public Library: Ruth Ruege

Kellogg Company: Deborah R. Moody

Kansas State University: John J. Vander Velde

Smithsonian Institution, National Museum of American History: Faith
    Davis Ruffins

The Colonial Williamsburg Foundation: Rosemary Brandau

Iowa Chapter, Victorian Society in America

The James Beard Foundation: Barbara Kafka and Marion Cunningham

Kent State University: Mary DuMont

Louisville Free Public Library

Hawaiian Historical Society: Katherine Knight

The Sarah Daft Home, Salt Lake City: Ramona Linnell

Utah Heritage Foundation: Dina B. Williams

Reed Memorial Library (Ohio): Cynthia Gaynor

University of Kentucky at Lexington

Lake Agassiz Regional Library (Minnesota): Joyce Pettengir

Dayton and Montgomery County (Ohio) Public Library

Julia Marcel Jewell

Los Angeles Public Library: Dan Strehl
    and to

The University of South Carolina Press for permission to quote from *The
    Carolina Housewife*

A Genuine American Cookbook

Amelia Simmons, "an American orphan," wrote and copyrighted the first genuine American cookbook in 1796, although American settlers had been refining many of the recipes contained therein for more than a hundred years before the signing of the Declaration of Independence. A few of these dishes were, of course, Native American concoctions that dated back much farther, and a few more were taken verbatim from an English cookbook by Susannah Carter. Yet the resourceful Simmons, about whom virtually nothing else is known, made a valuable contribution to American history.

She took her personal collection of paragraph-form receipts, household hints, and domestic advice to the prestigious printers Hudson & Goodwin in Hartford, Connecticut, where she is believed to have lived, and had them published at her own expense. As could be expected, the print featured the long *f* for *s*, so that the recipes for stuffing and roasting read to *ftuff* and *roaft* and so on. The books were sold at Isaac Beers's bookstore for two shillings, threepence according to advertisements in Connecticut newspapers. The tiny, 8vo, forty-seven-page "paperback" was given a comprehensive title: *American Cookery, or the art of dressing viands, fish, poultry and vegetables, and the best modes of making pastes, puffs, pies, tarts, pud-*

dings, custards and preserves, and all kinds of cakes, from the imperial plumb to plain cake; adapted to this country, and all grades of life.

It was welcomed by other American cooks and homemakers and enjoyed eleven reprintings by various publishers—and at least two plagiarisms—throughout New England during the next forty years. A third edition was auctioned in 1991 for $22,000, and some facsimiles are scarce and variously valuable, so it can be safely stated that Amelia Simmons's investment in her own talent was, and is, an extraordinary one for all concerned. The only personal insights about her that we glean from the first edition's text are contained in the Preface. She states that the book "is calculated for the improvement of the rising generation of *females* [her italics] in America," particularly for "those females in this country, who by the loss of their parents, or other unfortunate circumstances, are reduced to the necessity of going into families in the line of domestics, or taking refuge with their friends or relations, and doing those things which are really essential to the perfecting them as good wives, and useful members of society."

This survival manual for waifs could also have been intended for the use of orphanages because some recipes are given in mess-hall proportions, but Simmons did not use the phrase "adapted to this country" without specific intent. Early settlers definitely had problems adapting. Corn, squash, pumpkin, cranberries, turkey, bear, and strange new seafoods were culinary challenges, complicated by the task of cooking at a hearth with very few kitchen utensils and without servants. Actually, half the recipes in one edition of *American Cookery* contain "Indian meal," what we now call cornmeal, a native food that would someday become a staple ingredient in an infinite number of national dishes—many of them more authentically American than apple pie. One-third of Simmons's recipes are for what we would now call entrees, while the rest of the manual is dedicated to desserts rather liberally spiked with brandy or wine. Herbs are used creatively. But what makes this document singular in the eyes of historians is that it was the first tangible evidence to prove exactly what was—and what was not—stored in American larders compared with those in the mother countries in 1796.

This charming glimpse into colonial domestic life also gives us an idea of the (thankfully forgotten) exertion that it took to run a household. For example, "to have sweet butter in dog days, and through the vegetable seasons, send stone pots to honest, neat, and trusty dairy people, and procure it packed down in May, and let them be brought in the night, or cool rainy mornings, covered with a clean cloth wet in cold water, and partake of no heat from the horse, and set the pots in the coldest part of your cellar, or in the ice-house."

Ironically, these instructions were contained in the first seventeen pages of text that Simmons haughtily disavowed in the next edition of her book, allowing us to see additional aspects of an intriguing character. Choosing another publisher in Albany, she publicly berated the first effort for "egregious blunders, and inaccuracies . . . wich [sic] were occasioned either by the ignorance, or evil intension [sic] of the transcriber for the press." She further explained that "the author . . . not having an education sufficient to prepare the work for press" hired someone to help her. Yet, regardless of the violation of trust of these alleged blithering or sinister collaborators, the fact remained that practical advice such as that inadvertently included in her book was not featured in the Victorian English cookbooks conveyed across the Atlantic, nor could it be, because English cooks didn't have a clue about what was going on in American kitchens. The need for good, all-American instruction was great, and Amelia Simmons shouldered the responsibility to answer that need.

During the decades before Simmons's native cookbook appeared, several English-produced cookbooks were available. William Parks brought over a fifth-edition copy of *The Compleat Housewife; or Accomplished Gentlewoman's Companion* by Eliza Smith, which had been published in England in 1727, and subsequently reprinted it in his Williamsburg, Virginia, publishing house in 1742. As a kitchen aid it was little more than inspiring under such differing culinary circumstances, but it became a best-seller in only a few months' time. Among the most popular imports was Hannah Glasse's classic *The Art of Cookery Made Plain and Easy*, published in London in 1747. Some notoriety was attached to her success, however, because rumor had it that no such person existed.[1] Susannah Carter of Clerkenwell was England's *The Frugal Housekeeper: or, Complete Woman Cook.* Her book, printed in London, was reprinted in Boston in 1772, with plates on carving engraved by Paul Revere. In 1803 it was reprinted with "an appendix, containing several new receipts adapted to the American mode of cooking" although no recipes actually developed by colonists were included.

---

1. Madeleine Hope Dodds, a historian from Newcastle-Upon-Tyne, claims Hannah was the half-sister of Sir Lancelot Allgood and that she eloped with John Glasse, had eight children, and truly was, as later editions of her book stated, "Habit-Maker to her Royal Highness the Princess of Wales." (See Coyle, *Cooks' Books.*)

In 1814 the Colonies were treated to *The Universal Receipt Book, or, Complete Family Directory . . .* by a Society of Gentlemen in New-York, published by Isaac Riley (later identified as the work of Englishman Richard Alsop). The second edition in 1818, a *Compendious Repository of Practical Information . . .* , was reorganized by one Priscilla Homespun (perhaps a pseudonym for the unfortunate Alsop). By this time, several other English cookbooks had been washed to the shores of the New World and given new title pages or authors. The only thing American about these books was the word itself in the title. English cooking was the basis of the early American cuisine on the eastern seacoast, however, just as English law was the basis of our judicial system.

The first fully developed household encyclopedia and cookbook, *A New System of Domestic Cookery, Formed Upon Principles of Economy: and Adapted to the Use of Private Families*, was published in London some time after 1800, by a Lady. Its author was also victimized by confusion, being Mrs. Helene Rundell or Mrs. Maria Rundle or Rundell, whose maiden name was suggested as Ketelby. Her cookbook was retitled (you guessed it) *American Domestic Cookery, Formed On Principles, etc.* by New England publishers (just as rascally as their English counterparts), who described her as an "Experienced American Housekeeper"! The book contains a sentence that is plagiarized repeatedly (and who knows where it actually originated) in nineteenth-century American cookbooks by female authors whose indiscretion is, well, forgivable: "Many families have owed their prosperity full as much to the prosperity of female management, as to the knowledge and activity of the father."

Richard Briggs's *The New Art of Cookery, According to the Present Practice . . .* was reprinted in Philadelphia and Boston in 1792, Briggs having been "many years cook at the Globe Tavern, Fleet-Street, the White Hart Tavern, Holborn, and now at the Temple Coffee-House, London." *The French Cook*'s author, Louis Eustache Ude, had even more impressive credentials as former chef to Napoleon's mother, "ci-devan [formerly] cook to Louis xiv and the Earl of Sefton, and steward to his late Royal Highness the Duke of York." Ude left France, according to Leonard Beck (See bibliography), "because of differences of opinion on the arithmetic of his bills." *The French Cook* was the first English-language cookbook reprinted in the United States that was devoted completely to French methods of cookery. It was published first in London in 1815 and again in Philadelphia in 1828.

Many other cookbooks of varying description and quality were brought over, and in other languages such as German, Spanish, and

Italian, but I have chosen not to linger over their importance (while acknowledging it at the same time). By 1796, America was becoming preoccupied with establishing its own identity in all things domestic—including cookbooks—and this book is about American cookbooks—those by Americans, for Americans, and using American natural resources.

About a dozen libraries have a first-edition copy of American Cookery, *including the American Antiquarian Society (AAS) in Worcester, Massachusetts, and in the "west," Northern Illinois University (NIU) in DeKalb. The AAS does not permit viewing of their "fragile beauty," however they have several reprints and facsimiles that can be lovingly paged through. NIU does permit viewing, at least for now.*

Detailed bibliographic information on who has republished scarce, original cookbooks, and when, can be obtained through the On-Line Computer Library Center (OCLC) searching system used in most major libraries. The printout will also tell you, among other enlightening things, where in the United States each copy can be viewed and whether it is an actual book or on microfilm. Some reprints of American Cookery *since 1900 include:*

1937: Windham, Conn.: Prospect Press (commemorative edition, copy in Connecticut State Library).

1958: New York: Oxford University Press (essay by Mary Tolford Wilson, glossary included). Same edition republished in 1984 by Dover Press and currently available.

1965: Grand Rapids, Mich.: Eerdmans.

1966: Johnsbury, N.Y.: Buck Hill; Harriman, Tenn.: Pioneer Press.

1984: Westport, Conn.: Silverleaf Press (hardback and paperback, with brief introduction).

Thanksgiving Menu

Taken from various editions of our nation's first cookbook, *American Cookery* by Amelia Simmons (1796). This cookbook records, among many firsts, the first use of pearl ash for leavening, and the first recipes for pumpkin pie, Indian pudding, and cookies. It was the first time in print that turkey was served with "cramberry" sauce.

Roast Turkey, Stuffed with Bread or Potatoes
Butter Gravy
Cranberry Sauce   Relish Tray
Boiled Onions   Boiled Cabbage
Butter Biscuits
Pumpkin Pie   Indian Pudding
Flavored Whipped Cream
Cookies

To Stuff and Roast a Turkey or Fowl

[NOTE: The colonial turkey was about eight pounds in weight.]

One pound soft wheat bread, 3 ounces beef suet, 3 eggs, a little sweet thyme, sweet marjoram, pepper and salt, and some add a gill of wine; fill the bird therewith and sew up, hang down to a steady solid fire, basting frequently with salt and water, and roast until a steam emits from the breast. Put one third of a pound of butter into the gravy, dust flour over the bird and baste with the gravy; serve up with boiled onions and cramberry sauce, mangoes, pickles or celery. 2) Others omit the sweet herbs, and add parsley done with potatoes. 3) Boil and mash three pints potatoes, wet them with butter, add sweet herbs, pepper, salt, fill and roast as above.

To Boil Cabbage

If your cabbage is large, cut it into quarters; if small, cut it in halves; let your water boil, then put in a little salt, and next your cabbage with a little more salt upon it; make your water boil as soon as possible, and when the stalk is tender, take up your cabbage into a cullender, or sieve, that the water may drain off, and send it to the table as hot as you can. Savoys are dressed in the same manner.

Butter Biscuit

One pint each milk and emptins, laid into flour, in sponge; next morning add one pound butter melted, not hot, and knead into as much flour as will with another pint of warmed milk, be of a sufficient consistence to make soft—some melt the butter in the milk.

Emptins

Take a handful of hops and about three quarts of water, let it boil about fifteen minutes, then make a thickening as you do for starch, strain the liquor; when cold put a little emptins to work them, they will keep well cork'd in a bottle five or six weeks.

Pompkin Pie

One quart of milk, 1 pint pompkin, 4 eggs, molasses, allspice and ginger in a crust, bake 1 hour.

A Nice Indian Pudding

3 pints scalded milk, 7 spoons fine Indian meal, stir well together while hot, let stand till cooled; add 7 eggs, half-pound raisins, 4 ounces butter, spice and sugar, bake one and a half hour.

Whipt Cream

Take a quart of cream and the whites of 8 eggs beaten with half a pint of wine; mix it together and sweeten it to your taste with double refined sugar, you may perfume (if you please) with musk or Amber gum tied in a rag and steeped a little in the cream, whipe it up with a whisk and a bit of lemon peal tyed in the middle of the whisk, take off the froth with a spoon, and put into glasses.

Cookies

[NOTE: The word *cookie* is a uniquely American borrowing of the Dutch *koekje* and first appears in print in Amelia Simmons's *American Cookery.* The English referred to these morsels as *cakes* or *biskets* (biscuits), and still do.]

One pound sugar boiled slowly in half pint water, scum well and cool, add two teaspoons pearl ash dissolved in milk, then two and half pounds flour, rub in 4 ounces butter, and two large spoons of finely powdered coriander seed, wet with above; make rolls half an inch thick and cut to the shape you please; bake fifteen or twenty minutes in a slack oven—good three weeks.

Manuscript Cookbooks

*I*n the meantime, while the New World anticipated Amelia Simmons's inevitable endeavor, American cooks were anything but idle. Proud and enterprising women were already developing and refining their own favorite "receipts" and writing them out, one by one, in blank-page handbooks destined in most cases to be handed down from mother to daughter.

America, during the Colonial Period, was a strange mixture of European sophistication and primitive backwoods survival, and the manuscript cookbooks that have survived were almost exclusively the products of upper-class English families. The cuisine was rich and varied, and most, if not all, herbs and spices used in today's gourmet cooking were evidenced. Before marriage, a daughter would copy from her mother's manual, adding and deleting at her own discretion cherished bits of information that enabled her to supervise the preparation of delicious meals, preserve foods and libations, keep a sanitary domicile, ease pain, and perhaps even save a life—tasks that were all too often performed with such quiet expertise that they were taken for granted. Nevertheless, some women achieved fame, if only through the political exploits of their husbands and sons, thus propelling modest meals into superstar suppers.

Supper Menu

Taken from manuscript cookbooks, 1700–1800.
Supper was served at about nine o'clock in the evening,
in place of—or a few hours after—tea, on such special
occasions as holidays, anniversaries, or birthdays.

Stewed Oysters
French Bread
Mashed and Browned Potatoes
Rolls, Butter
Water, Cider, Wine
Spruce Beer
Apple Fritters   Carrot Pudding
Sugar Cakes

The following two recipes are from manuscript pages held by the Historical Society of Pennsylvania at Philadelphia, hand-titled "My Mother's Recaipts for Cookerys Presarving and Chyrurgery [Surgery]—William Penn." The cooking recipes occupy sixty-one pages, transcribed by a family friend on October 25, 1702. Also included were cures, particularly for eye ailments, which have been attributed to Penn's maternal grandmother, who was renowned for her doctoring. The occasion of this compilation was the younger Penn's scheduled departure for the forty thousand square miles in America that King Charles II had granted his father in payment for a debt.

In her excellent rendering of these *Penn Family Recipes* published in York, Pennsylvania, by George Shumway in 1966, the author and editor Evelyn Abraham Benson gives the original cookbook author, Gulielma Springett Penn, her just due: "Although she never left England, she contributed substantially to the founding of Pennsylvania—materially, with her estate, and spiritually with her undeviating sympathy and support for her husband's noble aim to establish a government in which tolerance and freedom of conscience should be basic principles."

The courtship and marriage of the elder William and Guli is briefly but sensitively presented in *Penn Family Recipes*, as well as tales of the insults, tribulations, and jailings these Quakers endured in England. It is a vivid portrayal of the circumstances that caused wealthy Britons such as the Penns to brave the unknown in order to obtain freedom from religious tyranny and to write eloquent farewells and practical wills, "lest the sea be my grave, and the deeps my sepulchre."

It is fitting that Gulielma Penn's recipes should be her legacy, because she spent her entire life caring for family, friends, and neighbors and was extraordinarily talented at doing so.

To Stew Oysters

Take a quart of oysters, and put them into a skilett with ther Liquor, and sett them one the fire to boyle puting in to them a hole oynion, a blade or 2 of mace, sum hole peper, so Lett them boyle, then take them up and Drain the Liquor from them, then put to them almost a pint of white wine, and when they have stewd a while in the wine putt into them fouer Anchovis, and so stew them untill the Liquor bee thick, then Rubb the botam of the dish with half a pound of butter, then pore the oysters into the Dish, sturing them a bout till the butter bee melted—then Ring into them the juce of a Lemon so send them up with sipets of frentch breed—

Too Make French Bred

Take half a bushall of mele if it bee good, ale yeist a poringer full, wett it with warme water, but not boyled, kneded it not too stife—sett it by the fire 2 or 3 houers Covered with a Cloath then mold it in to Loves, and Lett it stand til the oven bee hott, wash it with the yeolke of an egg and a spunfull or 2 of bere, Lett it stand an houre and a halfe—

The following recipe comes from a large, leather-covered paperbound manual written in England and brought to America by its author, Elizabeth Mead, in 1697. It is inscribed "Finis Coronat Opius [the finish crowns the work] 1693" after fifty-one entries. An additional thirteen recipes are written in two more hands. The book was exhibited at the Groton Heights, Connecticut, Centennial Exhibition in 1881, loaned by Miss Annie E. Beckwith of New London. In

1905, the Reverend Frank H. Nelson received the book in his Cincinnati home, as he was deemed in her will, "a descendant of Mrs. Elizabeth Hallam." Was Mrs. Hallam née Elizabeth Mead? Nelson's wife presented the book to the Cincinnati Historical Society Library in 1943.

Pickled Mushrooms

Take the first white bottoms you can get and cut the stalks off pretty close and throw them into water and let them take water and salt and when it boiles, put them in and lett them boile a quarter of an hour then take some wine vinegar and boile it with a little mace, ginger and whole pepper and a little salt, then lett it cool and put them in and put some oile on the top of them.

Although the origin of the "Martha Washington" cookbook is in question, there are two undisputed facts concerning this beguiling document: Martha Washington used it while she was First Lady (1789-97), and her family brought the cookbook from England to America. It is a small volume bound in brown leather and divided into two parts: "A Booke of Cookery" with 205 recipes and "A Booke of Sweetmeats" containing 326 recipes. Belonging to the Historical Society of Pennsylvania at Philadelphia, the legible, handwritten pages have been studied by many, but never so assiduously until historian Karen Hess commenced her research. She titled her interpretation, with "historical notes and copious annotations" (no overstatement), *Martha Washington's Booke of Cookery and Booke of Sweetmeats: being a Family Manuscript, curiously copied by an unknown Hand sometime in the seventeenth century, which was in her Keeping from 1749, the time of her [first] marriage to Daniel Custis, to 1799, at which time she gave it to Eleanor Parke Custis, her granddaughter, on the occasion of her Marriage to Lawrence Lewis* (Columbia University Press, 1981).

To Make Fritters

Take a pinte of very strong ale, put it to a little sack & warme it in a little scillet; then take 8 youlks of eggs & but 2 whites, beat them very well; y^n put to them a little flowre & beat them together, y^n put in y^r warme ale; you must put noe more flower to ye eggs after ye ale is in. Y^r batter must be noe thicker then will just hang on y^r apples. season ye batter with ye powder of nutmegg, cloves,

and mace; then cut your apple into little bits & put them into y^e
batter; y^n set on ye fire a good quantety of tryed suet or hoggs lard,
& when it is very hot drop in y^r apples one by one with y^r fingers
as fast as you can. when they are fryde, lay y^m on trencher plates,
& strow on y^m sugar & cinnamon.[1]

This dessert selection from the receipt book of Harriott Pinckney Horry was used in her home in Charleston and on the Hampton
plantation in South Carolina where she and her first cousin Sarah
Rutledge, who wrote *The Carolina Housewife*, grew up. The manuscript is owned by the South Carolina Historical Society in Charleston; an excellent transcript, with history, was published in 1984 by
the University of South Carolina Press under the title *A Colonial
Plantation Cookbook: The Receipt Book of Harriot Pinckney Horry, 1770*
by Richard J. Hooker. Hampton Plantation State Park is forty miles
north of Charleston, and the mansion is still there.

Carrot Pudding

*Take a large Carrot, boil it Tender then set it by to be cold
and grate it through a hair sieve very fine, then put in half a
pound of melted Butter beaten with Eight Eggs leaving out half
the Whites, two or three Spoonfulls of Sack and Orange flower
Water, half a pint of good thick cream a little grated Bread, a
Nutmeg and a little salt, sweeten it to your tast, and make it of
the thickness of an Orange Pudding [very thin].*

From the manuscript cookbook of Elizabeth (Miller) Hart, Saybrook, Connecticut (1825), housed in the Connecticut Historical
Society in Hartford, are presented the following dainties. Information about the family can be found in Marion Hepburn Grant, *The
Hart Dynasty of Saybrook* (Old Saybrook Historical Society, 1981).
The book is small and covered in greenish cardboard with red
leather trim. Approximately three-fourths of the pages contain recipes. The spine is coming apart, which allows the viewer to see that

---

1. The y in y^e, y^t is a relic of the runic thorn, signifying *th* and in y^r abbre-
viates *your*. It is now used only in fun, as in Ye Olde Shoppe. When the Washington manuscript was written, y^e, y^r, and other quick forms such as w^ch, were
as commonly used as *thru* and *tho* today.

the pages were attached in about four places with twine. Next to many of the entries are the names of people who gave Elizabeth Hart recipes: cakes, puddings, breads, and diet breads (given by a doctor). Her own recipes are short and sweet.

Sugar Cakes

2 lb of flour, 1 lb of butter, 1 lb of sugar, 3 eggs, mace, rosewater, and caraway seeds, turn them round like a ring—

Drop Biscuits

7 eggs, 1 pint of cream and as much flour as will make a thick batter, drop them into a bake pan, butter and eat them warm—

Early New England Classics

During little more than a century, the thirteen original colonies that formed the nucleus of the United States were settled and declared as states. Cities were formed, attracting tradespeople of all types including printers and publishers who were relatively slow to pick up on the potential of genuine American cookbooks. But by the 1830s authors were warmly received or actually sought out to coordinate volumes of household hints and domestic advice, cures, and preventions, within pages numbering from a few to the hundreds. How many pages of cookery were included would depend upon whether the author was, as most were, a homemaker or a domestic herself, or a physician with cautions from his practice, a farmer with advice on crops and husbandry, a chemist, a brewer, or a minister. In the case of the male authors, food entries were usually, but not always, minimal. Entrepreneurs in New York, Philadelphia, and Boston led the way in numbers of volumes, followed by Baltimore, Hartford, and the Federal District of Washington. These population centers were separated from each other and from other towns by wide stretches of wilderness, thus necessitating local activity elsewhere, such as in Providence, Charleston, Walpole, Watertown, Bath, Troy, Albany, Newhaven, Harrisburgh, Salem, Monpelier, Woodstock, Bellows Falls, Brattleboro, and, of course, Williamsburg.

These ambitious authors wrote for the middle class rather than the gentry (although food legends, mentioned in correspondence, diaries, and newspaper accounts, particularly in the South where slaves did the work, speak of outlandishly lavish meals), vying to outdo each other in practicality, newness (whether new or not), efficiency, patriotism, healthfulness, and—sometimes—frugality. Christian observances were noted casually throughout. English cooking was the basis of this cuisine, but, again, it was only a basis. Ethnic influences other than English and French were already apparent in recipes, particularly Native American (e.g., Indian Pudding and Succotash à la Tecumseh) and African, although black influence would be more evident in New Orleans than in all of the original Territory of Virginia. But these cultures would not be expressed, beyond recipe, into a genuine American cookbook until the middle of the twentieth century.

The American copyright law was passed in 1790, but not all books were copyrighted, and recipes were "borrowed" whether copyrighted or not. Foreign books and recipes were routinely plagiarized despite moans of protest on the other side of the Atlantic until foreign copyrights were recognized. Most cookery books were paperbound, with or without boards, or clothbound, that is, plain calico cloth, dyed and coated, sometimes embossed to simulate grained leather. A few grandiose editions from such established authors as Eliza Leslie were bound in leather, and these often featured a portrait frontispiece with the title page. Pages were handprinted, one at a time, using various types of printing presses, and illustrations were rare. Book size was 8vo, 12mo, 16mo, or 24mo, resulting from folding a sheet into, for example, twelve leaves (twenty-four pages) by means of right-angle folds. The book was bound and sold with these folds, or the top fold, still intact. To sample its contents, the buyer would slit the pages open with the fingers, a "bone folder" similar to a letter-opener and made of bone, ivory, or tusk, or a dull knife. (Sharp metal instruments tend to tear sideways.)

The next American cookbook of significance, after Simmons's in 1796, was *The Virginia House-wife; Method is the Soul of Management*, created by Mary Randolph in 1824. Born August 9, 1762, at Ampthill, Virginia, "Molly" was a direct descendant of Pocahontas, a cousin to Thomas Jefferson, and sister-in-law of his daughter, Martha. She was also cousin to George Washington's stepson George Washington Parke Custis, who had Arlington House built on that part of the property now known as the Arlington National Cemetery. Marrying yet another cousin once-removed meant her name did not change, but her position in this social milieu did as a result of her husband's politics.

David Meade Randolph was appointed a U.S. marshall by President Washington for his service in the Revolutionary War, but President Jefferson had him removed because of his Federalist sympathies. The Randolphs had to sell their splendid home in Richwood, Virginia—Moldavia (Molly-David)—and move to modest surroundings, where Mrs. Randolph, like many foremothers who found themselves in dire financial straits, inaugurated a boardinghouse. Her mealtime expertise and social repartee soon became the talk of the town, and her establishment was considered quite fashionable. She was an adventuresome cook, and when compiling recipes for *The Virginia House-wife* she introduced to America not only what would become the basis for traditional southeastern cuisine, but also the international influences, for example, those of France, Africa, and India, that were already affecting it. The book was printed by Davis and Force on Pennsylvania Avenue in Washington, D.C., and the author inscribed a copy and generously sent it to "Mrs. Randolph, Monticello": Jefferson's daughter, who had been hostess of the White House while he was president. Thomas Jefferson (theoretically) used the blank pages at the back of this copy to write down some of his favorite recipes (see Recipe, page 00).

Later subtitled *Methodical Cook, The Virginia House-wife* was printed again and again, and recipes were brazenly lifted from the text to enhance other cookbooks (such as this one). The Randolphs had eight children, four of whom lived to maturity. Molly Randolph was living in Washington, D.C., at the time of her death on January 23, 1828. The Custis family allowed her burial at Arlington not only because she was a relative, but also because of her affection for the estate itself—thus hers was the first burial at Arlington Cemetery. The beautiful stone that graces Mary Randolph's tomb was provided by her youngest son, Burwell Starke Randolph, who had been a midshipman in the U.S. Navy when he fell from a mast and suffered severe permanent injuries. He believed that his mother's death was hastened by her tireless caring for his needs. The stone reads in part: "a victim of maternal love and duty. As a tribute of filial gratitude this monument is dedicated to her exulted virtues by her youngest son. Requiescat in pace."

Most famous of the early-nineteenth-century cookbook authors was Eliza Leslie. Her cookery books and reprints outnumber those of any writer of this period, but she was also an artist known for her copies of the masters. Leslie was anonymously introduced in 1828

Miss Eliza Leslie
(1787-1857)

as "a lady of Philadelphia," offering *Seventy-Five Receipts, for Pastry, Cakes, and Sweetmeats* in eighty-eight pages, a collection gleaned from the notebook she kept while studying at America's first cooking school in Philadelphia (see chapter 5).

She was born in Philadelphia on November 15, 1787, of Scottish, Swedish, and English descent. Her father, a prosperous watchmaker and a self-taught mathematician, was a friend of Benjamin Franklin and Thomas Jefferson. The eldest of five children, Leslie was privately tutored. The family spent six active years in London while her father set up an export business, but while they were abroad his partner badly mismanaged the American side of their mutual endeavor. Upon return, the family's style of living was altered dramatically. When Mr. Leslie died a few years later, Mrs. Leslie and Eliza were forced to open their home to boarders to support themselves and the younger children. Eliza Leslie taught drawing, sold copies of masterworks, and attempted to sell (unappreciated) poetry. In the mid 1820s she and her mother moved to West Point with her brother, Thomas Jefferson Leslie, who was serving as treasurer of the U.S. Military Academy. It is said that his advice prompted her to write down and sell those seventy-five recipes, a decision that positively changed her destiny.

The success of the book encouraged Eliza Leslie to try her hand at other facets of writing, and the critical acclaim for *The Young Americans: or, Sketches of a Sea-Voyage, and a Short Visit to Europe* (1829) enabled her to drop the cloak of anonymity. She wrote children's books, compiled tomes on behavior and etiquette, put together articles for magazines, and edited gift books—all in spite of weak eyes and debilitating headaches. Her books on domestic interests were her greatest source of income, however: *Domestic French Cookery* (1832), a translation supposedly from one Sulpice Barue, whose existence no one has been able to verify; *The House Book* (1840); the *Indian Meal Cook Book* (1846), issued to help with relief work during the potato famine; and *Directions for Cookery* (1837) of more than five hundred pages, about which *Ladies National Magazine* scolded, "No woman ought to be without." The advice was apparently heeded, because the book went into fifty printings. Leslie's repertoire had expanded to include entrees and vegetables, even exotic items such as Irish stew, kabobs, and East Indian pickle, and her talent for the culinary arts in general was elaborately exhibited on every page. A century later James Beard would describe her as "the best cook of her time."

Grown portly and walking with difficulty, Leslie lived out the last decade of her life at the United States Hotel in Philadelphia, where she was treated as the celebrity she was. A sarcastic tongue and heady opinions sometimes offended strangers, but she was warmly affectionate to relatives and friends and so generous to the needy that at the end of her life she had to lean on assistance in return. Eliza Leslie was seventy when she died; she is buried in St. Peter's Churchyard in Philadelphia.

Robert Roberts, a "Negro,"[1] wrote *The House Servant's Directory, or a Monitor for Private Families*, published in Boston and New York in 1827. A cheery dissertation on servants' behavior toward their employers, Roberts addresses his "young friends Joseph and David, as they are now about entering into gentlemen's service" as well as other interested readers, patiently revealing his own thorough instruction and accomplished upbringing. The *Directory* is not actually a cookbook, but it contains recipes and is full of historical insights. It is also the first book by a black American to be published by a commercial publisher. Charles S. Francis in New York and Munroe and Francis in Boston boast that "this valuable Work was written by a servant in one of the most respectable families" in Boston. Testimony in a letter from Roberts's recently deceased employer, Christopher Gore, who was governor and state representative from Massachusetts and U.S. representative and senator from same (variously, 1788–1816), follows: "I have read the work attentively, and think it may be of much use. The directions are plain and perspicuous; and many of the recipes I have experienced to be valuable. Could servants be induced to conform to these directions, their own lives would be more useful, and the comfort and convenience of families much promoted. Consider me as a subscriber for such number of copies as six dollars will pay for, and I think that many more would be subscribed for in Boston."

The publishers elaborate on the woeful problem of the "inferior" manners, deportment, and knowledge of duties of American servants compared to servants from abroad (see Chapter 5), pointing out that "school-learning" was better in America, however. No other biographical material is attached; unfortunately neither is there any in the Gore Place Society facsimile (1977), or the Applewood Books reproduction (1988) retitled *Roberts' Guide for Butlers and Household Staff*.

---

1. As noted in Lowenstein, *Bibliography of American Cookery Books 1742–1860*.

Sarah Josepha (Buell) Hale
(1788–1879)

The early life of Sarah Josepha Hale, née Buell, who was born October 24, 1788, in Newport, New Hampshire, was no less tragic than Eliza Leslie's. She was primarily educated at home by her mother, who used the Bible, Shakespeare, and Milton as texts that were eventually supplemented by a reading program initiated by her brother, who taught at Dartmouth. Hale was around twenty-four when her mother and her sister died and her father's business failed. She married David Hale with every hope of a rosier future, eagerly embracing the challenge of a lifetime homemaking career. The couple had five children and experienced what she would later describe as perfect domestic bliss, but the union ended abruptly when pneumonia took her husband four days before the birth of their youngest child.

Sarah Hale opened a millinery shop and began writing to support her family. Her first book of verse, *The Genius of Oblivion* (1823), published with the help of her husband's Masonic friends, poignantly reveals her state of mind and a philosophy that would permeate her writings for the rest of her life: A woman's fulfillment comes as queen of the home ruled by her husband, "creation's lord." *Poems for Our Children* (1830) included "Mary's Lamb," the rhyme cherished by youngsters to this day.

Her literary efforts gained momentum, and in 1827 the Reverend John Lauris Blake, principal of Boston's Cornhill School for Young Ladies, offered her the job of "editress" (a title she preferred) of *Ladies Magazine* (after 1834, *American Ladies Magazine*), and Hale moved to Boston to oblige. Thirteen years later she moved to Philadelphia to propel to fame and fortune (Louis) *Godey's Lady's Book*, which she headed until her retirement after fifty years in the magazine trade.

Although she was not the first woman editor in America, she was the first to raise the standard of women's reading. She drastically cut back on the dreamy poetry and fiction that monopolized women's literature to concentrate on enlightening the "female intellect." In 1830 she launched a fund-raising campaign to complete the Bunker Hill Monument. She was later successful in establishing Mount Vernon as a national shrine and having Thanksgiving Day declared, by Abraham Lincoln, a national holiday. Thus she is called the "Mother of Thanksgiving."

Although editing was her forte, she still found time to write more than fifty nonfiction books, among them *The Good Housekeeper, or the Way to Live Well and to be Well While We Live* (1839); an adaption of Englishwoman Eliza Acton's *Modern Cookery* (1847); *The Ladies' New Book of Cookery* (1852), later expanded and retitled *Mrs.*

Hale's New Cook Book (1857); and, also in 1852, the encyclopedic *Mrs. Hale's Receipts for the Million: Containing Four Thousand Five Hundred and Forty Five Receipts. . . .* At this point in her life Hale had become a living paradox. Like many other early feminists, she enjoyed a family life while she maintained a career but condemned other women for aspiring to do so. Yet she totally encouraged women's "high calling" as wives and mothers, proudly supporting the growth of the female seminary movement by publishing the contributions of Emma Willard, Mary Lyon, and Catharine Beecher. Sarah Hale died in 1879 at age ninety-one and is buried in Philadelphia's West Laurel Hill Cemetery.

Described by Alcott biographers as "prissy" and "a stuffy little boy," a cousin and kindred spirit of Louisa May Alcott's egotistical father wrote several stuffy books on marital and premarital advice in general, and specific culinary advice about what not to do in the kitchen. In 1838 William Andrus [not Alexander] Alcott wrote both *Vegetable Diet,* and *The Young Housekeeper or Thoughts on Food and Cookery,* which progressed to a twentieth edition in 1855. Neither had many actual recipes. It is believed that Alcott, as a young man, was responsible for officially changing the family's name from *Alcox,* hoping, according to Alcott specialist Odell Shepherd, "to prevent obscene jokes."

A childhood friend of Louisa May Alcott's mother was also a cookbook author, who became known more for her antislavery activities than her culinary expertise. Lydia Maria Child, née Francis, was born in Medford, Massachusetts, on February 11, 1802; her father was a baker, whose Medford Crackers were famous. (Fannie Farmer also grew up in Medford, during the 1860s.) Child was twelve when her mother died. She first went to keep house for her elder sister's family, then joined her brother, who had graduated from Harvard Divinity School and taken a parish in Watertown. As in the case of Leslie and Hale, another wise brother recognized and nurtured his sister's literary talent and soon Child's first novel, *Hobomok,* a love story between an Indian brave and a white woman, was published. Child was twenty-one. Two years later came *The Rebels,* which contained a stirring but fictitious speech attributed to the American Revolutionary orator James Otis, a speech long reproduced in history textbooks as genuine!

Lydia Maria (Francis) Child (1802–1880)

Child was also renowned as a journalist, a great lover of nature, and in 1826 founded *The Juvenile Miscellany,* the first American periodical for young people. It was for the *Miscellany* that she wrote

"Over the river and through the woods . . . " a ditty later set to music anonymously, sung as a traditional Thanksgiving tune, and glitteringly set to canvas by Grandma Moses.

Taking advantage of her altered circumstances as the wife of David Lee Child, she wrote *The Frugal Housewife, Dedicated to Those Who Are Not Ashamed of Economy* (1829), in 1832 changing the title to *The American Frugal Housewife* to avoid confusion with the Englishwoman Susannah Carter's volume. In 1837 a medical supplement, *The Family Nurse*, was added. As cookbooks go, Child's was a compact little gem packed with basic information on thrift and self-reliance in the kitchen and elsewhere. It appealed particularly to Puritan-Protestant migrants going west to flee the depression and sold steadily. The couple existed almost solely on Lydia Child's income because her husband was an idealistic lawyer who took on any client with a good cause, whether they could pay or not—and they usually could not. Both the Childs extolled high personal values and became impassioned supporters of the American Indian cause and later the emerging antislavery movement. But abolition was not yet a popular topic of conversation in the North. As one of only two women having legal access to the Boston Athenaeum's library,[2] Child researched many shocking and eye-opening articles that were eventually accumulated in a book titled *An Appeal for That Class of Americans Called Africans* (1833), an exposé that would cost her her her journalism career. Her cherished task of writing for children was destroyed because parents considered her a bad influence. *An Appeal* was published eighteen years before Harriet Beecher Stowe's series on the same subject appeared in periodicals, which later resulted in the fictional but widely endorsed *Uncle Tom's Cabin*.

The Childs lived in poverty for many years, ostracized from society, their marriage strained; however she continued writing and helped launch many first-time authors into print. She lived to see the hostile opinions that had greeted her valiant words condemning slavery turned into homage. Maria Child died in 1880 and is buried with her husband in Wayland, Massachusetts.

Sylvester Graham, born in West Suffield, Connecticut, on July 5, 1794, was inadvertently the most famous of all early cookbook

---

2. The other woman was Hannah Adams, historian. The exclusion of female membership from the library was a "protection" measure, because the building's iron spiral stairs might cause members of the full-skirted sex to trip and tumble to their death.

authors because his appellation appears on boxes of Graham Crackers in kitchen cabinets all over America. He would abhor the product, however, as it in no way resembles his meticulously described whole-wheat recipe and, worse, is contaminated with the abominable sugar. His cautions against using refined white flour went far beyond suggesting simple whole wheat as an alternative. In his revolutionary little book *A Treatise on Bread, and Bread-Making* (1837), Graham demanded that consumers use unbolted wheat flour coarsely ground from berries home-grown without manure fertilizer. The 131-page diatribe alerted housewives and mothers to their failed nutritional habits, and, as a consequence, Graham bread was served at every conscientious table, whole-wheat flour was commonly called Graham Flour, and recipes for Graham biscuits, Graham gems, Graham crackers, steamed Graham bread, Graham prune bread, Graham muffins, Graham puddings, Graham cake, Graham flour wafers, Graham diamonds, and Graham cookies were featured in cookbooks all across the nation. Certain rusks in Finland were called *grahamkorputs*.

Gifted with oratory, Graham survived a disastrous childhood to study evangelism. He was the seventeenth child of a father who died at seventy-four when Graham was two years old, and a mother who was declared unfit as a parent when he was six. From then until he was in his twenties he seems to have been shuffled from relative to neighbor, working as farmhand, clerk, and teacher, all the while showing increasingly severe symptoms of tuberculosis. He was in ill health when he began his preaching career, and, after one long siege, married his nurse, a Miss Earls, by whom he had several children.

In 1830 the Pennsylvania State Society for the Suppression of the Use of Ardent Spirits involved Graham in the temperance cause, and he began to study the affects of diet and drink on his own ill health. Soon he was popularizing in sermons the advanced health teachings of the day, filling lecture halls by challenging the existing medical establishment, which was none too popular at the time. The more successful his lectures, the more opinions he shared, recommending fresh foods and roughage (his vegetarianism was spurred by a belief that meat eating aroused unmanageable carnal desires), pure drinking water, cold showers, looser and lighter clothing, hard mattresses, fresh-air exercise (he swam in a river 365 days a year), and cheerfulness at meals. Although his ideas were basically sound, he was a fanatic for detail, yet vague enough in his recipes not to be accused of an error in measurement. At the peak of his popularity, Graham boardinghouses were erected in Boston and New York, where young adults could live in a wholesome environment that reflected his teachings. At this time he was claiming that being a "Grahamite" would prevent cholera, but the bogusness of the boast was not the reason for his imminent downfall. That came about when in his talks to encourage sexual abstinence in the married as well as the single state to conserve precious body fluids, he mentioned unspeakable nocturnal "vices" by name in mixed company.

Graham was ridiculed as a filthy-mouthed zealot, and subsequently a mob of butchers and bakers in Boston who had enough of his exhortations against meat and sugar were only too eager to attack. Soon after this dismal experience his precarious health began to fail. He wrote several other noncooking publications, all published by Light and Stearns of Boston who advertised both these works and those by Grahamite William Andrus Alcott on the end-pages of both authors' works.

Graham died at the age of forty-three after taking a tepid bath in his Northampton, Massachusetts, home. It was said that he went back to eating meat and sipping stimulants to try to revitalize his body, and his early demise was often cited as evidence of the total failure of his health program. Yet given what we now know of nutrition and exercise, notwithstanding the ominous effects of early and severe physical and mental abuse, it is likely that Sylvester Graham's personal habits added a decade or two of life to his ravaged young spirit.

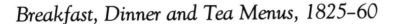

Breakfast, Dinner and Tea Menus, 1825-60

Fresh Fruit or Apple Sauce
Codfish Cakes or Clam Pancakes
Toast and Butter
Indian Pudding, fried in slices with Molasses
Tea, Coffee

Dinner was usually served about one o'clock in the country,
two o'clock in Northern cities, and three o'clock in
Southern cities. Thomas Jefferson dined at three-thirty
in the afternoon.

Beef à la Mode
Potatoes
Stewed Spinach   Parsnips
Graham Bread and Lemon Butter
Quaking Plum Pudding with Better Sauce
Peach Ice-Cream

Tea was usually served between five o'clock and six o'clock
in the evening; and if the family was entertaining or
otherwise staying up late, tea was followed a few hours
later by a supper.

Doughnuts   Scones
Almond Cake
Sliced Ham or Tongue
Rye Drop Cakes
Bread, Butter and Jam
Tea

Apple Sauce

Pare, core, quarter and wash one dozen russet apples; stew them twenty minutes in half a tea-cupful of water over a slow fire; stir into them one table-spoonful of sugar, one table-spoonful of butter, a pinch of cinnamon, and a little nutmeg; dish and serve.

—*The Practical Cook Book Containing Upwards of 1000 Receipts . . .*
by Mrs. Bliss of Boston
(Philadelphia: Lippincott, Grambo, 1850)

"It is the best cook book we have ever seen."
—Saturday Evening Post

"We have no hesitation in pronouncing it the best work on the subject of cookery extant."
—Ladies National Magazine

"It is worth a dozen times its price."
—Public Ledger

Codfish Cakes

Wash the fish, and after remaining in water all night, boil it. Take out all the bones, and mash it fine with some potatoes, a piece of butter, cayenne, and a little more salt, if necessary. Then make it out into small round cakes, and fry in lard, a light brown on both sides.

—*Widdifield's New Cook Book; or, Practical Receipts for the Housewife*
by Hannah Widdifield
(Philadelphia: S. & M. Widdifield, 1856)

Clam Pancakes

Make a thick batter of flour and milk; clam liquor does not make them so light as milk; put to each pint of milk two eggs and a few clams; the clams may be put in whole after being first stewed, or they may be only taken out of the shell and chopped fine.

—*The Improved Housewife or Book of Receipts*
by a Married Lady
[Mrs. A. L. Webster]
(Hartford, 1844)

"The true economy of housekeeping is simply the art of gathering up all the fragments, so that nothing be lost. I mean fragments of time, as well as materials. Nothing should be thrown away so long as it is possible to make any use of it, however trifling that use may be; and whatever be the size of a family, every member should be employed either in earning or saving money. . . .

In this country, we are apt to let children romp away their existence, till they get to be thirteen or fourteen. This is not well. It is not well for the purses and patience of parents; and it has a still worse effect on the morals and habits of the children. Begin early is the great maxim for everything in education. A child of six years old can be made useful; and should be taught to consider every day lost in which some little thing has not been done to assist others.

Children can very early be taught to take all the care of their own clothes. They can knit garters, suspenders, and stockings; they can make patchwork and braid straw; they can make mats for the table, and mats for the floor; they can weed the garden, and pick cranberries from the meadow, to be carried to market. Provided brothers and sisters go together, and are not allowed to go with bad children, it is a great deal better for the boys and girls on a farm to be picking blackberries at six cents a quart, than to be wearing out their clothes in useless play. They enjoy themselves just as well; and they are earning something to buy clothes, at the same time they are tearing them."

—The American Frugal Housewife. . .
by Mrs. [Lydia Maria] Child
(Boston: Carter and Hendee, 1836,
20th edition)

Parsnips

Scrape and split them, and boil until quite soft, either in salt and water, or with meat; they are very good served up in this way, with plenty of butter. They may, when boiled, either be baked with a few slices of salt meat, and require no seasoning but pepper, or made into small round cakes, seasoned with butter, pepper and salt, and fried.

—Domestic Cookery, Useful Receipts, and
Hints to Young Housekeepers
by Elizabeth Elliott Lea
(Baltimore: Colburn, 1845)

Beef à la Mode

Take a round of fresh beef and cut deep slits in it; grate a loaf of stale bread, mix with it thyme, sweet marjoram, one onion chopped fine, cayenne pepper, salt, cloves, more to your taste—an egg boiled hard and chopped fine, and one-quarter of a pound of butter: stuff the beef, and brown it with a sufficient quantity of butter. When brown, add water enough to stew it. When nearly done, add one glass of wine, or the juice of a sweet orange. It will take four or five hours to stew.

—Mrs. Hale's New Cook Book
by Mrs. Sarah J. Hale
(Philadelphia: T. B. Peterson, 1857)

To Pickle One Hundred Pounds of Beef to Keep a Year

Put together three quarts salt, six ounces salt petre, one and a half pints of molasses and water sufficient to cover your meat after laid into the barrel. Sprinkle the bottom of the barrel with salt, and also slightly sprinkle between the layers of meat as you pack, when done, pour on your pickle and lay on a stone or board to keep the whole down. Beef salted after this method during the fall or winter may be kept nice and tender through the summer by taking it up about the first of May, scald and skim the brine, add three quarts of salt, when cold pour back upon the beef.

—The Cook Not Mad, or Rational
Cookery
Anonymous
(Watertown, Mass.: Knowlton & Rice,
1830; Canada's first printed cookbook,
a reprint, 1831)

To Dress Potatoes

Wash your potatoes well and peal them. Let them lay 15 minutes in cold water. Take them out and throw them into as much boiling water and salt as will boil them tender, soft. When done take them out of the water and mash them with a spoon, add cream and butter equal quantities, enough to make them liquid (one-fourth pound of butter to two quarts of potatoes) with a little nutmeg. Stir them until perfectly light and white. If too stiff they may be liquefied with good milk.

—Thomas Jefferson's handwriting in
the endpages of *The Virginia
House-wife*.[3]

---

3. There is, in the 1927 edition of *The Congressional Club Cook Book* (see chapter 11) a short frontmatter section entitled "The Jefferson Cook Book" written by Laura Kay Cramton. It is an intriguing story, one that ends in mystery. According to Cramton, there existed one copy of Mary Randolph's *The Virginia House-wife* with additional favorite recipes jotted in the blank pages by Thomas Jefferson himself. The flyleaf carries the inscription "For Mrs. Randolph, Monticello, from her affectionate friend and sister," the book being sent to Thomas Jefferson's daughter, who acted as hostess in the White House while he was president. The two women were sisters-in-law (and cousins). When putting together the 1927 edition of *The Club Cook Book*, the authors learned that this unique volume had been sent to Mrs. Theodore Roosevelt in 1904 as a most generous gift from George A. Satterlee, a resident of the Los Angeles County Soldiers Home. An accompanying note stated in part: "Honored Madam: Understand you are collecting . . . souvenirs of the different administrations. I beg leave to offer you . . . a copy of the first cookbook published in America . . . but more valuable from the fact of containing about 45 recipes in Mr. Thomas Jefferson's handwriting. It has been handed down to me through a gifted kinsman. . . ." The Congressional Club goes on to explain that Mrs. Calvin Coolidge, the "present mistress" of the White House, allowed them access to book and letter and gave permission for some recipes to be photographed and others copied for publication. Although the cookbook was not America's first, the reprinted handwriting looks genuine to me. Unfortunately, a search through the several *Virginia House-wife* editions held by the Library of Congress and Joan Higbee's continued hunt through various other libraries in Washington and at Monticello produced nothing. Indeed, some called the story an old wives' tale. To further confound the researcher, in 1938 Marie Kimball wrote *The Thomas Jefferson Cook Book*, a compilation of his personal recipes and those connected with Monticello. Some of the aforementioned recipes were included, but no bibliography. I am, however, convinced the book existed, or exists. But where is it?

Seminole Soup

Take a squirrel, cut it up and put it on to boil. When the soup is nearly done add to it one pint of picked hickory-nuts and a spoonful of parched and powdered sassafras leaves—or the tender top of a pine tree, which gives a very aromatic flavor to the soup.

Ground-nut Soup

To half a pint of shelled ground-nuts, well beaten up, add two spoonsful of flour, and mix well. Put to them a pint of oysters, and a pint and a half of water. While boiling, throw on a seed-pepper or two, if small.

Stewed Spinach

When your spinach is nicely picked and boiled, press it well in a cullender; then add some pepper and salt, a spoonful of fresh butter, and put it back in the skillet, and let it stew gently a little longer, adding a small teacup of sweet cream, or, in its stead, a little beef or veal gravy.

—*The Carolina Housewife, or House
and Home*
by a Lady of Charleston
(Charleston: Babcock, 1847)

"The Carolina Housewife by a Lady of Charleston *was published in 1847, followed by other editions, all anonymous. For until about 1920-odd the name of a Charleston woman appeared in print but thrice—when born, when married and when buried— the legal necessities. Of course 'everyone' (everyone being her friends and relations) knew that the book had been compiled by Sarah Rutledge. . . ."*

—Introduction of 1847 Facsimile
Edition
by Anna Wells Rutledge (cousin)
(Columbia: University of South
Carolina Press, 1979)

Receipt 11

Greens and salads are stringy and indigestible. Besides, they are much used, as condiments are, to excite or provoke an appetite—a thing usually wrong. A feeble appetite, say at the opening of the spring, however common, is a great blessing. If let alone, nature will erelong set to rights those things, which have gone wrong perhaps all winter; and then appetite will return in a natural way.

But the worst thing about greens, salads, and some other things, is, they are eaten with vinegar. Vinegar and all substances, I must again say, which resist or retard putrefaction, retard also the work of digestion. It is a universal law, and ought to be known as such, that whatever tends to preserve our food—except perhaps ice and the air-pump—tends also to interfere with the great work of digestion. Hence, all pickling, salting, boiling down, sweetening, etc. are objectionable.

—*Vegetable Diet*
by Dr. William [Andrus] Alcott
(Boston: Marsh, Capen & Lyon, 1838)

Graham Bread

For it is infinitely better that the family should even do without bread one day, and eat roasted potatoes, than that they should eat poor bread three or four days; and if, from any cause, the bread should be poor, it is incomparably better to throw it away, than to set it upon the table, to disgust the whole family with bread, and drive them to make most of their meal on something else. If a lady can ever find a good excuse for having poor bread [one day], she certainly can find none except perhaps extreme poverty for setting her poor bread on the table a second time. Yet, too generally, women seem to think that, as a matter of course, if they, by carelessness or any other means, have been so unlucky as to make a batch of poor bread, their family and friends must share their misfortune, and help them eat it up; and by this means, many a child has had its health seriously impaired, and its construction injured, and perhaps its moral character ruined by being driven, in early life, into pernicious dietetic habits. . . . Take then such a quantity of meal, in a perfectly clean and sweet bread trough, as is necessary for the quantity of bread desired, and having made a hollow in the centre, turn in as much yeast as a judgement matured by sound experience shall deem requisite; then add such a quantity of water, milk and water, or clear milk, as necessary to form the meal into a dough of proper consistency. . . .

—A Treatise on Bread, and
Bread-Making
by Sylvester Graham
(Boston: Light & Stearns, 1937)

Lemon Butter or French Honey

Take a half a pound of butter, melt it in an earthen dish and squeeze in the juice of six lemons; beat twelve eggs with two pounds of brown sugar, stir it in with the rind of two lemons grated, mix it all together, and let it boil twenty minutes, when it will be about the consistence of honey; the flavor is agreeable, and it may be eaten on bread, or as a sauce for boiled pudding.

—Domestic Cookery, Useful Receipts, and
Hints to Young Housekeepers
by Elizabeth Elliot Lea
(Baltimore: Colburn, 1845)

Carrying Tea and Coffee Around

When placing your cups and saucers on the tray, be particular and have them all uniform and not crowded; with your sugar and cream in the centre, and the sugar tongs and handle of the cream toward the company. Have, on another tray, your cake, wafers, toast, bread and butter, &c. all neatly arranged to take round after you have served tea and coffee to all the company. But if you have a large party, you should have some person to hand round the cake, &c., at the same time that you are serving round tea. When you first enter the room with the tea, cast your eyes around the company to observe where the most elderly lady is seated, then proceed forward and help her first, observing to lower the waiter [tray], that the ladies may take off their tea with ease. When the ladies are all served, then proceed to help the gentlemen, beginning as with the ladies.

—The House Servant's Directory, or a
Monitor for Private Families . . .
by Robert Roberts
(Boston: Munroe and Francis, 1827)

Blackberry Cordial

To two quarts of juice of blackberries add one pound of loaf sugar, half an ounce of nutmegs, half an ounce of cinnamon pulverized, one-fourth of an ounce of cloves, one-fourth of an ounce of alspice, pulverized; boil together for a short time, and when cold add a pint of fourth-proof French brandy.

—The Southern Gardener and
Receipt Book
by P. Thornton
(Camden, S.C., 1840)

Quaking Plum Pudding with Better Sauce

[NOTE: It is a great tribute to Maria Child that the founders of Old Sturbridge Village, the living history museum of early nineteenth-century New England life located in Sturbridge, Massachusetts, used editions of her book *The (American) Frugal Housewife* to guide the reconstruction and interpretation of domestic life portrayed there. The recipes provided in the *Old Sturbridge Village Cookbook*, nicely edited by Caroline Sloat, are based on "the experiences of the Village staff in finding out just how the recipes in Mrs. Child's book should be prepared, and how the results should taste." Three recipes are included for each entry: (1) Mrs. Child's original; (2) the modern method of cooking that recipe; and (3) an explanation of how to use the hearth when fixing the recipe. The book is a valuable resource for any person or group wishing to attempt hearth cooking or to create meals as they were accomplished by our brave and imaginative foremothers.]

ORIGINAL RECIPE

Take slices of light bread and spread them thin with butter, and lay in the pudding dish layers of bread and raisins, within an inch of the top; then take five eggs and beat them well, and mix them with a quart of milk, and pour it over the pudding; add salt and spice to suit your taste; you may put in a cup of sugar, and eat it with butter, or you may omit the sugar, and serve it up with sweet sauce. Bake it twenty or twenty-five minutes. Before you use the raisins, boil them in a very little water, and put it all in.

1 cup raisins
½ cup water or brandy
½ loaf rye bread with a firm crust
¼–½ cup butter
5 eggs
4 cups milk
½ teaspoon salt
1 teaspoon cinnamon
¼ teaspoon freshly grated nutmeg

Cook raisins in water or brandy for 15 minutes. Slice bread, butter slices, line a 2-quart baking dish with a layer of slices. Sprinkle with raisins. Continue to build layers until all bread and raisins are used. Beat eggs, add milk and remaining ingredients. Pour over bread. Bake one hour in 350-degree oven.

¼ pound butter
½ cup sugar
1 tablespoon wine or brandy
¼ teaspoon nutmeg

Cream butter and sugar. Stir in wine or brandy and mold into a ball. Chill for two hours or more. Sprinkle grated nutmeg over hard sauce before serving. Yield ¾ cup.

Hearth Method

Cook raisins and water or brandy in a small pan on a trivet over coals near the fire for 15-20 minutes or until raisins are plump. Follow recipe above. Bake in a preheated Dutch oven up to an hour. Cooking time will vary depending on the shape and thickness of the baking dish. If it is cooking very slowly after 45 minutes, change the coals above and beneath the Dutch oven. Serves 8.

—*Old Sturbridge Village Cookbook*
by Caroline Sloat
(Chester, Conn.: Globe Pequot Press,
1984)

Ice Creams

When ice creams are not put into shapes, they should always be served in glasses with handles.

Peach Cream

Get fine soft peaches perfectly ripe, peel them, take out the stones, and put them in a China bowl; sprinkle some sugar on, and chop them very small with a silver spoon—if the peaches be sufficiently ripe, they will become a smooth pulp; add as much cream or rich milk as you have peaches; put more sugar, and freeze it.

Coffee Cream

Toast two gills of raw coffee till it is a light brown, and not a grain burnt; put it hot from the toaster without grinding it, into a quart of rich and perfectly sweet milk [or cream]; boil it, and add the yelks of eight eggs; when done, strain it through a sieve, and sweeten it; if properly done, it will not be discolored; [freeze it]. The coffee may be dried and will answer for making in the usual way to drink, allowing more for the quantity of water, than if it had not gone through this process.

"Management is an art that may be acquired by every woman of good sense and tolerable memory . . . the prosperity and happiness of a family depend greatly on the order and regularity established in it."
—Mrs. Mary Randolph (1824)

Oyster Cream

Make a rich soup, strain it from the oysters and freeze it.

—*The Virginia House-wife*
[by Mrs. Mary Randolph]
(Washington: Davis and Force, 1824)

Rye Drop Cakes

To a pint of sour milk, or butter-milk, put two or three eggs, not quite a teaspoonful of saleratus, a little salt, and sifted rye meal (this is much better than rye flour), enough to make a batter that will spread a little, but not run. Drop them in muffin-rings with a spoon.

They will require about twice as much time to bake as common griddle cakes. They will bake very nicely in a stove in fifteen minutes. Graham flour may be substituted for rye if preferred, but is not quite as good.

—*The Young Housekeeper's Friend; or, a Guide to Domestic Economy and Comfort* by Mrs. Cornelius [Mary Hooker] (Boston: Charles Tappan, 1846)

Rose-water

When the roses are in full blossom, pick the leaves carefully off, and to every quart of water put a peck of them. Put them in a cold still over a slow fire, and distill very gradually; then bottle the water, let it stand in the bottle three days, and then cork in close.

—*The New England Economical Housekeeper and Family Receipt Book* by Mrs. E. A. Howland [Esther Allen] (Worcester: S. A. Howland, 1847)

Talents

"Dig them up—bring them to the light—turn them over, polish them, and they will give light to the world. You know not what you are capable of doing; you cannot sound the ocean of thought within you. You must labor, keep at it, and dig deep and long before you will begin to realize much. Be inactive—mourn because you were not created a giant in intellect, and you will die a fool."

—*The Skillful Housewife's Book, or Complete Guide to Domestic Cookery, Taste, Comfort, and Economy* by Mrs. L. G. Abell (New York: D. Newell, 1847)

Almond Cake

2 ounces of blanched bitter almonds, pounded very fine
7 ounces of flour, sifted and dried
10 eggs
1 pound of loaf-sugar, powdered and sifted
2 tablespoonsful of rose-water

Take two ounces of shelled bitter almonds or peach kernels. Scald them in hot water, and as you peel them, throw them into a bowl of cold water, then wipe them dry, and pound them one by one in a mortar, till they are quite fine and smooth. Break ten eggs, putting the yolks in one pan and the whites in another. Beat them separately as light as possible, the whites first, and then the yolks. Add the sugar gradually to the yolks, beating it very hard. Then by degrees, beat in the almonds, and then add the rose-water. Stir half the whites of the eggs into the yolks and sugar. Divide the flour into two equal parts, and stir in one half, slowly and lightly, till it bubbles on the top. Then the other half of the white of eggs, and then the remainder of the flour very lightly.

Butter a large square tin pan, or one made of paste-board which will be better. Put in the mixture, and set immediately in a quick oven, which must be rather hotter at the bottom than at the top. Bake it according to the thickness. If you allow the oven to get slack, the cake will be spoiled.

Make an icing with the whites of three eggs, 24 tea-spoonsful of loaf-sugar, and eight drops of essence of lemon. When the cake is cool, mark it in small squares with a knife. Cover it with icing, and ornament it while wet with nonpareils dropped on in borders, round each square of the cake. When the icing is dry, cut the cake in squares, cutting through the icing very carefully with a penknife. Or you may cut it in squares first, and then ice and ornament each square separately. Eat it while fresh.

—Seventy-Five Receipts for Pastry, Cakes, and Sweetmeats
by a lady of Philadelphia [Eliza Leslie]
(Boston: Munroe and Francis, 1828)

"*The receipts in this little book are, in every sense of the word, American; but the writer flatters herself that (if exactly followed) the articles produced from them will not be found inferior to any of a similar description made in the European manner.*"
—Eliza Leslie (1828)

4

The Great Western Expansion

*I*f the mountains were the barriers that confined the first settlers to the Atlantic seaboard, the rivers that broke through the mountain passes were the silver threads that guided the bold pioneers of later generations through the gaps and across the plains from the Atlantic to the Pacific. The Mississippi Valley soon became known as the Great West, beckoning frontiersmen who learned that the fertile earth would grow not only Indian corn and tobacco, but cotton and grains and vegetables as well. The grasses that grew so abundantly on these plains would sustain cattle and sheep by the million. The pioneers became settlers rather than rovers; they were farmers who also took the opportunity to trade in furs and outfit canoes, boats, and, eventually, covered wagons to accommodate the great expansion. After the discovery of gold in California in 1848, settlement west of the Mississippi River increased faster in fifty years than it had east of the Mississippi during the preceding 250.

Once they reached their destination, these families could, if need be, produce their own food, weave cloth for clothes and linens, and make soap and candles; they were virtually self-sufficient. Men (and a few women) went into business, establishing city and town centers. Women, acting in their ancient role as custodians of the cultural identity, launched a social and community repartee. Education for children and men was a high priority, but women, too, were eager to learn and to share what they were fast comprehending about frontier life.

Some idealistic women, traveling alone as professionals, went west to bring to their sisters the latest theories on housekeeping, cooking, and child-rearing. Their goal was to earn higher respect for "women's work," to enlighten people on the powers of domestic strength at home and in the community. They envisioned women working to their full capacity in harmony with men, as each had a different path in the pursuit of happiness. Some women achieved financial independence as teachers and lecturers; however, most confronted unforeseen physical hardship as well as insult and ridicule in their efforts to further a separate, balanced civilization because their "castles" were built on the sands of chauvinism.

One of these idealistic women was Catharine Esther Beecher. The instrument she used to unleash women's powers to participate in the new democracy, as she and so many others before her had envisioned their destiny of equality to be, was the cookbook.

Catharine Esther Beecher was the first child of the Presbyterian minister Lyman Beecher and his first wife, Roxana Foote. Beecher was born on September 6, 1800 in a two-story frame house in the little seacoast village of East Hampton on Long Island. In her biographical sketch, her younger sister Harriet Beecher (later Stowe) stated that Catharine was endowed with an intellect "beyond most men's" that was greatly influenced by their father, a religious zealot and disciplinarian. But in later years it was to her versatile and gentle mother that Catharine Beecher attributed the formation of her best traits, and she was, without doubt, her own woman.

Catharine Beecher
(1800–1880)

When Beecher was sixteen, her mother died, and the burden of helping her aunt raise her seven sisters and brothers, of which Harriet was sixth, became her responsibility for a year until her father remarried. During this period she was allowed to forsake her schooling, which she was never enthusiastic about anyway, preferring instead to play and go horseback riding. In her newfound duties she discovered a propensity for domestic tasks, which she performed with a positive disposition that somewhat diluted the Calvinistic "thou shalt nots" that heavily influenced her Presbyterian family.

When she reached marriageable age she was not a handsome woman: blue eyes, long brown hair with little bouquets of corkscrew curls at her ears, there was nothing dainty about her facial features, and she was tactfully referred to as "homely." She did, nevertheless, meet a strikingly attractive young man at one of her father's sermons, fall in love, and succeed in becoming engaged. Alexander Metcalf Fisher, a professor of mathematics and natural philosophy at Yale College, found in Beecher an intellect as promising as his own, and the two reveled in their ability to accomplish masterful duets on the piano. Fisher vowed to marry his beloved after a year's sabbatical to Europe, where he planned to study European teaching methods. In the spring of 1822 he sailed for England, but he never returned. The ship *Albion* was wrecked off the coast of Ireland, and the sole survivor from the vessel was not Alexander Fisher.

Beecher was shocked and deeply grieved at the news. Her loss was made worse by the fact that Fisher had not converted to Presbyterianism at the time of death—a fate literally worse than death in Lyman Beecher's mind—and the cruel senselessness of this tenet tormented her for many years. She never seems to have contemplated marriage again, but in spite of her father's increasingly dire warnings did not ever convert to Calvinism herself, a decision that would have far-reaching consequences.[1]

It was with intense gratitude that the bereaved young woman soon learned that her fiancé had left her $2,000 with which she managed to pull herself out of depression through her own educational scheme. Along with her sister, Mary, she opened a school in a Hartford, Connecticut, storefront in 1923, planning to educate young girls "beyond the rudiments." Thus began a sixty-one-year career devoted to guiding women. Knowing her own formal education to be wanting, Beecher took on the challenge of educating herself and her young charges at the same time, barely keeping ahead of them in her determination to teach, and learn, Latin. Although eleven-year-old Harriet, entrusted once again to Catharine's care, would consider it a piteous fate boarding at the school with her dominating sister, she would lean on Catharine's intelligence and maternalism for the rest of her life.

The Hartford Female Seminary, as it was known in 1827, prospered, offering Italian, French, Latin, art, mathematics, music, rhetoric, and, uniquely, calisthenics. Its pupils were prodded toward "intellectual, physical and moral perfection." Later, Beecher would seek to replace the "fainting, weeping, vapid, pretty plaything," as she perceived girls to be in *An Essay on the Education of Female Teachers* (1835), with energetic, capable, kind personalities endowed with a sacred vocation.

---

1. It is believed she burned all correspondence with her lover in a poignant frenzy of privacy when, during her seventies, she visited Fisher's relatives.

In 1832 the Beechers became enchanted with the Christian climate flourishing around Lane Seminary in Cincinnati, Ohio and decided to move to the place her father referred to as "the London of the west." They bought a home in Walnut Hills (now the Harriet Beecher Stowe Museum on Gilbert Avenue). At Fourth and Sycamore streets Beecher established the Western Female Institute; tuition was $18 per fourteen-week term. But if the Christian climate pleased her, the intellectual climate of Cincinnati did not. She would spend much of her energy arguing with city fathers over money-raising ventures, extolling temperance, and penning hotly defensive letters, under the pseudonym "Christus," to the *Cincinnati Daily Gazette*, whose editors ridiculed her for wasting everyone's time educating women, who were only going to "end up" homemakers anyway. Cincinnatians also feared that Eastern intellectuals were taking over the city, advocating abolition and causing dangerous unrest between Northerners and Southerners at this line of demarcation. By the time Beecher spoke out against the abuse of American Indians in Georgia, her whole family was being shunned. Eventually they sold home and belongings at a loss and went their separate ways. But it is speculated that Beecher's courageous decision to stick it out in the West was one reason she is not as well known as such academically minded eastern counterparts Emma Willard, who founded the Troy (New York) Female Seminary, and Mary Lyons of Mount Holyoke (Massachusetts).

Thankfully, her days in Cincinnati were not devoted entirely to the school, or the London of the West may have aborted many female careers. Beecher had written religious materials and two textbooks while in Connecticut, and she added four more to her credit while living in Walnut Hills, as well as collaborating with the Reverend William H. McGuffey on his *Eclectic Fourth Reader* in 1837. She was now launched on a second career, that of writing—Cincinnati had become a major publishing center in the midwest. She began assembling material for what proved to be her most popular book, *A Treatise on Domestic Economy, for the use of young ladies at home, and at school.* Obsessed with the need for decent "teachers for our country," and in spite of the fact that teaching was not yet considered a suitable job for women, Beecher began a life of travel upon leaving Cincinnati, establishing schools in Quincy, Illinois and Dubuque, Iowa, and the Milwaukee College in Wisconsin, the only one that survives. She also lectured in other major cities on women's education and health. She used the excuse of wishing to discuss a book in progress to stay as uninvited guest in the homes of locally

"Let the young women of the nation find that domestic economy is placed in schools on equal or superior grounds to chemistry, philosophy, and mathematics, and they will blush to be found ignorant of its first principles."
—Catharine Esther Beecher (1841)

prominent families, where she often offended her hosts with her "radical" views, or she stayed in homes of members of the Beecher clan.[2]

Her fame spread through the popularity of *A Treatise on Domestic Economy*, which included hundreds of recipes in the common paragraph form and was published in New York by Harper & Brothers and in Boston by Marsh, Capen, Lyon & Webb in 1841. In time this book was sold door to door in every state in the Union, and Ralph Waldo Emerson endorsed it, using it as a text in his private school in Boston. Calling the homemaker a "domestic scientist," Beecher emulated Child in recommending frugality, and Leslie in offering grace and respectability, but she added an outspoken militancy that attracted women of unusual grit and determination. Although standard measurements were being suggested in England, she was the first American author to point out that "it is a good plan to have a particular measure cup kept for the purpose," and that the cook should make note of the weight of certain staple ingredients.

Miss Beecher's Domestic Receipt Book, "designed as a supplement" and published in 1846 by Harper & Brothers, was likewise a nationally successful endeavor. Years later, when her funds were low primarily due to travel and reinvestment in her brand of female education, her sister Harriet came to the rescue. In 1869 Catharine and Harriet (who had also written a few domestic essays under the pseudonym Christopher Crowfield, a sage, benevolent old man, while at the same time maintaining her notoriety as the abolitionist H. B. Stowe) put together *The American Woman's Home, or Principles of Domestic Science*, another common-sensical manual filled with recipes. It was an enlarged version of Catharine's two books, with some quotations from Stowe's *House and Home Papers* and some new material. The book was published by J. B. Ford in New York and was beautifully bound and lavishly illustrated. It was immediately successful and is highly collectible because of its connection to Harriet. In 1873 Ford published *The New Housekeeper's Manual* and *The Handy Cookbook* bound together (with five hundred recipes); and in 1884 Harper & Brothers brought out *Miss Beecher's Housekeeper and Healthkeeper*. Both editions were practically identical to the 1869 publication.

"You may make houses enchantingly beautiful, hang them with pictures, have them clean and airy and convenient; but if the stomach is fed with sour bread and burnt meals, it will raise such rebellions that the eyes will see no beauty anywhere."
—Catharine E. Beecher and Harriet Beecher Stowe (1873)

2. When she was seventy, she not only demanded to be allowed to take a course at Cornell University that was, surely, open only to men, but she also moved into the male dormitory, stating to the dean that the residents "will not trouble me in the least." They loved her.

The reasons for Beecher's initial appeal as a writer and lecturer on the domestic front were simple: Her advice was new and valid. Furthermore, no one had ever expressed themselves so eloquently on behalf of women's physical health.[3] The concept that the homemaker, whether wealthy, poor, or hired, should actually take into consideration her own stamina and hygiene among her other responsibilities was embraced gratefully. Ironically, although she would never marry or have an actual home of her own, Beecher became the ultimate spokeswoman for the "Happy Housewife."

She believed that women who were tending the nation's children were also shaping the world to come, and she intended that they assume the role responsibly and with eyes wide open. In her published *Letters* to housewives, she was specific about ways to keep the kitchen clean, advising frequent scalding of the sink; she even offered an efficient kitchen design. She recommended opening windows to air the house and bed linens on a regular basis. She was the first to advocate washing of the teeth with a brush and to warn against the dangers of going outdoors in cold weather while covered with perspiration (such as on wash day), the dangers of leaky shoes, murderous fashions, and excessive use of tea and coffee to interfere with a good night's sleep.

The schools she founded in Illinois and Iowa failed to thrive for lack of funding, primarily because she refused to bind their philosophy to any one religious denomination. Graduates were sent to barely civilized lawless regions, often returning completely demoralized. The physical hardships they experienced while living in the pitiful homes of their charges, as well as the weakening effects of confronting poverty, prejudice, ignorance, and illness, were overwhelming. The women were paid less than their male counterparts, if they were paid at all, and their efforts to educate their already exhausted species to accept their "true professions" as chief ministers of the family unit, teachers, and "saviors" of society were at best endorsed only halfheartedly.

Back in New England, Beecher defended her views against her critics but refused to relax efforts to improve living standards wherever she went. It did not occur to Catharine Beecher, or almost anyone else at the time, that home duties could be shared with a spouse. Women and children continued to exist in a substandard life-style, fulfilling their dawn-to-dusk responsibilities.

---

3. Because she was a woman, she chose to let one of her brothers do the actual speaking, while she sat approving from the audience, for many years.

Like so many of the bright, talented women before her time and after, Beecher was torn when contemplating the possibility of women merging their careers with that of wife and mother. She desperately feared the actuality would destroy family life. In the meantime, the woman's suffrage movement, led by women much younger than she, was gaining momentum, and suffragettes were exasperated that the high-profile Beecher sisters refused to endorse their case—nay, they preached loudly against it! Some historians theorize that Beecher did not embrace suffragism in order not to hinder the already difficult task of raising money, primarily from men, for women's education, and her sister followed suit. But there is no question that in her heart Catharine Beecher believed men's and women's roles to be different, that each would lose by the other's betrayal, and that women were subservient to men by nature. She was surely conservative on the issue, yet, in the sublime faith she had in the capabilities of her own sex, she was absolutely radical.

Hers was a life of example and inspiration, holding out the role of homemaker as an exciting responsibility, a completely satisfying, dignified career choice for which women must constantly seek up-to-date information in order to perform to the best of their abilities. By rejecting Calvinism, and every other religion for all practical purposes, she freed a host of the faithful, her siblings included, from the debilitating threats of an unforgiving, wrathful, paternalistic God. She was not the first woman from whom other women would gain inspiration by imitating what she did rather than what she said, nor would she be the last.

Catharine Esther Beecher suffered a nervous breakdown when she was thirty. She also battled stress and depression throughout life and sought relief for chronic sciatica through established medicine, psychiatry, water cures, clairvoyance, and a multitude of chemical bath spas. Stricken with "apoplexy" in May of 1880, she died two days later. Two weeks before her death, she wrote a column for the newspaper in Elmira, New York, where she had been living with her brother Tom, the kindest of her seven brothers who became ministers, and his wife, Julia: "To the Christian women of Elmira . . . The President of the Board of Education states that there are in this city 1,719 children of legal school age who attend no school, most of whom it is fair to suppose are growing up to ignorance and vice. . . ."

Beecher's death was widely noted throughout the country. The day following, the editor of the Elmira newspaper wrote an eloquent eulogy and an impassioned plea for assistance to those seventeen hundred children as fitting tribute to "Miss Beecher's Legacy." Her unfinished tasks would be left in other hands, just as homage to her deserving spirit remains in ours.

The Hunter's Delight

Cut slices from the ham of a deer, lay them on a dresser, beat them as you would beef-steak, season them with salt, pepper, cloves, mace and nutmegs, then dip them in a rich egg batter. Take soft bread-crumbs, some of the venison minced fine, a little beef-suet, sweet butter, and strew all these over the collops; roll them up, put them on skewers, and roast them. Make a rich gravy with more minced meat and herbs, some butter, pepper, salt, cloves, and pour it over the roasted delights.

—*Mrs. Collins' Table Receipts: Adapted to Western Housewifery*
by Anna Maria Collins
(New Albany, Ind.: Nunemacher, 1851)

"To the Ladies of the West I offer this little volume [144 pages] with full confidence that it will be properly appreciated and well received, and should it in any manner add to their comfort or convenience I shall be full compensated for the employment of my leisure hours."
—Anna Maria Collins
(1851)

Pot au Feu

[NOTE: Charmingly illustrated by Harper Pennington, this book is a well-meaning (however racist), affectionate tribute to the political Eustis's family of "colored" folk.]

Take two pounds of round of beef, cutting off all the fat very carefully, put it in a good sized saucepan, add cold water enough to cover the meat well, put the lid on half way to allow the steam to evaporate, let it simmer by a fire of live coals an hour, and skim carefully as the scum arises. While your broth is cooking, prepare your vegetables, have them nice and fresh, wash and scrape them carefully (requisite care must be taken), throw them into a pan of cold water until the time to use them. Cut three carrots in half, two leeks the same way, or half an onion, a small piece of cabbage and a bit of garlic, a piece of celery, parsley and pepperpod. Put all these vegetables in your broth, adding two or three tomatoes, or two spoonfuls of tomatoes; let it simmer for two hours, skimming it carefully. It can be served with or without vegetables. Without vegetables it can be served as bouillon, to which you add rice, vermicelli, or macaroni or any other Italian paste, or bread dried in the oven, or drop in a poached egg, one for every person, if your dinner is a little short. These receipts were given to me by an old colored cook who was brought up in James Madison's family, and she said they were served on Mr. Madison's table when he entertained the distinguished guests of his day.

—*Cooking in Old Créole Days*
by Celestine Eustis
(New York: Russell, 1903)

The Buckeye Cookbook

The Centennial Buckeye Cook Book (1876) *was patriotically published in Marysville, Ohio (the Buckeye State) by the Buckeye Publishing Company. It was a compilation of recipes created and collected by the women of the First Congregational Church, mainly Estelle Woods Wilcox, although she remained anonymous at the time.*[4] *This edition was the only one to be issued as a fund-raiser. Under Wilcox's authorship, the book was re-issued from Marysville in 1877 without the celebratory title, as* Buckeye Cookery and practical housekeeping, *with pages 305 to 320 of 464 left blank. Four editions were put forth in 1883. The* Buckeye Cook Book *(which was what everybody called it anyway) in English and German and* Practical Housekeeping, *both with the subtitle* a careful compilation of tried and approved recipes, *were published by Buckeye Publishing, now located in Minneapolis, Minnesota and Dayton, Ohio; The* Dixie Cook Book, *based on this book but "carefully compiled from the treasured family collections of many generations of noted housekeepers . . . supplemented by tested recipes . . . contributed by well-known ladies of the South," was published by L. A. Clarkson & Company of Atlanta, Georgia. (An abridged facsimile of one of the northern editions was published in 1975 by Dover Press.) Instructive, discriminating, and thorough in its recipe renditions, most editions contain drawings of such "Kitchen Luxuries" and "Household Conveniences" as the Dover eggbeater (mentioned in chapter 5's dish-washing instructions). The* New Practical Housekeeping, *a 689-page revision, came out in Minneapolis in 1890, published by Home Publishing. Wilcox wrote* The Housekeeper Cook Book *in 1894, which was more of the same, 759 pages, for the Housekeeper Publishing Company of Minneapolis. Anonymously and redundantly, Wilcox dedicated her work to "those plucky housewives who master their work instead of allowing it to master them."*

Yankee Pork and Beans

Pick over carefully a quart of beans and let them soak over night; in the morning wash and drain in another water, put on to boil in

---

4. I could not discover if Wilcox was the owner or the wife of the owner of Buckeye Publishing, but it is likely that there was a connection.

cold water with half a teaspoon of soda; boil about thirty minutes (when done the skin of a bean will crack if taken out and blown upon), drain, and put in an earthen pot first a slice of pork and then the beans, with two or three table-spoons of molasses. When the beans are in the pot, put in the center half- or three-fourths of a pound of well-washed salt pork with the rind scored in slices or squares, and uppermost, season with pepper and salt if needed; cover all with hot water, and bake six hours or longer in a moderate oven, adding hot water as needed; they cannot be baked too long. Keep covered so that they will not burn on the top, but remove cover an hour or two before serving, to brown the top and crisp the pork. This is the Yankee dish for Sunday breakfast. It is often prepared the day before, allowed to remain in the oven all night, and browned in the morning. Serve in the dish in which they are cooked, and always have enough left to know the luxury of cold beans, or baked beans warmed over. If salt pork is too robust for the appetites to be served, season delicately with salt, pepper, and a little butter, and roast a fresh spare-rib to serve with them.

—*The Buckeye Cook Book* (1883)

To Roast a Sparerib of Pork

[NOTE: Mrs. Bryan's excellent cookbook is notable for its articulate recipes and the hospitable manner in which she suggests accouterments.]

Saw the ribs across in several places, for the convenience of carving. Roast it before a clear brisk fire, but be careful not to roast it too brown and hard. Make a rich gravy for the rib, of scraps or trimmings of the fresh meat, butter, flour, parsley, pepper, cream and any kind of catchup you choose. Serve with it apple jelly, a dish of baked sweet potatoes, and one of raw tomatoes, which have been peeled, sliced and highly seasoned with salt, pepper and vinegar.

Kitchen Catchup

Chop fine two quarts of ripe tomatoes, sprinkle them with salt and put them into a pan with one dozen minced onions, a handful of scraped horseradish, and boil them gently for one hour, adding no water, but stirring them frequently. Then strain them, put the liquid into a pan with an equal portion of red wine; add half an ounce of black pepper, half an ounce of nutmegs and half an ounce of cloves.

Cover the pan and boil it gently till reduced to half the original quantity; then cool and bottle it.

—*The Kentucky Housewife*
by Mrs. Lettice Bryan
(Cincinnati: Shepard & Stearns, 1839)

Beef Tournedos

[NOTE: In 1878 Naomi A. Donnelley, wife of publisher R. R. Donnelley of Chicago, started, anonymously, what would become a series of limited-edition cookbooks with "The Lakeside Press" imprint. The book was titled *The Lakeside Cookbook No. 1.* Our entries come from a later book of this series, *Favorite Old Recipes* by Joseph Leiter (1927). A thousand copies were printed, and each cookbook was bestowed "only to my friends who are interested enough to have contributed by suggestion to the conspiracy which led to its hatching."]

A L'EGYPTIENNE: Cut up the noisettes of a filet of beef, let cook on a hot fire, with salt and pepper. Take some slices of egg-plant about two centimetres thick which you have cooked in butter in a stewpan. Dress on each slice of egg-plant, your filets and a small tomato stuffed with egg, bread crumbs and mushrooms, which you pose on your filets. Cover the lot with a good demi-glace.

CHORON: Stew the tournedos in butter. Cover the tournedos with a spoonful of Bearnaise Sauce finished with tomato preserve. Garnish with bottoms of artichokes filled with small peas or asparagus tips. Madeira Sauce.

VIVIENNE: Let the tournedos cook in clarified butter. Dress them on toasted crusts of the same size and which have been passed through melted butter. Place on top of each tournedo an artichoke bottom garnished with puree of tomatoes. Enclose the tournedos in small potato croquettes around the edge of the plate.

Anonymous to Pseudonym

"Marion Harland" was the androgynous pseudonym chosen by Mrs. Mary Virginia (Hawes) Terhune of South Ninth Street in Brooklyn, New York, who wrote several sensationally successful cookbooks and novels from the 1850s to the 1870s. Both her first novel Alone *(1854) and her magazine series-turned-cookbook titled* Common Sense in the Household *(1871) sold more than a hundred thousand copies in ten years, although they were*

felt by some to be "tiresomely chatty." According to a biographical sketch in The Ladies Home Journal (August, 1887), Terhune was the "descendant of a cultivated Virginia family, of a mother gentle, refined and born and bred with quiet domestic and literary tastes," inheriting from her father "the pith and earnestness for which . . . life is distinguished."

Perhaps this traditional southern upbringing was the reason she began writing under the protection of obscurity, but it was unusual that she did not reveal herself publicly even after the entire country was on to her deception. Did she like her pen name and the independence her alter ego afforded her? Or perhaps she did not want to upstage "the popular pastor of the Bedford Avenue First Reform Church," as her husband is described in the same article: "a genial, magnetic man of splendid physique, standing six feet in his stockings and broad-shouldered in proportion. He is a specimen of muscular Christianity good to see" declares the author, Florine Thayer McCray.

Terhune considered motherhood "three halves" the reason for her existence, raising three of four children to adulthood. Two daughters followed her with outstanding literary careers of their own, but a third died a somewhat mysterious death. Reportedly, a servant dressed as a ghost frightened the imaginative child and threw her into convulsions from which she never rallied. Terhune was described as a "medium sized woman, with a sweet, piquant face, dark hair and eyes sparkling with kindliness and a hopeful view of life." She made time to take charge of the social interests of the parish as a faithful pastor's wife should, doubtless remaining throughout her life "one of the busiest women in the country."

Mrs. Mary Virginia (Hawes) Terhune, aka Marion Harland (1830–1922)

Asparagus Biscuit

Scrape the crumb from the inside of stale biscuits, leaving a thin wall on all sides, except the tops. These should be carefully cut off and set aside. Rub the inside of each biscuit with butter, also the under part of the crust-cover, and set them, open, the crusts beside them, in a moderate oven. Heat in a saucepan a cupful of boiled asparagus, chopped and prepared with drawn butter. Do this when the biscuits are crisp and hot, and so soon as the asparagus-mixture is heated throughout, smoking as you stir it, fill the prepared cavities with it, fit on the tops, and send hot to the table.

—The Cottage Kitchen
by Marion Harland
[Mary Virginia Terhune]
(New York: C. Scribner's Sons, 1883)

Grilled Shoulder of Lamb

Score it each way an inch apart and brush the surface with melted butter and the beaten yolk of an egg. Sprinkle with grated bread crumbs, salt, pepper and sweet herbs. Roast until tender. For the gravy, take a tablespoon of flour made smooth with water for the required amount, and a tablespoon of tomato catsup and grated rind and juice of a lemon and salt and pepper to taste.

—Mrs. [Frances E.] Owens' New Cook
Book and Complete Household Manual
(Chicago: Owens, 1899)

Cutlet Surprises

Cut slices from leg of lamb. Over each spread turkey stuffing, then three large oysters. Roll and pin with toothpicks. Place in pan with lumps of butter and a little water around them. Cook one hour and baste often. Add Worcestershire sauce to gravy.

—Tennessee Cookbook
by Mrs. Reese Lillard
(Lebanon, Tenn.: McQuiddy, 1912)

Artichoke Fricassee

Clean young artichokes, cutting off the stalks, all the outer leaves and thorny ends; then cut in thin slices, throw them into fresh water, drain, and place in a saucepan with butter, parsley, a little minced garlic, and salt to taste. Cook slowly until tender; before drawing from the fire add the yolks of two or more eggs, that you have first beaten together with a little water, some lemon juice and grated Parmesan cheese. Be careful to stir constantly and not allow the egg to burn. Serve when it is of a creamy consistency.

—High Living, Recipes from
Southern Climes
by L. L. McLaren
(Published for the benefit of the
Telegraph Hill Neighborhood
Association, San Francisco, 1904;
published again in 1907 to benefit
victims of the 1906 earthquake.)

Potatoes

A good roasted potato is a delicacy worth a dozen compositions of the cook-book; yet when we ask for it, what burnt, shriveled abortions are presented to us! Biddy rushes to her potato-basket and pours out two dozen of different sizes, some having in them three times the amount of matter of others. These being washed, she tumbles them into her oven at a leisure interval, and there lets them lie till it is time to serve breakfast, whenever that may be. As a result, if the largest are cooked, the smallest are presented in cinders, and the intermediate sizes are withered and watery . . . In the same manner we have seen boiled potatoes from an untaught cook coming upon the table like lumps of yellow wax— and the same article, under the directions of a skillful mistress, appearing in snowy balls of powdery whiteness. In the one case, they were thrown in their skins into water, and suffered to soak or boil, as the case might be, at the cook's leisure, and after they were boiled to stand in the water till she was ready to peel them. In the other case, the potatoes being first peeled were boiled as quickly as possible in salted water, which the moment they were done was drained off, and then they were gently shaken for a moment or two over the fire to dry them still more thoroughly. . . . As to fried potatoes, who that remembers the crisp, golden slices of the French restaurant, thin as wafers and light as snowflakes, does not speak respectfully of them? What cousinship with these have those coarse, greasy masses of sliced potato, wholly soggy and partly burnt, to which we are treated under the name of fried potatoes in America?

—Miss Beecher's Domestic Receipt Book
(New York: Harper & Brothers, 1846)

Foreign-language Cookbooks Published in the United States

"The earliest French language work was La Petite Cuisinere Habile by Mme. Utrecht-Freidel (New Orleans, 1840); the first German, Hochst Nüzliches Handbuch uber Kochkunst [by Dr. G. Girardey] (Cincinnati, 1842); and the first Spanish, Novisimo Arte de Cocina (Philadelphia, 1845). Recent schol-

arship . . . indicates that the Spanish book was simply published in the United States but was actually intended for Mexican distribution."

—*American Cookbooks and Wine Books 1797-1950,* an outstanding bibliography by Janice Bluestein Longone and Daniel T. Longone (Ann Arbor, 1984)

Spanish Omelette

Chop into dice one fourth pound of breakfast bacon, a small tomato, four mushrooms, mince very fine a small onion; add pepper to taste, put in a frying pan and cook slowly until the bacon is done; take off and put in a warm place to keep hot. This is sufficient for six eggs.

—*Clayton's Quaker Cook Book* by H. J. Clayton (San Francisco: The Women's Co-Operative Printing Office, 1883)

Bishop

Rub a fresh lemon on 2 pounds of hard loaf sugar, add 1-2 ounce cinnamon broken in small pieces, 3 dozen cloves, the juice of 4 oranges and 3 quarts claret wine; put all in a bowl, cover it and let it stand for 24 hours; then filtrate it through a cloth. If strong port wine is used, this drink bears the name of Cardinal.

—*The North American Compiler . . .* by Dr. G. Girardey (Cincinnati, 1844, printed in the formidable fraktur)

Meat Pies

Considering the popularity of these dishes, few make their appearance on the table nicely prepared. When the meat is cooked in the pastry, I do not think they are healthful for anyone. Make a nice pastry and line a pan with it, lay broom straws over the pan, then put on the top crust; put it in the oven and bake. Cut up a steak into small pieces (cold, underdone steak, or roast may be used), put into a stewpan and cook until tender. Season with pepper and salt to taste and a little butter; thicken the gravy with a little flour. When the pastry is done, lift off the cover and pour the meat in and serve at once, or the under crust will become soggy. Rabbits and squirrels make nice pies. Cut them into pieces and stew until the meat will fall from the bones; season and thicken the gravy. Potatoes and a little tomato catsup or wine may be added to these pies.

—*Housekeeping and Dinner Giving in Kansas City*
by Mrs. T. F. Willis and
Mrs. W. S. Bird
(Kansas City: Ramsey, Millett & Hudson, 1887)

"The kitchen is the most important room in the house, as the comfort of the household depends on the management and order of the kitchen."
—Mrs. T. F. Willis and
Mrs. W. S. Bird (1887)

Chicken Tamales
(Submitted by Mrs. Charles Stevens)

One cup minced chicken, one tablespoon chile, chopped fine (omit seeds), three spoons chicken stock, one-half cup chopped olives. Mix well. Take a large spoonful of rather stiff corn meal mush, flatten to half an inch, put on a spoonful of the mixture and roll this in a clean, smooth corn husk, fold the ends over and tie securely. Drop these in boiling fat the same as doughnuts, cook about the same length of time.

Chiles Rellenos de Queso
(Green peppers filled with cheese, contributed by A. O. H.)

Toast green peppers and wrap them in a towel a few minutes to loosen the skin; skin them and take out all the veins with great care; wash the peppers in salt and water; dry them and fill with grated cheese. Beat separately three eggs, more may be needed if there are many chiles; dip each chile in the egg, the yolk and white together with a little salt added; then in flour and fry in hot lard. The lard should be very hot and the chile removed as soon as it is well browned.

—*El Paso Cookbook*
by the YMCA Ladies Auxiliary (1898)

Orange Pudding

[NOTE: This recipe is taken from a small handbook that is recorded in Waldo Lincoln's bibliography and declared in Katherine Golden Bitting's to be "the first book treating on cookery printed in the Middle West." While the husbandman's information is thorough and interesting, the housewife's section is not imaginative; perhaps more for the former's use the book was highly popular, and copies are held in many libraries throughout the country. Barnum and Roff were members of the Ohio Historical and Philosophical Society in Cincinnati and officials of the Hamilton County Fair.]

Grate the rind of a Seville orange: Put to it six ounces of fresh butter, six or eight ounces of lump-sugar pounded: beat them all in a marble mortar, and add as you do it, the whole of eight eggs well beaten and strained; scrape a raw apple, and mix with the rest; put a paste at the bottom and sides of the dish, and over the orange mixture put cross bars of paste. Half an hour will bake.

—*Family Receipts, or, Practical Guide for the Husbandman and Housewife* by H. L. Barnum (Cincinnati: A. B. Roff, 1831)

Rocky Mountain Cake

1 scant cup of sugar
½ cup butter
½ teaspoonful of baking powder
¼ teaspoonful of salt
½ cup of milk
3 eggs
1¾ cups of flour
flavoring

Cream the butter and the sugar, add flavoring of any kind, the well-beaten eggs, part of the flour (with the salt and baking powder sifted in it), the milk and the rest of the flour; beat thoroughly for ten minutes. Loaf or layer cake; bake in gem pans if you like.

Make "Rocky Mountain" Cake; mix melted chocolate with one-third of it; put in the pan a layer of the plain cake, then the chocolate mixture, after that the remainder of the mixture. A very nice way to make marble cake is to take one-third of the mixture of "Rocky Mountain" cake and mix with it spices, currants and citron, or a little preserved orange or lemon peel.

The greatest difference between sea level cooking and here is in the cakes. Most of the sea level receipts can be used here by adding another egg to them, that gives a delicious, moist, rich cake. Water boils at sea level at 212 degrees. In Denver, where the air is much lighter, it boils at 202 degrees; therefore, it does not reach as great a heat here, so vegetables or anything boiled requires a little longer cooking.

—*The Rocky Mountain Cookbook*
by Caroline Trask Norton
(Denver: W. F. Robinson, 1903)

LaFayette Cake

[NOTE: Although this little fifty-eight-page booklet, The Cake Baker, is subtitled A *book of practical recipes for making cake, as made by Mrs. Crawford at her celebrated Bakery, New York City, and at the Bakery, No. 32 Steuben St., Albany, established by Mrs. Crawford, and at present known as Cooper's Bakery*, it is suggested in Lowenstein's bibliography to be the first cookbook published west of Indiana. The only known surviving copy is housed in the Newberry Library in Chicago, Illinois.]

8 ounces of white sugar
6 ounces of butter
½ a nutmeg
5 eggs
½ a gill of brandy
½ a pound of flour
1 pound of jelly or jam (88 cents worth)

Grate the nutmeg into the sugar and add the butter; rub them to a fine cream, beat the eggs well and add them, keeping it well stirred to prevent the mixture from curdling—then the brandy. Now sift in the flour and mix carefully; bake in thin sheets on paper; this should make four about 8-inches in diameter and half an inch thick. When baked, take them carefully off the paper and divide the jelly into three parts; spread one part on the first cake, and put the next cake on that, spread the jelly again on the top and cover it with a cake, and so on till all are used, leaving the top and bottom without jelly.

—*The Cake Baker*
by Mrs. Crawford
(Chicago: Isaac A. Pool, 1857)

Wedding Fruit Cake

2 pounds raisins stoned, 2 pounds currants, 1 pound sliced citron, a few figs cut in small pieces. Pour over this 1 goblet sherry and port wine, ½ goblet brandy or whiskey, let stand over night and in morning pour on what liquor has not soaked into fruit. 1 pound butter, 1 pound sugar, yolks 12 eggs, 2 tablespoons mace, 1 tablespoon cinnamon, 2 nutmegs, 1 pound browned flour and (the beaten) whites of 12 eggs. Dissolve 1 teaspoon soda in a little water, add just before putting in fruit.

Prunes in Ambush

Boil one cupful of rice in milk, sweeten to taste and pour into a ring mold. When cold turn out on a platter and fill the center with stewed prunes. Pour some of the prune juice over the rice and cover the prunes with whipped cream.

—*The Kentucky Cook Book*
by a Colored Woman [Mrs. W. T. Hayes, Emma Allen]
(St. Louis: J. H. Thomkins, 1912)

"This book is the work of a colored cook of many years' experience and who has had ample opportunity for experimenting and testing the recipes presented. They are simple and easily made, and have proved to be excellent. The book will be found a most useful addition to any kitchen."
—Mrs. W. T. Hayes (1912)

Egg Lemonade

Grate over the sugar the peel of half the lemons you intend to use, and squeeze the lemon into it with a squeezer. Then beat up as many eggs as you intend glasses of lemonade. If you are making a quantity you may take one or two eggs less. Beat up the lemons and the sugar, next add water in proportion and then shake or beat the whole vigorously for a few seconds. Fill the tumblers half full of broken ice. Before serving shake again.

Yum-Yums

Beat the whites of two eggs to a stiff froth, adding gradually one cup of confectioners sugar and one heaping cupful of desiccated cocoanut, and two heaping teaspoonfuls of arrowroot. Drop from the teaspoonful upon buttered paper in a large baking pan. Drop an inch apart. Bake in moderate oven fifteen minutes.

—*"Aunt Babette's" Cookbook*
by Mrs. Bertha F. Kramer
(Cincinnati: Bloch, 1891)

To Make a Hen's Nest

Get five small eggs, make a hole at one end, and empty the shells, fill them with blanc mange; when stiff and cold take off the shells; pare the yellow rind very thin from six lemons, boil them in water till tender, then cut them in thin strips to resemble straw, and preserve them with sugar; fill a small deep dish half full of nice jelly; when it is set put the straw on in form of a nest, and lay the eggs in it. It is a beautiful dish for a dessert or supper.

—*Cookbook of the Northwest*
compiled by the Ladies of the
Westminster Presbyterian Church
(Keokuk, Iowa, 1875)

Female Obstructions[5]

Take one tablespoonful tincture of guaiacum in half a cup of milk, at the full moon; or, Take a strong tea made of Seneca snakeroot, as much as the stomach will bear; or, Take of borax, saffron, myrrh, each 10 grains; salt of amber, four grains; this may be taken at one dose.

---

5. Although I have chosen to concentrate on recipes of cookery and not the various formulas for other household chores and medicinal cures, it would be remiss not to make special note of the one female cookbook author who dared speak outright to "sister, mother, and wife" on the most delicate of subjects: female complaints. This cause was alluded to by husbandmen and doctors in their manuals, but they usually had more to say about cows' teats than women's breasts, and the advice was so vague that a cure for menstrual problems, for instance, did not specify whether the menses would be brought on or shut down by a certain prescription. I did not test these cures; nevertheless, common sense indicates that the remedy for sore nipples would work.

Menstrual Discharges

In order to check the too free discharge, take of burnt alum, three drachms, dragon's blood one drachm; and make into pills. Dose, four or five, night and morning; or, Make a tea of snakeweed, or yarrow, and drink freely; or, In order to help the discharge, take one teaspoonful of the tincture of gum guaiacum in a tumbler of new milk on going to bed, two or three nights before the full moon; and at the same time, make a strong tea of snakeroot, and drink in the course of the day as much as the stomach will bear. This may be depended upon as an infallible remedy.

Sore Nipples

Spread a plaster of fir balsam, and apply it to the breast after the child has nursed.

—Ladies Indispensable Assistant
by E. Hutchinson
(New York, 1850)

Teaching the American Tradition

Regional cooking accelerated after the Civil War, and by 1900 cooking schools were in every major city in America. The most prolific authors, however, were in Boston, Philadelphia, and, to an extent, New York, educating women (who would not have otherwise dared to apply anywhere as chefs, a "man's profession") to (1) work in or run school, hospital, prison, and asylum kitchens; (2) open confectionery shops and tearooms; (3) manage small catering services; (4) give public lectures on cookery and diet; (5) design, on a limited basis, utensils and cooking vessels, tableware, appliances, and even kitchens; (6) create recipes and demonstrate new products for food manufacturers; (7) teach in public schools, clubs, settlement houses, and some colleges; and, of course, (8) write magazine articles and cookbooks. Later on, cooks and cookbook authors would invade the air waves as radio personalities on daily and weekly "kitchen" shows, discussing everything from lumpy mashed potatoes to the repasts of Hollywood stars. Hundreds wrote textbooks published by school boards and designed for use in public schools (and it is a strange phenomenon that so many of these authors were named Ida, Edna, or Isabel), with tremendously varying results. Almost all of these opportunities for women offered secure employment where very little had existed before, and cookery-related jobs became the first (virtuous) field of endeavor—outside homemaking—in which women outnumbered men.

Many of these early career women did not marry or did not remarry after being widowed. The fact that their chosen profession was centered in the home did not spare them from the hypocrisy of a society that viewed ambition as unfeminine and educating women as a waste of time. But their contribution could not be denied, and they were supported by the group that needed them most: other women.

As cooking schools gained prestige, their principals and superintendents became national celebrities. They knew each other and shared the applause on lecture circuits. Their lectures were well attended and reported in lengthy and adoring detail in daily newspapers and magazines. Church and club cookbooks reprinted recipes from cooking school cookbooks and lectures, and credited them graciously. Indeed, as any cookbook collector knows, some women cut additional recipes or lessons from the newspaper articles and pasted them on the blank pages of their own cooking school cookbooks.

Competition among these ambitious celebrities was not acknowledged, but it was inevitable and exploited when industry tried to tempt them away from nutritional objectivity, to cajole them into shelving common sense—to compete, to succeed, to make money, to invent new "secret methods." At the same time, religious leaders began to take their assumed duty as social reformers seriously, arming themselves with nutritional truths certain to bring health and happiness into every home (see chapter 6). What finally occurred a few decades later was that the creative art of cooking a delicious meal at home took on a bullying aspect, which resulted in sillifying a natural science (e.g., one-eighth teaspoon pepper) that put off many homemakers, confusing and confounding them.

However, women with creative urges had very little opportunity or encouragement to act on such talents anywhere except in their homes, and whether they were paid or not, they constantly found themselves coming back to the pots and pans for fulfillment.

Fundamentally, the legacy of the women of America's cooking schools is one of dedication, generosity, accomplishment in spite of tragic personal adversity, love and respect for one another as capable professionals, and yes—unusual culinary talent. The authors refined the technique of writing concise cooking instructions for beginners and experienced cooks, as well as for people who did not and would never have a propensity for cooking. At worst, the authors only temporarily thwarted the talent and curiosity of a gifted but yet untutored cook, giving her techniques to survive, perhaps even to flourish. At best, they saved women's lives, bestowing positive reinforcement and practical, orderly example.

The efforts of these women have lately been viewed cynically by women who criticize such faulty nutritional habits as the so-called disproportionate amount of dessert (sugar) recipes contained in the cookbooks. But any skilled everyday cook would pounce upon the probable excuse for this occurrence. Cakes, pies, and quick breads— with their more complicated ingredients—eggs, leavening, various grinds of flour, fresh or soured milk, and selected baking powder chemistries—were not remembered as easily as recipes for vegetables, fruits, grains, and seasonings. In other words, you could make a fool of yourself more easily at dessert time, and beginning cooks welcomed foolproof formulas in print. Cookbook authors were— and still are—chastised for selling out to industry in the field of product endorsement when they had no hope of earning the salary of other professionals who perhaps studied less and worked fewer hours. There is also a temptation to poke fun at the bizarre, too-cute recipes that can certainly be found among the multitude of sensible ones in the cooking school cookbooks, although these eye-catching entries in no way represent the totality of the contribution these early teachers made. Judging them without taking into account the complexities of the society that surrounded them including years of war rationing and the effect of the draft on farm output, is grossly unfair.

Master Chef James Beard dedicated *James Beard's American Cookery* (1972) to "my favorite great ladies of the American kitchen," a tribute he was often wont to make: "The written record of our cuisine is in many ways more complete than that of any other country. Beginning with Amelia Simmons we have the wisdom of such notables as Eliza Leslie, Catharine Beecher, Mrs. T. J. Crowen, Marion Harland [Mary Virginia (Hawes) Terhune], Maria Parloa, Mrs. Sarah Tyson Rorer, Mrs. Mary Lincoln, and Fannie Merritt Farmer."

Beard, labeled posthumously as the "Father of American Cooking," was correct in his assessment that our written food record is awesome, but the existence of that history must be seen for what it is: proof that our national cuisine was conceived, developed, penned, and conserved almost entirely by women. It is not a record that can be judged by a few books or the comparison of a few recipes. Rather, the essential American cuisine—the product of these and other women of wisdom—is a living, changing, improving discipline reflected in the average American's relative eagerness to try new foods, to be concerned with nutrition and yet retain cherished family traditions. It is a history that sustains us, and we can be proud of it.

The history of the Boston Cooking School must start with the woman who would claim (in the same year Fannie Merritt Farmer entered it) that she was "founder of the original Cooking School in Boston." Although misleading, that title page credential was as authentic as the many others Maria Parloa held when *Miss Parloa's Kitchen Companion* was published in 1887.

Having acquired expertise with private families and as a pastry cook in several New Hampshire summer resorts including the Appledore House on the Isles of Shoals, she took friends' advice and opened a cooking school in Boston but left a year later to teach in Mandarin, Florida, where Harriet Beecher Stowe had a home. In March of 1879 Parloa returned to Boston as one of two teachers at the Woman's Education Association's newly opened Boston Cooking School. She was invited to take charge but declined. Fees as a lecturer and royalties from the *Appledore Cookbook* (1872), *Camp Cookery* (1878), and *First Principles of Household Management and Cookery* (1879) were adding to her personal wealth, and Parloa shied away from a routine commitment. Nevertheless, she did agree to lecture every other Saturday, and because of her reputation the school was off and running. A two-year course was offered that would train women to earn a living, from the rudiments into the realm of expert. The first building was located at 158 Tremont Street; later the address was 372 Boylston Street. Johanna Sweeney, an Irish girl, was hired as director on a temporary basis until Mary Johnson (Bailey) Lincoln was approached. (Sweeney's dismissal may have been attributable to racism.) With no experience but with average talent and potential, Lincoln steered the school farther forward, lecturing throughout the country, and accomplishing cookbooks of her own: *The Peerless Cook-Book* (1886) and *New England Cook Book* (with Parloa, 1894). In 1894 she also wrote *The Boston Cook Book* (237 pages), a friendly but preachy manual with few actual recipes and not at all a forerunner to Farmer's classic as some believe.

After finishing her own two-year stint as a student gloriously, Fannie Merritt Farmer stayed on as assistant principal, becoming director five years later. Coming from "untainted New England stock," the bookish, Unitarian Farmer was lame from a childhood disease now believed to be polio. She was an exacting instructor, testing and retesting each dish until satisfied that it was as perfect as it could be, much to the exhaustion of her disciples in their stiffly starched aprons and lacy caps. These students, most of whom came from Ireland, were taught, in groups of eight, basic cooking, advanced cooking, presentation, serving, care for the kitchen, and personal grooming at about $1 a lesson.

In 1896, exactly one hundred years after Amelia Simmons published the first American cookbook, Farmer finished her 831-page

Fannie Merritt Farmer
(1857–1915)

masterpiece. She had to pay Little, Brown and Company (who had published a few cookbooks, perhaps unprofitably, as early as 1831) the initial cost of publishing, and correct the galleys herself with pen dipped in India ink.

Although many cooks have since hailed *The Boston Cooking-School Cook Book* as the last of the "luxurious" cookbooks until long after World War I, it has recently come under attack for its concise rather than long-drawn-out explanations. But it must be remembered that the text was written to accompany cooking classes. It was completely modern in the concept that it was to be consulted not read, respecting the ultimate truth that most cooks learn from watching and doing, rather than reading. There may have been a certain assumption of expertise, yet the tested recipes were still instruction enough for novices to create a decent meal on the very first try. Farmer respected the truth that some women didn't have cooking talent, didn't want to learn but inherited the responsibility nonetheless, didn't have the time, or simply didn't want to spend their life in the kitchen like their European counterparts. She invented the short "formula" recipe to enable these busy women to perform the task quickly, almost without thinking.

Although she was not the first to recommend specific measurements as some believe, she and Mary Johnson Lincoln were the first to tabulate ingredients at the head of the recipe and designate, for instance, that a teaspoonful be level.[1] The ingredients were not yet listed in order of use, but this method made it infinitely easier for the cook to check whether she had the necessary groceries on hand to fulfill a planned meal.

American women at the turn of the century recognized Farmer's talent and serious dedication to "women's" responsibilities and responded in the appropriate fashion. They bought the book—by the

---

1. Specific measurements (e.g. one cup or two teaspoonfuls) were being used in England long before the first American cookbook was printed. In a diatribe against formula recipes, precise measurements, and white sauce, Karen and John Hess, authors of *The Taste of America* (New York: Grossman, 1977), sexistly dismiss Fannie Farmer as the "maiden aunt of home economists." Laura Shapiro, in an otherwise informative history of American cooking schools, *Perfection Salad: Women and Cooking at the Turn of the Century* (New York: Farrar, 1986), pits one cookbook author against another, and about Farmer snipes "she left behind a kitchen she had helped, crucially, to redirect toward social homogeneity and American cheese." Such comments are typical of the type of criticism cookbook authors experience at the hands of journalists attempting to gain notoriety as food wits.

thousands. It was prized as a "married cookbook," one that could be confidently bestowed upon a bride about to set up housekeeping. It was reprinted twice in 1897 and annually for decades; in 1906 it was revised to incorporate gas and electric cookery. It was also reprinted in England and is believed to be the first American cookbook translated into French, Spanish, and Japanese.

In the meantime, the book's success propelled the school and its subsequent *Boston Cooking-School Magazine* Company to unparalleled heights. Graduates contributed to the magazine, and, in turn, the magazine published their cookbooks and pamphlets. Boston Cooking School credentials seemed to be the passport to publication: graduates Lucy A. Allen, Alice Bradley, Anne Barrows, Mary D. Chambers, and Janet McKenzie Hill, editor of the magazine for several years, produced multiple titles, as did Parloa and Lincoln. Farmer's subsequent five major titles were *Chafing Dish Possibilities* (1898); *Food and Cookery for the Sick and Convalescent* (1904), her personal favorite based on lectures at Harvard Medical School; *What to Have for Dinner* (1905); *Catering for Special Occasions* (1911); and *A New Book of Cookery* (1912). She also wrote pamphlets that were attractively printed and illustrated by famous contemporary artists. One door that was left ajar to all was that of the amazed Little, Brown and Company. Fannie Farmer's cookbook had turned out to be their second-best seller, going through twenty-one printings before her death.[2]

Farmer resigned her position in 1902 to lecture and open her own Miss Farmer's School of Cookery, catering more to housewives and society girls than cooks-for-hire. The Boston Cooking School closed its doors in 1903, the year after she left. For ten years, from 1905 to 1915, Farmer edited a page on cooking in the *Woman's Home Companion* with her sister Cora Dexter (Farmer) Perkins.

In her later years Fannie Farmer was a striking figure, slender and firmly corseted, a gold-rimmed pince-nez emphasizing her vivid blue eyes, her red hair graying handsomely. When she could no longer walk, she continued to lecture from a wheelchair, her legs

---

2. First place went to Henryk Sienkiewicz's *Quo Vadis*. Little, Brown also eventually published another classic in *Ruth Wakefield's Toll House* cookbook (1930), an extension of the Toll House restaurant in Whitman, Massachusetts, where New England cooking school fare was refined, and Toll House cookies invented. The book, revised several times, went through thirty-two printings. Whitman's recipe-writing style may have influenced Irma Rombauer.

covered and straight out in front of her. Like her cookbook, her school outlived its founder and was supervised from 1915 to 1944 by Alice Bradley. Fannie Farmer was a wealthy woman at the time of her death, having invested in utilities, railroads, and a chocolate company. Her savings were distributed among nineteen bank accounts.

And what happened to Parloa? In 1881 she opened a school near Stuyvesant Square in New York City; went on to write the first cookbook for the Washburn Crosby Company, a flour milling concern later called General Mills; and thus became the only live woman ever to receive author credit from Betty Crocker country. She also became part-owner of a magazine that she hoped would prosper. It was called *The Ladies Home Journal.*

By the end of the nineteenth century, immigrants were flooding into America, many unable to speak the language and all unfamiliar with the culture. When Mrs. Simon Kander (Lizzie Black), a member of a Milwaukee, Wisconsin, Reformed Jewish congregation, learned of the problems of Jewish arrivals to her hometown, she became active in the newly formed Ladies Relief Sewing Society, whose goal was to repair used clothing to give to the needy. The organization became the Milwaukee Jewish Mission, and the women expanded their charity to include teaching young children sewing and other marketable skills. The women also gave sermons on cleanliness that clients found insulting.

Mrs. Simon (Lizzie Black) Kander (1858–1940)

In 1900 they united with the Sisterhood of Personal Service to form a social "settlement" and rented a house on Fifth Street. Soon the Settlement was bursting with creative energy. There was special instruction for mothers and night classes in English and American history for adults. Clubs such as the Arbeiter Ring, Poalay Zion Singing Society, Yiddish Dramatic Society, Newsboys Literary Circle, Boxing Club, and Campfire Girls all thrived within these walls, welcoming native Jews as well as newcomers. A savings bank and gymnasium were opened, and by the time the Settlement moved to larger quarters in 1904, approximately seventeen thousand adults and children a year were spending a few cents each to suds up in their public baths.

One of the most popular courses was a domestic lesson taught by Kander and her colleagues; they instructed in modern house-keeping methods and how to prepare simple, nutritional meals using American products. As the lesson grew into a series of classes, it became apparent that a workbook would make things easier for all concerned. The girls would not have to spend so much time copying the recipes and instructions from the blackboard, and the women would not have to write them out in the first place, only to have them erased for another class. The volunteers applauded the idea, but the men of the Settlement board refused to invest the needed $18 to print such a book, advising volunteers to subsidize it on their own. It is said that the board laughingly told the women that it would be willing to "share in any profits from your little venture," however.

Kander and four other women went ahead, gathering recipes from volunteers and their friends (many were noted Milwaukee hostesses) and favorite European dishes from the students and their families and later from a few noted chefs. They obtained sufficient advertising to offset the printing cost and arranged with a local department store to place extra copies on sale for 50 cents each. In 1901, a thousand copies of *The Way to a . . . Man's Heart (sic)*; *"The Settlement" Cook Book* were published with no author given. A second printing was done under the same title in 1903, but the title page reveals that the book was compiled by Mrs. Simon Kander and Mrs. Henry Schoenfeld. Several printings later it would be called simply *The Settlement Cook Book*. As her colleagues retired or died, Lizzie Kander became more closely associated with the book's progress and fame, editing and revising it personally from 1914 until her death in 1940.

Because the text was expanded so greatly over the years, many believe it to have been a huge manual. It was not. *The Settlement Cook Book* was a modest 174 pages of appetizingly basic cooking, indicative of the good, hearty Russian-German fare produced in the Upper Midwest, where winters are long and cold. Twenty-four lessons are stipulated at the beginning of the manual, with page-numbered recipes designated to guide students through the rigors of preparing eggs, fish, soup, meats, and so on.

When the Settlement Committee took possession of its newly built Abraham Lincoln House in 1911, the trustees of *The Settlement Cook Book* contributed $5,560 toward the building's cost of $18,000. They also donated a monthly stipend of $150, all from the "little venture."

The Settlement Cook Book holds the record as the country's most profitable fund-raising cookbook. The classic original was updated, revised, and expanded (but not always improved) through forty editions, selling almost two million copies. Nearly thirty editions of the cookbook can be viewed at the Milwaukee Public Library, including perhaps the only existing copy of the original. (In 1984 a facsimile of this original was produced by Hugh Lauter Levin Associates in

New York and distributed by Scribner's.) Cookbook historians acknowledge those determined women and their accomplishment, but it is also a tribute to Lizzie Black Kander and her friends that the multifaceted Jewish Community Center of Milwaukee exists today.

According to the Census of 1900, there were twenty-nine million wage-earners in America. Ninety percent of the nearly two million who were women were listed as domestics. This was a conservative estimate, not including the large numbers of workers who hired out part time. Although no one listed the job of "millionaire" on the census form, there were quite a few, more than there ever were or have been since. Every family that could afford help had it. Kitchen help, child-care, and laundry workers were the most frequently sought after, and folks such as the Astors, Rockefellers, Vanderbilts, Belmonts, and Longworths managed their mansions only with the assistance of a dozen or more servants.

This country was formed upon principles of personal freedom, however, and American domestics—no matter what their country of origin—did not like being "servants." Quite outspokenly, most considered domestic employment as a temporary situation while they amassed the fortune or made the connections or patented the invention that would propel them into a better life. This attitude, and servants' notorious undependability, gave rise to an industry of domestic employment agencies called "intelligence offices." Butlers, maids of all kinds, valets, footmen, chauffeurs, laundresses, liverymen, gardeners, and cooks were marketed. Mrs. Seely's Intelligence office would eventually be one of the very few established firms; most were as fly-by-night as their employees.

Lida was born Eliza Campbell in Canada in 1854. She married a bank cashier named Holly Seely, and the couple set up housekeeping in Manhattan. It is probable that Seely herself hired out before deciding to become an entrepreneur and set up an intelligence office on 22nd Street off lower Fifth Avenue. When her manual appeared in 1902, published by Macmillan (it was reprinted in 1908 by Grosset & Dunlap), it was apparent that this kind and wise woman possessed an astonishing knowledge about this complicated field of expertise. More important, she had an extraordinary ability to define and defend the problems and concerns of families both "upstairs and downstairs."

Mrs. Lida A. Seely
(1854–1928)

Mrs. Seely's Cook Book, a Manual of French and American Cookery with Chapters on Domestic Servants, their Rights and Duties, and Many Other Details of Household Management spells out those rights and duties in rational terms, including a detailed expected pay scale in

Part 1 (forty-two pages). Chapters 5 and 6 contain lists of don'ts for employer and servants, respectively, and the lists are almost equal in length. She admonishes the mistress to give servants some privacy, be clear about her expectations, never to spy on them, and not expect perfection. Employees are enjoined to listen, refrain from hiding breakage, never spy, and not think their mistress unbearable when she is a little short-tempered: "ladies often have worries and responsibilities of which servants have no idea."

The remaining 350 pages of this superior book feature sixteen chapters of lavish, delectable European-American recipes graciously presented within alphabetized chapters. The whole provides an authentic, fascinating look into the world from which turn-of-the-century television miniseries are fashioned.

The 1984 "facsimile" of this book, published by American Antique Cookbooks, Oxmoor House, Inc., Birmingham, Alabama, with special historical contents, is a singularly beautiful and informative reproduction of an old cookbook, probably the finest currently available.

Seely's venture was extremely profitable until her retirement. She died in 1928 at the age of seventy-four, never knowing of the stock market crash and depression that would change American society, as she knew it so well, forever.

Others in New York received classes in food wisdom from a talented woman whose short life was dedicated primarily to the underprivileged. Born in 1841 in Roxbury, Massachusetts, one of Juliet Corson's first jobs was working in a girls' library, where she was paid a small stipend and given a sleeping room. This firsthand experience with poverty instigated within her a social conscience that matured into significant productivity. When she was thirty-three, she organized a cooking course at the Free Training School for Women, lecturing while a chef did the actual preparations, because she could not cook.[3]

But Juliet Corson was a quick study; she opened the New York Cooking School in her home at St. Mark's Place in November 1876. The school averaged one thousand students annually; the rich paid full fees, the middle class five cents a lesson, and the poor were welcomed without charge.

---

3. The chef was probably Pierre Blot, a Paris-trained chef who organized a tour of lectures throughout the eastern states in the 1860s.

Cooking Manual (1877) was written to help working-class wives and daughters learn to fix a decent meal or get a job as a cook. Corson's most interesting book, *Practical American Cookery* (1885), was the result of a joint effort with the U.S. Department of Education to tout authentic regional cookery. As unemployment continued to rise in the 1870s she wrote and self-published a controversial pamphlet, "Fifteen-Cent Dinners for Families of Six," distributing fifty thousand copies, most of them free of charge. The pamphlet, a huge success, was reprinted by the *Baltimore Daily News* and the *Philadelphia Record* and translated into several languages, yet criticized by some who feared that proof of how cheaply people could live would cause a lowering of wages. Meeting this challenge head-on a year later, she composed "Twenty-Five Cent Dinners for Families of Six."

Corson never married, preferring instead to live in austerity with her pets. She wrote other cookery publications for the Department of Education and set up programs dealing with domestic economy in Washington D.C., Oakland, California and other cities until her death at fifty-six.

America's first cooking school is believed to have been Mrs. Elizabeth Goodfellow's Cooking School. She arrived in Philadelphia in 1806 as the widow Eliza Coane and opened a confectionery at 68 Dock Street. By 1809, she was married to the clock-maker William Goodfellow and had already enrolled students in her classes, which she conducted at the shop. Of the graduates who wrote cookbooks, the most famous was Eliza Leslie who became one of Goodfellow's most outspoken advocates in support of using pure foods, and in the development of an essentially American cuisine. Because of the former mandate, many of Goodfellow's students were Quakers.

Apparently Goodfellow did not write a cookbook herself, although recipes from the school do exist, but one beautiful composition representing the school was copyrighted in 1853, revised and enlarged in 1855, and titled *Cookery As It Should Be* "by a practical housekeeper, and pupil of Mrs. Goodfellow." In 1865 the same work was titled *Mrs. Goodfellow's Cookery As It Should Be*.[4] The reci-

---

4. The former title is held at the Texas Woman's University in Denton, and a fine copy of the 1865 edition can be viewed at the American Antiquarian Society. Philadelphia experts do not believe this opinionated, competently and confidently put together document was written by Eliza Leslie anonymously, but the matter is under consideration, as it would raise the value of the cookbook considerably if that were the case.

pes, mostly sweets, are mouth-watering, but the Introduction is a virtual tirade on the necessity of woman self-sacrificing to the point of evading any education other than domestic in her "holy" role as homemaker—perhaps Catharine Beecher's influence.

Almost forty years later, another woman would organize the Philadelphia Cooking School, adding her culinary treats to that illustrious city's larder. The record of these achievements would be recorded in her numerous cookbooks and magazine articles, but her private life would also remain frustratingly elusive, as her personal papers were reportedly destroyed by a sickly and reclusive son.

Sarah Tyson (Heston) Rorer came from a poor family, and although she was one of only a few early career culinary experts who married, hers was not a happy union and would end in separation. The frail health of her first son, the early death of her daughter, and her own digestive difficulties drew her attention to questions of diet, but Rorer remarked in one of her regular articles about homemaking in *The Ladies Home Journal* ("How I Cured My Own Ill-Health," June 1905) that she was "not especially interested in either cooking or housekeeping" before 1879. In that year, however, she enrolled in the recently formed New Century Club Cooking School in Philadelphia (the New Century Guild is still located across the street from the Library Company on Locust Street) and instantly became enamored of the craft. The following year there was a vacancy in the teaching staff, and Sarah Rorer took advantage of the opportunity. During the next three years she attended lectures at the Woman's Medical College of Pennsylvania, where she began to develop her lifelong interest in "household chemistry," primarily dietetics. She left New Century in 1883 to open her own Philadelphia Cooking School, for which she wrote a small-sized but dense handbook of recipes in 1886: *Mrs. Rorer's Philadelphia Cook Book: A Manual of Home Economics* (581 pages). The school rated the approval of physicians in Philadelphia who felt lectures on nutrition and diet within the cooking craft would greatly benefit public health.

In all her classes Rorer taught wise marketing, food preparation, and serving. She also clarified the chemical principles (as they were understood at the time) involved in the various tasks of cooking and cleaning. She was a popular speaker, chastising the folly of consuming the twelve-course dinners that other authorities, such as Fannie Farmer, condoned. Fannie Merritt Farmer, Maria Parloa, Mary Johnson Lincoln, Juliet Corson, Sarah Rorer, and their students interacted on the lecture circuit. Their personalities were diverse, and their techniques and food philosophies differed, yet they exchanged ideas freely. Dressed in a silk gown with a lace fichu

Mrs. Sarah Tyson (Heston) Rorer (1847–1937)

over her shoulders to prove that cooking need not be drudgery or messy, Rorer captivated her audiences, preparing a somewhat "healthier" six-course dinner in one hour.[5]

Through the years she wrote at least forty cookbooks including *Colonial Recipes* (1894), a pocketbook that capitalized on the revival of colonial-type recipes at the time; *Good Cooking by Mrs. S. T. Rorer of the Philadelphia Cooking School* (1898); and *How to Cook Vegetables*, a lovely, slim, hardbound volume published by W. Atlee Burpee & Company. Burpee customers received a paperbound copy with a $3 order, a clothbound copy with a $5 order of seeds. *Mrs. Rorer's New Cook Book: a Manual of Housekeeping* (1902, 730 pages) included chapters on Spanish, Creole, Hawaiian, and Jewish dishes, and the *World's Fair Souvenir Cook Book* was published by Arnold and Company in 1904. From 1893 to 1897 Rorer collaborated with a local merchant on a magazine titled *Table Talk* that did for Philadelphia what the *Boston Cooking-School Magazine* had done for Boston. Although *Table Talk* was less known elsewhere, some historians rank it as the outstanding culinary magazine of the period. Rorer also became editor and part owner of the *Household News*, which evolved into *The Ladies Home Journal*, penning lively instructions as its domestic editor until 1911, and three years later assumed charge of the culinary department of *Good Housekeeping*.

Sometime in the early 1900s yet another Philadelphia school not connected with the original, which folded in 1903 after twenty years, was established. In 1912 Marion Harris Neil, author of *The Story of Crisco* (see chapter 6), was principal of the Philadelphia (Practical) School of Cookery. One might speculate that Sarah Tyson Rorer would question the meaning of the parenthesis.

One of the more unusual culinary enterprises of this period branched out of the Chautauqua Movement founded by John Heyl Vincent, a Methodist minister and later bishop of New York, and Lewis Miller, a Sunday school lay teacher from Akron. Visitors to the first Lake Chautauqua, New York, outdoor assembly in 1874 were sheltered in white tents, but the meetings under sun and stars were so inspiring that the camp grew rapidly into a charming permanent summer colony. It started with instruction in Sunday school organization and management; in 1878 the Literary and Scientific

---

5. She did not, however, do it without help from the wings, nor did she do the dishes on stage.

Circle was formed, inaugurating a series of home-study courses. In the first year seven thousand people participated to be "awakened and instructed." As this number multiplied, more and more courses were added: mathematics, library training, music, arts and crafts, physical education, and domestic science. On the original grounds at Fair Point, lecture halls seating from two hundred to five thousand were built, as were clubhouses, gymnasiums, a nondenominational church, a theater, library, rustic bridges, playgrounds, and a colonial marketplace, all in quite remarkable architecture.

Vincent, a man of logic and vision, felt college life to be "the vestibule to a great temple" because education should be a lifelong pursuit. "Kitchen work," he maintained, "farm work, shop work, as well as school work, are divine. They hide rare pearls in their rough shells. They are means of discipline in the highest qualities of character, and through them come some of the greatest and mightiest energies from the heavens."[6]

For the next four decades, hundreds of small-town assemblies in the United States and Canada set up tents and created joyous revivals subsidized by local churches and civic and individual contributions, welcoming such orators as William Jennings Bryan and Chew Ng Poon (the "Chinese Mark Twain") and such trooping entertainers such as the ventriloquist Edgar Bergen with Charlie McCarthy and Laura, a girl dummy who was hopelessly upstaged by Charlie and later discarded.

Hundreds of thousands of Chautauquas completed the subsequent home-study courses to which they were committed. But at its height in the late 1920s the movement (as well as all American cooking schools) began to be adversely affected by two things: the depression, which deprived the movement of its charitable support, and the domination of universities and colleges as industries of financial competition. Vincent's idea that "college facilities are not the only opportunities for securing an education" became a naive dream as Chautauqua course recipients were rejected in the marketplace in favor of those with state-accredited degrees, regardless of how talented the applicants.

Emma P. Ewing, former superintendent of the Chicago Training School of Cookery, wrote *The Art of Cookery* in 1896 while serving as superintendent of the Chautauqua School of Cookery. The book was advertised in the *Boston Cooking-School Magazine*. Sarah Tyson Rorer succeeded Ewing at Chautauqua after her own school closed. One cookbook author who attended the domestic course one summer would go on to write the most popular cookbook of the 1900s. Her name was Irma R. Rombauer, and her book would sport that most recognized and plagiarized of titles: *The Joy of Cooking*.

---

6. John H. Vincent, The Chautauqua Movement (Boston, 1886).

A Full Course Dinner

Little Neck Clams

Consommé au Parmesan

Olives   Salted Pecans

Bouchées

Filets of Halibut à la Poulette with Mayonnaise

Tomatoes   Delmonico Potatoes   String Beans

Larded Fillet of Beef with Horseradish Sauce

Glazed Sweetbreads

Artichokes with Béchamel Sauce

Sorbet

Broiled Quail with Lettuce and Celery Salad

Bananas   Cantaloupes

Sultana Roll with Claret Sauce

Cinnamon Bars   Lady Fingers   Bonbons

Crackers   Cheese

Café Noir

FIRST COURSE: *Little Neck Clams or Bluepoints, with brown-bread sandwiches. Sometimes canapés are used in place of either. For a gentlemen's dinner, canapés accompanied with sherry wine are frequently served before guests enter the dining room.*

SECOND COURSE: *Clear soup, with bread sticks, small rolls, or crisp crackers. Where two soups are served, one may be a cream soup. Cream soups are served with croûtons. Radishes, celery, or olives are passed after the soup. Salted almonds may be passed between any of the courses.*

THIRD COURSE: *Bouchées or rissoles. The filling to be of light meat.*

FOURTH COURSE: *Fish, baked, boiled, or fried. Cole slaw, dressed cucumbers, or tomatoes accompany this course; with fried fish potatoes are often served.*

FIFTH COURSE: *Roast saddle of venison or mutton, spring lamb, or fillet of beef; potatoes and one other vegetable.*

SIXTH COURSE: *Entrée, made of light meat or fish.*

SEVENTH COURSE: *A vegetable. Such vegetables as mush-*

rooms, cauliflower, asparagus, artichokes, are served, but not in white sauce.

EIGHTH COURSE: *Punch or cheese course. Punch, when served, always precedes the game course.*

NINTH COURSE: *Game, with vegetable salad, usually lettuce or celery; or cheese sticks may be served with the salad, and game omitted.*

TENTH COURSE: *Dessert, usually cold.*

ELEVENTH COURSE: *Frozen dessert and fancy cakes. Bonbons are passed after this course.*

TWELFTH COURSE: *Crackers, cheese, and café noir. Café noir is frequently served in the drawing and smoking rooms after the dinner.*

For a simpler dinner, the third, seventh, eighth, and tenth courses, and the game in the ninth course may be omitted. For a home dinner it is always desirable to serve for first course a soup; second course, meat or fish, with potatoes and two other vegetables; third course, a vegetable salad, with French dressing; fourth course, dessert; fifth course, crackers, cheese, and café noir.

Where wines and liquors are served, the first course is not usually accompanied by either; but if desired, Sauterne or other white wine may be used. With soup, serve sherry; with fish, white wine; with game, claret; with roast and other courses, champagne. After serving café noir in drawing-room, pass pony of brandy for men, sweet liquor (Chartreuse, Benedictine, or Parfait d'Amour) for women; then Crême de Menthe to all. After a short time Apollinaris should be passed. White wines and claret should be served cool; sherry should be thoroughly chilled by keeping in ice box. Champagne should be served very cold by allowing it to remain in salt and ice at least one-half hour before dinner time. Claret, as it contains so small an amount of alcohol, is not good the day after opening.

—The Boston Cooking-School Cook Book
by Fannie Merritt Farmer
(Boston: Little, Brown, 1896)

Halibut à la Poulette

A slice of halibut, weighing
1½ pounds
¼ cup melted butter

⅛ teaspoon pepper
2 teaspoons lemon juice
Few drops onion juice

¼ teaspoon salt

Clean fish and cut in eight fillets. Add seasonings to melted butter, and put dish containing butter in saucepan of hot water to keep butter melted. Take up each fillet separately with a fork, dip in butter, roll, and fasten with a small wooden skewer. Put in shallow pan, dredge with flour, and bake 12 minutes in hot oven. Remove skewers, arrange on platter for serving, pour around one and one-half cups Béchamel Sauce, and garnish with yolks of two hard boiled eggs rubbed through a strainer, whites of hard boiled eggs cut in strips, lemon cut fan-shaped, and parsley.

Sorbet

2 cups water, 2 cups sugar, 1 can grated pineapple or 1 pineapple shredded, 1⅓ cups orange juice, ½ cup lemon juice, 1 quart Apollinaris. Prepare and freeze to a mush.

Sultana Roll with Claret Sauce

Line one-pound (metal) baking-powder boxes with Pistachio Ice Cream; sprinkle with sultana raisins which have been soaked one hour in brandy; fill centres with Vanilla Ice Cream or whipped cream, sweetened, and flavored with vanilla; cover with Pistachio Ice Cream; pack in salt and ice, and let stand one and one-half hours.

CLARET SAUCE

1 cup sugar, ⅓ cup claret, ¼ cup water. Boil sugar and water eight minutes; cool slightly, and add claret.

—*The Boston Cooking-School Cook Book*
by Fannie Merritt Farmer
(Boston: Little, Brown, 1896)

Collecting Boston Cooking School Cookbooks

All editions supervised by Fannie Merritt Farmer (before 1915) are much more collectible than those handled by her sister Cora (Farmer) Perkins. Perkins's books are considered superior to those prepared by their nephew, Dexter Perkins (1930-51), and later by his wife, Wilma Lord Perkins (after 1951). In 1979 a thirteenth revised edition was commandeered by Marion Cun-

ningham, a protégée of James Beard. Cunningham doubled the number of recipes and updated the entire text to the point that it is unrecognizable as a descendant of the original but still suffices nicely as a thorough, basic American cookbook. It is currently a best-seller, true to form.

"Our object has been to elevate this department of work; to show its bearing upon many vital questions; to impress upon girls that all work well done is honorable; and that it is as really a part of education to be able to blacken a stove, to scour a tin, or to prepare a tempting meal of wholesome food, as it is to be able to solve a problem in geometry, to learn a foreign language, to teach a school, to decorate a plaque, to make an elegant gown, or to interpret the melodies and harmonies of the great masters in music. . . . Youth is the time to begin to acquire this, as well as other knowledge. Many a young housekeeper overwhelmed with responsibility regrets that her mother did not require her to learn these things in her girlhood. No matter how high her social position may be no girl is sure of retaining it through life. Though in her youthful conceit she may boast of never scrubbing a floor, or washing a dish, and many think it commendable to be ignorant of the mysteries of the kitchen, the time may come when she will have harder work than this to do, and will be thankful if there is one thing she can [already] do well."

—The Boston School Kitchen
Text-Book
by Mary Johnson Lincoln
(Boston: Roberts Brothers, 1884)

Marguerite Salad

"Do not undertake to cook a new dish until you have carefully read the receipt at least once, and . . . do not be discouraged by failure in first experiments."
—Maria Parloa (1887)

Cut the whites of eight hard-boiled eggs into rings, and mix the yolks with half a pint of mayonnaise dressing. Arrange 16 small crisp leaves of lettuce on a flat dish in a tasteful way, having two leaves lie together in such a manner as to be round or almost round. Lay the rings of white upon these leaves, to simulate the petals of a daisy, and heap the yolks in the center. If one possesses a little originality, there is hardly a limit to the variety of salads that can be made during summer.

—Miss Parloa's Kitchen Companion
by Maria Parloa
(Boston: Estes and Lauriat, 1887)

Apple Snow

Pare, slice, and quarter ten good-size tart apples; steam them until tender, and then run them through the cullender, and set where they will get ice cold. When cold, add the grated rind and the juice of two lemons, one cup of sugar, and the whites of six eggs. Beat all to a froth, and serve immediately in a deep glass dish.

Tipsy Parson

Stick a large square of sponge cake full of blanched almonds, and then lay it in a deep glass dish; pour over it a tumbler of sherry, and when the wine has all soaked into the cake, fill the dish half full of soft custard.

—*The Appledore Cook Book*
by M. Parloa
(Boston: Groves and Ellis, 1872)

Serving the Breakfast in Detail

Grapefruit   Cereal
Dropped Eggs on Toast with Rashers of Bacon
Buttered Toast   Orange Marmalade
Coffee

1. *Remove fruit plate (right hand) and finger-bowl and doily together (left hand).*
2. *Place individual cereal dish on service plate (left hand).*
3. *Pass serving dish containing cereal with serving spoon in dish (left hand, napkin).*
4. *Pass cream and sugar (tray), sugar-spoon, when presented to the first person, upon the tray beside the bowl. Have handle of pitcher and handle of spoon for sugar in a position convenient for the person served.*
5. *Remove service plate with individual cereal dish (left hand) and place warm plate (right hand). Soiled plates should be removed to the pantry, not to the serving-table. Warm plates may be brought from the pantry or taken one by one from the serving-table, if previously placed there.*
6. *Place serving silver for eggs and bacon (right side, right hand, napkin or tray).*

7. *Place asbestos mat, fitted with linen cover, in front of host (left side, left hand).*

8. *Place platter containing eggs and bacon before host (napkin).*

9. *Bring warm plate (right hand) and place before host after taking up (left hand) filled plate.*

10. *Place filled plate (left hand) before person to be served, removing first (right hand) warm one already there, which take to host for serving.*

11. *Take cup of coffee from mistress (left hand), change to right hand and place (right side) before person to be served. Be sure that the cup is placed so the handle may be taken easily.*

12. *Repeat in the same manner until all are served. If tray or space before mistress is not large enough for all cups needed, after placing a filled cup go to serving-table for fresh cup (right hand), and place before mistress when the next cup is taken (left hand).*

13. *Pass plate of toast (napkin).*

14. *Pass marmalade in small dish with spoon in dish (napkin).*

—*Table Service by Lucy G. Allen*
of the Boston School of Cookery
(Boston: Little, Brown, 1914)

A Twelve O'Clock Company Breakfast

Orange and Malaga Grape Cocktail
Fish Soufflé   Lattice Potatoes
Deviled Kidneys and Mushrooms
Maryland Chicken   Rice
Cress with French Dressing
Toasted Crackers   Cream Cheese
Pineapple Parfait   Lady Fingers
Coffee

—*Breakfasts, Luncheons and Dinners*
by Mary D. Chambers
(Boston: Boston Cooking-School
Magazine, 1924)

Ice Cream à la Mexicana

Put two cups of granulated sugar in a saucepan over fire and stir constantly until it is melted; add two cups of English walnut meats and pour into a shallow, buttered pan to harden. When perfectly cold, grate or chop fine. Crumble two dozen macaroons into fine crumbs, then toast in hot oven a few minutes. Make a rich, boiled custard of yolks of four eggs, one-half a cup of sugar and two cups of cream, then pour over the stiffly beaten whites of two eggs and let cool. To one quart of cream add one-third a cup of sugar and beat until thoroughly mixed, add to the custard, and flavor with vanilla or maraschino, then freeze. When half-frozen add the macaroon crumbs and half of the grated walnut mixture and finish freezing. Let ripen two or three hours. Sprinkle remaining grated walnuts over the cream when serving. This is the typical ice cream of Mexico, just as it is served there.

> —*The American Cook Book; Recipes for Everyday Use*
> by Janet MacKenzie Hill
> (Boston: Boston Cooking School Magazine, 1914)

Charlotte Polonaise[7]

Beat together the yolks of six eggs which must be perfectly fresh, mix with them two tablespoonsful of flour, boil a pint and a half of cream and stir the eggs with it, great care being taken that the flour is not in lumps; the cream must be still kept over the fire, and it may boil slowly for ten minutes or more, stir it continually, and be sure the fire is not too hot; divide the mixture into two separate pans; scrape six ounces of chocolate quite fine, break up a pound of maccaroons and add them to two ounces of powdered sugar; mix this with the ingredients of one pan, boil it a few moments, stir as before, take it from the fire, stir a little longer and leave it to cool; blanch a dozen bitter almonds and four ounces of shelled sweet almonds; pound them in a mortar with a little rose water until they are quite fine, add an ounce of chopped citron and pound them again; pour the contents of the mortar into a dish and add to them

---

7. The reader might like to compare this recipe to Leslie's, page 37.

four ounces of powdered sugar; stir this mixture into the other half of the cream, and let it boil gently. Take it off and put it in a cool place; cut a sponge cake (it should be a large one) into slices about half an inch thick, spread alternately one with the chocolate cream and another with the almond cream; pile them evenly on a china dish until the slices have all been used; whip together the whites of six eggs until they become a stiff froth, mix with it six ounces of powdered sugar, twelve drops of oil of lemon, some persons prefer rose water, but it is not generally considered as good; pour this mixture lightly over the pile of cake, using a spoon to distribute it evenly, and then sift some sugar (not too finely powdered) over it. It should be left in a slow oven until the outside is browned; if the oven is too hot it will become deeply browned, and will not look well. It may be ornamented with slices of peaches or quinces cut in fanciful shapes, or drops of jelly, or raspberries preserved whole; should the chocolate cream be too thin, thicken it with crumbled maccaroons; should the cream be too thin add in more pounded citron; should either of the mixtures be too thick, dilute it with cream.

—*Cookery as it should be; a new manual of the dining room and kitchen for persons in moderate circumstances*
by a pupil of Mrs. Goodfellow
(Philadelphia: Willis P. Hazard, 178 Chestnut Street, 1855)
and
—*Mrs. Goodfellow's Cookery as it should be etc.*
by a pupil of Mrs. Goodfellow
(Philadelphia: T. B. Peterson & Bros., 306 Chestnut Street, 1865)

Ham Baked in Cider

Secure a small lean ham. Wash thoroughly and soak over night. Next morning wipe perfectly dry, and sprinkle over the flesh side a tablespoonful of chopped onion, a teaspoonful of ground cinnamon, the same of allspice, a quarter of a teaspoonful of mace, the same of ground cloves. Make a paste of flour and water, roll it out, cover it over the flesh side of the ham, packing it down close to the skin. Put the ham, skin side down, in a baking-pan; pour into the pan two quarts of cider, to which you have added half a teaspoonful of white pepper and half a teaspoonful of paprika. Cover with another pan, and bake in a moderate oven two hours, basting every 20 minutes. At the end of this time remove the upper pan, and allow the ham to cook two hours longer. When ready to dish, remove carefully the paste, then the skin. Trim the bone neatly, brush the skin side with beaten egg, dust it thickly with bread-crumbs and chopped parsely, and put it in a quick oven to brown. Skim off the fat from the cider, boil it down until you have one pint, which you may turn into the sauce-bowl. When the ham is browned take from the oven, garnish the bone with a quill of paper and serve it in a bed of cress. Slices of red-skinned apples may be placed here and there in the cress as a decoration.

—*Good Cooking by Mrs. S. T. Rorer of
the Philadelphia Cooking School . . .*
(Philadelphia: Curtis, 1898)

Winter Dinner Menu

Clear Soup with Croutons
Ham Baked in Cider   Apple Sauce
Mashed Potatoes   Stewed Cabbage
Browned Turnips
Lettuce Salad with French Dressing
Wafers   Cheese
Cerealine Blocks with Jelly
Coffee

—*How to Cook Vegetables*
by Mrs. S. T. Rorer
(Philadelphia: W. Atlee
Burpee, 1897)

Chili Vinegar

This is made by simply infusing fifty small peppers in one pint of best white-wine vinegar.

Horse-radish Vinegar

1 teacup of grated horse-radish, 1 quart of cider vinegar, 1 tablespoonful of granulated sugar. Put the horse-radish in two glass jars, bring the vinegar to the boiling point, add the sugar and pour over the horse-radish. Screw the tops on the jars, shake once a day for one week. Strain, bottle, and seal, and it is ready to use.

Onion Vinegar

1 quart of vinegar, 2 teaspoonfuls of granulated sugar, 1 teaspoonful of salt, 2 large onions. Grate the onions, mix with them the salt and sugar, let stand two hours and add the vinegar. Turn into bottles, shake every day for two weeks, strain through a fine cloth, bottle, cork, and seal. This onion vinegar may be used for salads and sour meat dishes where a very delicate onion flavor is desired.

Soup Flavor

Take of lemon peel, thyme, sweet marjoram and parsley each one ounce. Dry carefully on paper in a warm oven, then pound in a mortar and rub through a fine sieve. Add one teaspoonful of powdered celery seed, bottle and cork. One teaspoonful of this may be added to each quart of soup.

—How to Cook Vegetables
by Mrs. S. T. Rorer
(Philadelphia: W. Atlee Burpee, 1897)

Cracker or Matzos Balls

Butter the size of walnut
1 egg
chopped parsley
salt and cracker meal

Stir the butter, add egg, then as much cracker meal as it absorbs. Moisten with a little soup, add parsley and salt. Roll into marbles and boil in the chicken soup just before serving.

Pepper and Grape-fruit Salad

Remove the tops from six green peppers. Take out seeds and re-fill with grape-fruit pulp, fine-cut celery and English walnut meats mixed with mayonnaise dressing. To one cup and a half of the mixture add one-fourth a cup of heavy cream, beaten stiff. For each pepper use three halves of walnut meats and half as much celery as grape-fruit.

Casserole of Rice and Meat

Steam: 1 cup rice, 3 cups boiling water, 1 teaspoon salt.

2 cups cold cooked meat	1 teaspoon chopped onions
½ teaspoon salt	2 tablespoons cracker crumbs
¼ teaspoon celery salt	1 egg
⅛ teaspoon pepper	1 cup hot water or stock
⅛ teaspoon poultry seasoning	

Steam the rice twenty minutes. Chop the meat very fine, add all seasonings, then the beaten egg, cracker crumbs, and stock or hot water enough to pack it easily. Line the bottom and sides of a greased mould or small bread tin one-half inch thick with the cooked rice, pack in the meat, cover with rice, and steam 45 minutes. Loosen around the edge of mould, turn out upon a hot platter and pour tomato sauce around it.

—*The Way to a . . . Man's Heart;*
"The Settlement" Cook Book (1901)

Washing Dishes

Have a pan half filled with hot water. If dishes are very dirty or greasy, add a little washing soda or ammonia. Wash glasses first. Slip them in sideways, one at a time, and wipe instantly. Wash the silver and wipe at once, and it will keep bright. Then wash the china, beginning with the cups, saucers, pitchers, and least greasy dishes, and changing the water as soon as cool or greasy.

Rinse the dishes in a pan of scalding water, take out and drain quickly. Wipe immediately. Then wash the kitchen dishes, pots, kettles, pans, etc. A Dover egg-beater should not be left to soak in water, or it will be hard to run. Keep the handles clean, wipe the wire with a damp cloth immediately after using. Kitchen knives and forks should never be placed in dish water. Scour them with brick dust, wash with dish cloth, and wipe them dry.

Tinware, granite ironware should be washed in hot soda water, and if browned, rub with sapolio, salt or baking soda. Use wire dish cloth if food sticks to dishes.

Keep strainer in sink and pour all dish water, etc. in it, and remove contents of strainer into garbage pail. Wash towels with plenty of soap, and rinse thoroughly every time they are used. Hang towels up evenly to dry. Wash dish cloths. Scrub desk boards with brush and sapolio, working with the grain of the wood, rinse and dry. When scrubbing, wet brush and apply sapolio or soap with upward strokes. Wash dish pans, wipe and dry. Wash your hands with white (castile or ivory) soap, if you wish to keep smooth hands, and wipe them dry. Wash teakettle. Polish faucets. Scrub sink with clean hot suds.

—The Way to a . . . Man's Heart:
"The Settlement" Cook Book
compiled by Mrs. Simon Kander
and Mrs. Henry Schoenfeld (1903)

For a Dinner of Six

Oysters or Clams
Brown-bread sandwiches
Julienne Soup
Broiled Kingfish, Maître d'Hôtel Sauce   **Cucumbers**
Lamb Chops, Soubise Sauce
Potato Croquettes   Peas
Fresh Asparagus
Roast Capon   Romaine Salad
Apple Charlotte
Fruit   Dessert

Roast Capon with Truffles

Select a nice, meaty capon, singe and clean it, and fill it with truffles prepared as follows: Peel, slice, and remove the stringy part from one quart of truffles. Let them stand in their own juice. Melt one pound of butter with salt and pepper, three bay leaves, two sliced shallots, a clove of garlic, and a sprig of thyme. Stir while the butter is melting. Rub through a colander over the truffles. Mix them and let them stand until thoroughly cold. Fill the capon, make it a good shape, and sew both ends so the truffles will not come out. Cover with thin strips of larding pork. Wrap in a thick sheet of white paper which is well oiled, and bake in an oven for one hour and a half. Baste frequently with melted butter. Remove paper and pork. Serve with a gravy made of the strained liquid the capon was cooked in and a little broth.

Fried Parsley

Soak parsley in ice water for two hours, so it will be crisp. Dry thoroughly, arrange in frying basket, plunge in boiling hot fat, leave for a second, remove basket from fat, shake it. Plunge in fat once more, drain on brown paper, and serve.

—Mrs. Seely's Cook Book
by Mrs. L. Seely
(New York: Macmillan, 1902)

How to Make Good Sandwiches

In the first place have bread which is close-grained and one day old. Each slice should be cut evenly and about one-eighth of an inch thick. Spread each slice with butter before you cut it from the loaf. After cutting, spread the slice with any mixture you may desire and cover it with another slice. Cut off every bit of crust and press the sandwiches together firmly. Cut your sandwiches in half, each half in quarters, and each quarter diagonally. Trim off all protruding edges of filling. Cover the sandwiches with a cloth wet with a very weak solution of brandy and water and pack them in a tin box until ready for use. Fresh butter is preferable for sandwiches, as it is more dainty and delicate. If not obtainable, use best creamery butter. Many people when eating a sandwich spread with fish prefer Graham bread in place of white bread.

In making butters of various kinds for sandwiches, first rub the butter to a cream, then blend it with the flavor wanted—caviar, anchovy, sardine, lobster, cheese, parsley, chives, cress, chutney, chili, and horseradish are all used. A few drops of lemon juice improves any kind of fish sandwich. With an anchovy sandwich also add a few olives stoned and minced very fine.

Dates and figs chopped very fine and moistened with hot water and lemon juice may be spread on thin slices of bread and sprinkled with finely chopped nuts. Finely minced ginger and candied orange peel may be sprinkled on Neufchâtel cheese which has been moistened with a little butter or rich cream and spread on buttered slices of bread.

—*Mrs. Seely's Cook Book*
by Mrs. L. Seely
(New York: Macmillan, 1902)

Breakfast Menu

Strawberry Shortcake
Broiled Chicken   Creamed Hashed Potatoes
Vienna Rolls   Butter
Coffee

—*The Art of Cookery*
by Emma P. Ewing, super-
intendent of the Chau-
tauqua School of Cookery
(Meadville, Pa.: Flood
and Vincent, 1896)

Broiled Pompano

Have the fish scaled, drawn, and thoroughly washed in cold water; score it to the bone on both sides, making three or four cuts across the fish; season it lightly with salt and pepper, place it between the bars of a buttered double wire gridiron, and quickly broil it over a hot fire for about five minutes on each side, or until the flesh begins to cleave from the bones. Serve it on a hot platter, with a tablespoonful of butter spread over it, and a little salt and pepper dusted on it. Pompano is excellent when fried or boiled.

Cucumber Sauce

Cucumber sauce is delicious with broiled pompano; it is made by adding a very little juice squeezed from grated cucumber, or the cucumber itself, to a *mayonnaise* sauce. The cucumber-juice must be used with great caution, because it possesses decided medicinal properties.

> —*Miss Corson's Practical American Cookery and Household Management* by Miss Juliet Corson (New York: Dodd, Mead, 1886)

Crystallized Flowers

Candied Rose Petals: Dip large rose petals in a heavy sugar syrup made by boiling a cupful of sugar and a fourth cupful of water together for ten minutes. Drain, lay on waxed paper to dry for a few hours, then brush over with slightly beaten egg white and dust with granulated sugar. Dry in the sun on the radiator.

Candied Violets: Select English violets or the very sweet-scented bird's foot violets that grow wild, remove all the stem, then finish as directed for candied rose petals.

Candied Lilacs: Select very beautiful small clusters of purple lilacs, remove all the stem possible, and proceed as for candied rose petals.

Mrs. Ida Cogswell Bailey Allen

Candied Orange Blossoms: Select clusters of three or four orange blossoms each, remove as much stem as possible, and proceed as for candied rose petals.

Candied Mint Leaves: Select perfect mint leaves and proceed as for candied rose petals.

"Then marriage and motherhood—Food Editorships on Good Housekeeping, Pictorial Review, Woman's World, *and the help of their splendid Editors, special articles in many other magazines and newspapers—consequent letters from thousands of women asking for advice in feeding those dear to them—sick babies, disgruntled husbands, growing boys who could not be filled up, girls who would not eat. Other letters, too, from home-makers who had no leisure, who were always tired, or could not meet the bills. Then the war, and the inestimable privilege of addressing a half million men and women. The memory of those eager, enthusiastic faces will ever stay with me—a constant inspiration. Women needed, wanted, food help."*

—Mrs. Allen on Cooking, Menus, Service
by Ida C. Bailey Allen
(New York: Doubleday, Doran, 1929)

Perfection Salad

2 tablespoons gelatin soaked in:
  ½ cup cold water
½ cup mild vinegar
2 tablespoons lemon juice
2 cups boiling water
1 teaspoon salt

½ cup sugar
2 cups celery cut into ⅛-inch lengths
1 cup finely shredded cabbage
2 pimentos, cut fine

Add vinegar, lemon juice, boiling water, salt, and sugar to soaked gelatin. Strain and chill. When mixture begins to set, add remaining ingredients. Mold. Cut into squares or other shapes and serve on lettuce leaf with Mayonnaise. Any mixture of vegetables desired may be used. 12 servings.

Butter Curls

Butter curls are made with a special device known as a butter curler. Essentially this is a knife with a curved blade and notched edge. To make butter curls, start with an unbroken 1-pound or ¼-

pound print of butter of room temperature. Dip curler into hot water, then cool slightly. If too hot, butter will melt when it comes in contact with the metal. With a light stroke draw curler, held almost horizontally, lengthwise across surface of butter. Strip of butter so separated rolls into a curl with corrugated markings. Place finished curls in ice water to harden.

> —*Practical Cookery; and the Etiquette
> and Service of the Table*
> by the Kansas State College of Agriculture and Applied Science
> (Manhattan, Kan., 1941)

Toll House Chocolate Crunch Cookies

Cream

    1 cup butter, add

    ¾ cup brown sugar

    ¾ cup granulated sugar, and

    2 eggs beaten whole.

Dissolve

    1 teaspoon soda in

    1 teaspoon hot water, and mix

alternately with

    2¼ cups flour sifted with

    1 teaspoon salt. Lastly add

    1 cup chopped nuts and

    2 bars (7-ounce) Nestles yellow label chocolate, semi-sweet, which has been cut in pieces the size of a pea.

Flavor with

    1 teaspoon vanilla and drop half-teaspoons on a greased cookie sheet.

    Bake 10 to 12 minutes in 375-degree oven.

Makes 100 cookies.

> —*Ruth Wakefield's Toll House; Tried
> and True Recipes*
> by Ruth Graves Wakefield
> (New York: M. Barrows, 1930)

The American Woman's Cook Book

In the late 1890s the Butterick Publishing Co., Ltd. of London, Paris, Toronto, and New York offered to the public a series of twelve sizable pamphlets for sixpence, or fifteen cents a copy. Titles included "Correct Cookery," "The Correct Art of Candy-Making," "The Perfect Art of Canning and Preserving," "Dainty Desserts," "Mother and Baby Care," and "Fancy Drills for Entertainments." The pamphlets were well received and bound together to be sold in one volume after the turn of the century.

Then, in 1911, the cooking topics were removed and elaborated upon by Helene Judson for a new publication titled The Butterick Cook Book (360 pages); recipes were in paragraph form, and there were a few menus and illustrations. The New Butterick Cook-Book (733 pages) was an enlarged version of the book, revised, and with all recipes retested by Flora Rose, co-head of the School of Home Economics at Cornell University, assisted by a staff of no less than thirteen women. Among other modernizing touches, ingredients were listed at the start of recipes. There was a Preface by Martha Van Rensselaer, home-making editor of The Delineator magazine. Butterick, now home-based in the Butterick Building in New York, published this magazine (and perhaps the cookbooks) in French for its customers in Paris. Brief introductions opened each chapter, there was an explanation of herb usage although most recipes were rather bland, a glossary of foreign words and phrases "often used in connection with cooking," and a comprehensive index (situated in the front of the 1911 edition). However, the text was very dry and unfortunately "commended to the schools . . . as part of their course of study" by Van Rensselaer.

In 1928 the volume was once again revised as the Delineator Cook Book, this time by the Delineator Home Institute under the direction of Mildred Maddocks Bentley, edited by Flora Rose and Martha Van Rensselaer, now listed as co-directors of the School of Home Economics at Cornell, with Butterick still the publisher.

As its next incarnation the book was titled The American Woman's Cook Book, edited and revised by Ruth Berolzheimer, whose title was director of a nebulous enterprise called the Culinary Arts Institute, and published by Consolidated Book Publishers, Inc., Chicago, Illinois in 1938. Land O'Lakes provided the illustration on the jacket, and color plates were courtesy of the Carnation Company. A unique feature of this edition, and probably the biggest reason this book finally caught the fancy of the public at the time, was the thumb-indexing of chapters, which gave it the subtle authority of a reference work. Indeed, in 1941 and 1947 it was retitled The Encyclopedic Cook Book.

Berolzheimer's signature and the Culinary Arts Institute cameo would be connected with hundreds of titles based on these same and similar recipes—and numerous new ones—during the next two decades, with scores of industries—for example, the American Cranberry Exchange, Ball Brothers, Corning Glass Works, Heinz, the Idaho Potato Growers, Quaker Oats, Sealtest, Van Camp Sea Foods, and the Winter Pear Bureau—providing scores of black-and-white and color photographs. Ironically, the book would likewise be broken down by chapters (more or less) into fifty-page pamphlets—once again—with such names as "600 Ways to Serve Potatoes and Vegetables," "300 Recipes for Delightful Cooking," and why not? "Dainty Desserts."

It was the rare American kitchen library that did not have some item from Ruth Berolzheimer's vast outpouring in the 1940s and 1950s, and—perhaps not too surprisingly because most are in the public domain—some of these recipes are still in print! But few homemakers knew how far back these fat little books, and their slick offspring pamphlets, were actually rooted.

"How can any one tell how much a pinch is, Aunt Jane?" asked Rose. "Is it about as much as when you take a pinch of anybody's arm?"
—Six Little Cooks: or, Aunt Jane's Cooking Class by Elizabeth Stansbury Kirkland (Chicago, 1877)

The Lunch Box

Select a box that can be kept clean. Lunch boxes should be washed, scalded and aired daily. Those made of light-weight metal are best. Many attractive boxes are now made with a vacuum bottle which fits the box. These are highly desirable. A lunch box should not be air-tight, as a circulation of air prevents the mingling of odors. All food should be protected from dirt by wrapping.

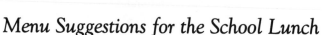

Menu Suggestions for the School Lunch

Cream of Spinach Soup (in vacuum container)
Crackers
Raisin and Nut Bread and Butter
Sandwiches   Apple Sauce

Scrambled Egg Sandwiches
Lettuce Sandwiches
Milk (in container)
Orange   Molasses Cookie

—*The New Butterick Cook-Book*
by Flora Rose (New York, 1924)
—*Delineator Cook Book*
by Mildred Maddocks Bentley
(New York, 1928)
—*American Woman's Cook Book*
by Ruth Berolzheimer
(Chicago, 1938)

Little Cookbooks with Motives: Ulterior and Avowed

I n 1906 surgeon John Harvey Kellogg turned a hard grain of wheat into a delicate, crunchy flake, thus revolutionizing breakfast menus throughout the Western world. His emphasis on wholesome foods (he, too, was a devotee of Sylvester Graham) caused Lenna Frances Cooper to tempt the region with her *One Hundred Recipes* (1909) dealing with nutritional theories. Not to be outdone by Battle Creek, Procter & Gamble in Cincinnati issued *The Story of Crisco* (1911), compiled by that ambitious graduate of Philadelphia (Practical) School, Marion Harris Neil. The Washburn Crosby Company, a flour milling endeavor in Minneapolis and soon to be known as General Mills, had published *Maria Parloa's Cook Book* in 1880, the *Gold Medal Flour Cook Book* in 1903, and in 1921 would introduce the most successful of all pseudo-domestics: Betty Crocker (see chapter 7).

This seemingly harmless competition accelerated rapidly. In time the "housewife's" attention was cunningly diverted away from using fresh, simple, natural resources to prepare her daily meals to a dependence on prepackaged, high-priced, complex products, a process that gave birth to lucrative new convenience food industries.

Propagandized but highly popular advertising booklets and pamphlets were either distributed free with the product or sent to the consumers by request; later a small fee was charged.[1] JELL-O-Co. first described their product as "ice-cream powder," and had been publishing recipe pamphlets since before the turn of the century, when output reached an annual fifteen million booklets in the early 1900s. JELL-O fast became the most frequently mentioned product name in American recipe lists of ingredients.

Again, these books and pamphlets of varying quality were prepared by specialists, but company owners and directors could not refrain from including their own particular brand as an absolutely necessary—but often ill-used—main ingredient in almost every recipe, thus detracting from an unbiased consideration of their product's merits as well as the esthetic objectivity of the document as a whole. But the value of books and pamphlets as instruments to introduce and spread knowledge about product or kitchen appliance use could not be overstated.

Good examples of these small, industrial cookbooks are especially noteworthy for their outstanding illustrations done by unknown artists and those as familiar as Norman Rockwell. The books also introduced color processing techniques in drawings and photographs, changing the way people chose household cookbook purchases, and groceries, forever. Color was used as an eye-catcher to promote products and whet the appetite for the depicted meal or recipe, and to deceive viewers into thinking that the product represented luxury, sophistication—or economy—in those times when it was most needed. Industry joined the "war effort" during World Wars I and II by commissioning known cookbook authors to compile recipes using substitutes for, limiting, or eliminating rationed foods, along with recommending meals for the War Department. Few cookbooks were published during the Civil War or during World War I or II with any other intent.

The decades between 1900 and 1940 were filled with upheaval. World War I and the stock market crash were followed by the Great Depression and a national surge toward forming and joining labor unions. A country that never wanted to engage in war again after its

---

1. Booklets and pamphlets have become very collectible, earning a place in the Smithsonian Institution's Collection of Advertising History. Currently most advertising cookbooks are profit-making in themselves; companies also profit by selling their mailing lists.

own Civil War found itself mired in yet a second world war that destroyed fathers and sons and took wives and mothers away from home to work in factories and die on the battlefields. The national depression between 1837 and 1844 had brought with it a soul-searching attitude toward charitable causes and social reform that was renewed in the 1930s and 1940s. At the same time, the farm population was dwindling as young couples left rural areas in droves to come to the cities in search of steady employment and work benefits, causing further crowding, unemployment, and squalor. Although blacks were free, racism toward all non-Caucasian people was rampant, and their already-dire problems would only worsen until well into the twentieth century.

The government attempted to meet the needs of some of these families and see to its own interests at the same time by issuing Department of Agriculture (USDA) bulletins (available in most city libraries) and putting together recipes from "Housekeeper's Chats," a radio service program begun in 1926. The role of housewife was elevated to a patriotic ideal as industry abetted first the cause of war; then the cause of keeping families down on the farm; and, finally, the task of wooing (and shaming) women back into kitchen workplaces that required less devotion to run than ever before—and keeping them there. High school girls were not given a choice in their destiny; the top 20 percent or so were allotted college preparatory courses while the rest were channeled into secretarial or home economics regimens. These controlling forces are blatantly apparent in the pointed introductions, prefaces, and preachy texts of the drab period cookbooks collected not for their culinary contributions but for their historical overview. The same nutritionists who lent their names to give credibility to products were sponsored on radio broadcasts, daily and weekly, coast to coast, to give voice to the traditional role of women in society. This trend toward confining woman to the kitchen was agreeable to the man who sat on a board of directors, because it was infinitely more convenient for him that his wife not be competing for his salary but rather be making his life easier and raising their children.

But some women weren't so easily swayed. What, asked Madison Avenue, were they thinking? For one thing, the adventurous Amelia Earhart was idolized and the internationalism of Eleanor Roosevelt envied. At the same time women's choices were being deliberately sabotaged by subtly manipulative advertising and debasing education, the machine age was making housekeeping chores easier than ever and allowing more free time to volunteer—and to wonder and desire.

All of these factors were affecting cookbook production, as did such political events as woman's suffrage[2], and the temperance movement which did not fail as many believe (except with recent European immigrants who simply could not believe that the wines of the gods were wicked) but was actually gaining momentum when liquor laws were repealed. Grahamism and other dietary theories exploded into a multitude of movements championing vegetarianism or specific restraint at the dinner table for reasons of health, religion, weight loss, and new curative regimens for various physical problems.

Thus another type of small and medium-sized, but basically unattractive, publication emerged during these periods of national stress, books and pamphlets produced to raise funds for nationally recognized charitable causes, be they political, health-related, or religious (see chapter 10 for the development of fund-raising cookbooks as regional treasures). They weren't free, although most were non-profit-making, but their causes were far more altruistic than capitalistic, and their reason for existence was certainly more apparent than that of the average advertising propaganda pamphlet.

"Meal planning is both an art and a science—a science when we serve the family with food which supplies their body needs, and an art when this food is selected so that it combines flavor, colors and textures in ways that are pleasing to the palate and the eye. The successful housewife aims for both."

—Dr. Louise Stanley, Chief of
Bureau of Home Economics, USDA
in *The Congressional Club Cook Book*
(1927)

JELL-O with Fruit

Dissolve one package of jell-o (any flavor) in a pint of boiling water. Pour into a bowl or mold. Just as jell-o is beginning to set, arrange in it, with the aid of a fork, sliced oranges and bananas, or

---

2. The first woman to claim the right to vote was Margaret Brent in 1647, but women were not "granted" the right to cast their vote in an American election until August 26, 1920, more than two and a half centuries later.

peaches and strawberries, or cherries and currants, or any other fruit that may be preferred for the purpose. Be sure to use jell-o with the name "JELL-O" in big red letters on the package.

—*Tennessee Cookbook*
by Mrs. Reese Lillard
(Lebanon, Tenn.: McQuiddy, 1912)

Club-House Sandwich

Butter toast well; arrange half the slices on a large platter; lay a lettuce leaf on each slice, and brush lightly with a French dressing seasoned with mustard. Then cover with pieces of two or three kinds of meat—cold breast of turkey sliced and a piece of freshly fried bacon, or cold sliced tongue and fresh fried ham. Add a slice of cucumber or green tomato pickle; cover with the remaining slices of toast and garnish with lettuce and olives. Keep as warm as possible. Fine for luncheons.

Short Process for Bread Making

One quart of potato water
One dried yeast cake, or ½ compressed, or ¼ cup home made
¼ cup sugar

Drain water from potatoes at Noon, let cool until lukewarm, add sugar and yeast cake dissolved in one-quarter cup warm water, leave this to raise in warm place until next morning. Then add one tablespoon salt and enough flour (about three quarts) to make a dough just stiff enough not to stick to the hands or board; let raise again 2½ times its size. Bake in a moderate oven. May knead dough down once if desired, but not necessary.

—*The Pillsbury Cook Book*
by Mrs. Nellie Duling, who won the
Medal of Honor for Perfect Bread at
the St. Louis World's Fair
(Missouri, 1914; 126 pages)

Conservation Cutlets

4 hard-cooked eggs, cut fine

½ cupful ham, cut fine

½ cupful chicken, cut fine

⅓ cup Crisco

½ teaspoon salt

¼ cupful cornstarch

1 cupful chicken broth

¼ cupful rich milk

½ teaspoon celery seed

½ teaspoon paprika

1 egg, uncooked

1 cupful bread crumbs

3 tablespoons melted Crisco

Combine the solid ingredients, which should be kept rather coarse, and set aside. Melt the Crisco, add the salt and cornstarch, and stir and cook until frothy; add the broth and milk and stir until boiling. Add the solid ingredients with the celery salt and paprika; mix and turn on a Criscoed plate. When cold, shape into 8 cutlets, dip in the egg beaten with its bulk of milk or water, and then into crumbs mixed with the melted Crisco. Set on a Criscoed tin and let bake in a hot oven until hot throughout. Serve with peas, asparagus or creamed potatoes.

"At the present time the patriotic woman, in planning her food supply for the week, keeps in mind the soldiers at the front. . . . She uses no butter for cooking purposes, but in its place makes use of a vegetable fat, such as Crisco."

—*War Time Recipes*
by Janet McKenzie Hill
(Cincinnati: Procter & Gamble, 1918;
96 pages)

Devils Food Cake

1½ cupfuls sugar

1½ cupfuls milk

½ cake chocolate

2 teaspoonfuls vanilla extract

2 eggs

2 cupfuls flour

½ cupful Crisco

1 teaspoon baking soda

3 tablespoonfuls boiling water

½ teaspoon salt

Put ½ cupful of sugar into small saucepan, add chocolate and one cupful milk. Put on stove and stir until it boils five minutes. Remove from fire, add vanilla and set aside to cool. Beat Crisco and remainder of sugar to light cream, then add eggs well beaten, and beat two minutes. Now add remainder of milk, soda dissolved in boiling water, flour, salt, and chocolate mix. Mix carefully and divide into two large greased and floured layer tins and bake in moderate oven 25 minutes. Turn to cool and put together with boiled frosting. Sufficient for two large layers.

—A *"Calendar of Dinners"* with 615
Recipes by Marion Harris Neil, including
The Story of Crisco
(Cincinnati: Procter & Gamble, 1920)

Scalloped Onions and Peanuts

6 medium onions   1 tablespoon flour

1 cup peanuts, ground   1 cup milk

1 tablespoon melted butter or fat   ½ teaspoon salt

1 cup buttered bread crumbs

Skin the onions, cook in boiling salted water until tender, drain, and slice. Make a sauce of the fat, flour, milk, and salt. In a greased baking dish place a layer of the onions, cover with the peanuts and sauce, and continue until all are used. Cover the top with buttered crumbs and bake in a moderate oven for about 20 minutes, or until the crumbs are golden brown. Serve from the baking dish.

—*Aunt Sammy's Radio Recipes Revised*
by Ruth Van Deman and Fanny
Walker Yeatman
(Washington, D.C.: U.S. Government
Printing Office, 1931)

Table Beer

To eight quarts of boiling water put a pound of treacle, a quarter of an ounce of ginger and two bay leaves, let this boil for a quarter of an hour, then cook, and work it with yeast as other beer.

—*Confederate Receipt Book*
(Richmond, Virginia, 1863; 28 pages)

"This book is planned for women who have been whirled into a dizzy series of readjustments. They are showing, nevertheless, dauntless spirit, courage, and the resolve to turn out delectable food with whatever materials may be available. They are resolved that good food, good cheer, and good neighborliness shall not vanish."

—*Cooking on a Ration*
by Marjorie Mills
(Boston: Houghton Mifflin, 1943)

Honey Apple Candy

Soak one tablespoon gelatin in ¼ cup cold water. Put in saucepan 1½ cups unsweetened apple sauce and 1 cup honey and cook until very thick, stirring constantly. Remove from fire, add soaked gelatin, and stir until dissolved. Then add 2 tablespoons orange juice and ¾ cup chopped nutmeats. Pour into an 8-inch square pan and let stand 24 hours or until firm. Cut in squares and just before serving roll in soy nuts, fine cocoanut, or powdered sugar.

—*Wartime Cooking*
by Alice Bradley, principal, Miss Farmer's School of Cookery
(Cleveland: World Publishing, 1943)

"They shall rise up and call her blessed—this woman, who—loving and thoughtful of future joy and health—secures the goodness of Nature at her best, and cans against the barren sameness of the Winter months. Well does she look to the ways of her household."

—*Ball Blue Book*
by the Ball Brothers Company
(Muncie, Indiana 1938)

Macaroni au Gratin

1½ cups macaroni[3] broken into 1-inch lengths
1 cup grated yogurt or Neufchâtel cheese
1 cup bread crumbs
3 tablespoons butter
3 tablespoons flour
2 cups milk
1 teaspoon salt

Cook macaroni in boiling salted water until tender; drain and pour over it a dash of cold water. Make a White Sauce of the last four ingredients and mix with the macaroni. Stir the grated cheese into the mixture. Turn into a baking dish, cover with bread crumbs and bake in a moderate oven until nicely browned. If desired, buttered crumbs may be used.

—*The New Cookery*
by Lenna Frances Cooper, director of
the Battle Creek Sanitarium School of
Home Economics
(Battle Creek: Modern Medicine,
1929)

---

3. See "Paste" in glossary.

Eugene Christian

Mollie Griswold Christian

The following articles compose three ideal
meals for a perfectly normal person:

BREAKFAST

One red apple with combination nut butter
One ounce protoid[4] nuts   Five or six black dates
One glass milk

LUNCHEON

Sauce dish Combination Cereal   One ounce Pecan Meats
Cold slaw with Olive Oil   Two cakes of Unfired Bread[5]
Four prunes with thick cream   Sweet butter
Glass of Egg-nog

DINNER

Two ounces Nut Meats
Vegetable Salad with Hygeia Dressing
Two or three cakes Unfired Bread   Combination nut butter
Very ripe Banana with thick cream
Pint of Whole Milk

> —*Uncooked Foods and How to Use Them*
> by Eugene Christian and
> Mollie Griswold Christian
> (New York: Passaic, 1904)

---

4. This word is not explained in the text and does not appear in either the
Oxford English Dictionary or *Dorland's*. It is the only word italicized in the
menu. The Christians refer to "proteins" elsewhere as "proteids"; perhaps
this was a commercial name for certain nuts that contain less fat and more protein, rather than the reverse.

5. A combination of coarsely ground grains and nuts moistened and sun-
dried or dehydrated in an incandescent electric-light oven.

Vegetable Salad

1 small Carrot,
A small piece of Green Pepper,
1 White Turnip,
A little Celery,

A little Cabbage,
A few Radishes,
1 small Onion,
Lettuce.

Grind or chop fine all vegetables. Serve on lettuce leaf with salad dressing.

Hygeia Dressing

2 Eggs,
½ Lemon,
2 tablespoonfuls Olive Oil,

1 cup Whipped Cream,
Sugar,
Salt.

To the yolks of the eggs, beaten very stiff, add the oil and juice of the lemon very slowly, beating hard all the while, until it has all been added and is quite thick. Then add the beaten white of eggs, salt and sugar to taste, and last, the whipped cream; whip all together until very stiff and set on ice until ready to serve.

—*Uncooked Foods and How to Use Them*
by Eugene Christian and
Mollie Griswold Christian
(New York: Passaic, 1904)

"If there were nothing else to recommend the use of uncooked foods except simplicity and economy, it would be quite enough. There is nothing more complicated—more laborious and more nerve-destroying, than the preparation of the alleged good dinner."
—Eugene Christian and
Mollie Griswold Christian
(1904)

Syllabub

Sweeten a quart of cream with loaf-sugar, grate nutmeg into it, milk your cow into the liquor very fast, that it may be very frothy. This is very good for evening entertainments, etc. Take a pint of cream, grate in the skin of a lemon, beat the whites of three eggs, sweetened, until light, put into your syllabub glasses, etc.

—*The Temperance Cookbook, containing 189 Receipts: Designed for the Use of Those Persons Who Wish to Exclude Spirituous Liquors from their Cookery*
by a Lady of Philadelphia
[Miss C. A. Neal] (1835; 160 pages)

Beef Olives

[NOTE: These morsels of complicatedness were used as decoration on, or accompaniment to, an entree; mentioned in several cookbooks of character.]

Take a slice of beef (from the round if possible) of the thickness of an inch; pound it out till it is only half an inch thick; cut it into four inch squares. Make some dressing of chopped beef, bread crumbs, cream, salt, and sweet marjoram; mix it with an egg, and sew it up in the bits of steak in the shape of an olive; lay them in a tin pan with a cup of brown stock (or water in which meat has been boiled) and set them in the oven. Cook them 20 minutes. Put them into a dish; add a little cream and flour to the gravy. While it is boiling, pour on a little water, and if you have it, add a little sugar or tomato catsup. Let this boil once and turn it over the olives when you are ready to send them to the table.

—*Christianity in the Kitchen; a
physiological cook book, by
Mrs. Horace Mann [Mary Tyler Peabody]*
(Boston: Ticknor and Fields, 1857)

Home Made Yeast
(Contributed by Lucy Stone)

[NOTE: This gem of a cookbook was published in aid of the Woman's Festival and Bazaar in Boston, December 13–19, 1886, with contributors including "many who are eminent in their professions as teachers, lecturers, physicians, ministers, and authors,— whose names are household words in the land."]

Boil a heaping quart of loose hops (or if they are pressed, two ounces) in one gallon of water, strain it, when it is cold put in a small handful of salt, and a half pound of sugar, then take a pound of flour and rub it smooth with some of the liquor, after which make it thin with more of the same liquid and mix all together, let this stand 24 hours; then boil and mash three pounds of potatoes and add to it, let it stand 24 hours or more; then put it in a bottle or a tight vessel, and it is ready for use. Shake the bottle before using. It should be kept in a warm place while it is making, and in a cool place afterward.

Coffee Cakes
(Contributed by Mrs. Dr. Flavel S. Thomas, M.S.)

Beat three eggs very light, add two cupfuls brown sugar, one cupful butter, one cupful sweet milk, one teaspoonful soda, two teaspoonfuls cream of tartar. Make a stiff dough by kneading in flour, roll out to about one-half inch thick, sprinkle with powdered sugar and cinnamon, roll up as if for jelly rolls, and cut off slices about half an inch thick, dip in granulated sugar and bake.

> —*The Woman Suffrage Cook Book*
> by Hattie A. Burr
> (Boston, 1886; 148 pages)

"As soon as I heard of the proposed plan of this book I became positively frantic to co-operate in it. The idea of a cookery book which should contain Allied Recipes and Allied Recipes only, struck me at once as one of the finest ideas of the day. For myself I have felt for some time past that the time is gone, and gone for ever, when I can eat a German Pretzel or a Wiener Schnitzel. It gives me nothing but remorse to remember that there were days when I tolerated, I may even say I enjoyed, Hungarian Goulash. I could not eat it now. As for Bulgarian Boosh or Turkish Tch'kk the mere names of them make me ill. For me, the rest of my life, it must be Allied Food or no food at all."

> —*Allied Cookery*
> from the Preface written by Canadian
> satirist and humorist Stephen Leacock
> (New York: G. P. Putnam Sons, 1916)

7

The Joy and the Myth

Irma Louise (von Starkloff) Rombauer was fifty-four years old when she wrote *The Joy of Cooking* and quick to admit to her publisher that her daughter Marion, an artist, was her "collaborator and Rock of Gibraltar" during the years she spent readying the original manuscript for Bobbs-Merrill. The Rombauers were a close-knit family with diverse intellectual interests, and the whole project started as a remedy for the "keen unhappiness" Rombauer had experienced when her husband died. To divert her, Marion and Rombauer's son, Edgar, cajoled her into writing down the recipes for the delicious meals they had grown up eating. What began as a family enterprise never veered from that original intent, even when the "family" grew into hundreds of thousands of readers across the nation.

Born on October 30, 1877, in St. Louis, Missouri to professionally distinguished parents, Irma von Starkloff was educated at boarding schools in Switzerland and learned to converse in German and French as well as she did in English. During her European travels she met Mark Twain, and, while staying with relatives in Indianapolis, the strikingly beautiful young woman flirted with Booth Tarkington, who never forgot her. She majored in fine arts for a time at Washington University, but when she married Edgar Roderick Rombauer at age twenty-two she found herself accomplished in every facet of living except homemaking. It was her husband, an enthusiastic outdoorsman, who taught Irma to cook while the couple was on camping trips. Her curiosity aroused, she added to her expertise by attending a Chautauqua seminar and to delve into the techniques applied in French and German cookbooks and indulged in her unusual flair for cake decorating.

As Edgar Rombauer's political career in the Urban League gained momentum, she complemented him by being a capable and highly entertaining hostess; her future publisher described Irma Rombauer as "incapable of being boring." Her children would remember feeling that their dinner table was like a lecture with a participatory audience because the Rombauers considered social intercourse just as important as food.

Irma Louise (von Starkloff) Rombauer (1877–1962) and Marion Rombauer Becker

Rombauer was only fifty-three when she was widowed. Marion and Edgar, both married and with households in other states, were concerned about her acute loneliness. It so happened that she had already engaged in one cookbook effort, a sheaf of seventy-three recipes gathered for a Unitarian Church-sponsored cooking course she taught in the 1920s, so the "home-made" cookbook idea seemed a natural.[1] With Edgar's encouragement, the mother-daughter team went into action. In St. Louis, Irma created and wrote, assisted by a family friend who typed and criticized. Marion tested recipes and concentrated on production as the pages were sent to New York. With her husband, John Becker, she returned to St. Louis to direct the Art Department at the John Burroughs School about a year later, a move that made the whole project easier to accomplish.

The two shared a sense of savoir faire and an abundance of energy, but it was obvious from the outset that Rombauer's wry wit and literary talents were unique and should not be disposed on family alone. In the end, she decided to go ahead and bankroll a substantial printing herself. Three thousand copies of *Joy of Cooking* were published in 1931 by the A. C. Clayton Co., 395 pages, with Marion's illustrations included.[2] The book contained five hundred recipes, both easy and fancy European-influenced.

---

1. Marion Rombauer Becker could locate no copy of this book and neither could I.

2. Ten copies are itemized on the OCLC listings, from the Atlantic City Free Public Library to Indiana University to Bishop College in Dallas. This is the most collectible *Joy*, referred to as the true first edition; the 1936 edition is called the first "commercial" edition.

Sales were lively thanks to words of praise from family and friends, but Rombauer wasn't satisfied. She went to Chicago to consult with Adolph Kroch, founder of Kroch's International Bookstore, who sent her home with a dubious compliment, "Two thousand copies privately sold in two years, woman, and you come to me?" It was only by chance (or so they say) that she met Lawrence Chambers, president of Bobbs-Merrill, at a bridge game. He agreed to look at the book after the recommendation of a mutual friend whose cooking he greatly admired. He agreed to publication only if the text were refined and the recipes were retested. Once again, Marion assisted her mother in this time-consuming and expensive task.

The Joy of Cooking; A Compilation of Reliable Recipes with a Casual Culinary Chat, published in 1936 (345 pages), did not become a best-seller overnight, but it sold steadily with generous encouragement from St. Louis Post-Dispatch food writers. However, in the 1943 revision (628 pages) Rombauer incorporated another cookbook she had written in 1939, Streamlined Cooking, and crystallized her style of recipe writing, imitated to this day. This larger volume, with its 3,500 recipes, hostessing tips, and many charts and tables, caught the nation's interest immediately. The timing of its release coincided with the needs of war brides and women who worked in defense plants. The book was more fun than Fanny Farmer et al., and its recipes were written in a far more user-friendly fashion. Although ingredients were not listed at the start of recipes they were easy to identify, and entered as used in the dish.

Rombauer did not have a corporate budget available to her, but by this time she knew that she had mastered the myriad details of the cooking craft, was able to impart this knowledge with an I-did-it-you-can-do-it-too attitude, and could race any chef through the fields of imagination. For instance, she was a fan of Chinese cooking and was the first to suggest that its efficient techniques be applied to American ways. Often referred to as a bible of sorts, the only consistent criticism about Joy of Cooking through the years has been that its typography is small and dull, and that it contains no glossy pictures, facts that only point out the remarkableness of its success.

In 1952 the book went through a third revision, and Marion Rombauer Becker was named as coauthor. This enabled Irma Rombauer to go back to traveling, which she dearly loved, and turn over most of the responsibility of the book's progress to her daughter. She answered fan letters in longhand as she always did, and broadcast optimistic speeches for the Voice of America. Irma Rombauer died in St. Louis in 1962 of a heart attack. Marion Rombauer

Becker continued what she referred to as the Family Business, moving with her husband to Cincinnati. She corresponded with thousands of enthusiasts, leading many readers to believe erroneously that the cookbook originated in Cincinnati.

Aside from its chattiness and the testimony from satisfied cooks, who reassured each other that "it even has" certain favored recipes, *Joy* was more remarkable than any other twentieth-century cookbook for one specific reason: It peddled no products, nor was it sponsored by any magazine or newspaper with the publicity the latter allows. In later years Becker became almost fanatical in her desire to remind the public that the family owed no allegiance to anyone but their readers, but one cannot blame her for wanting to boast about an achievement that sets the book above almost all competitors because its success is solely attributable to its own merits as a cooking tool. Marion Becker also revised the book twice on her own, displaying a vast understanding of international cuisine, and although the editions were not as well received by some critics, the new *Joy* soared in sales.

In *Little Acorn: The Story Behind The Joy of Cooking, 1931–1966*,[3] Becker regrets that her mother always meant to write her memoirs but never got around to it. As Irma S. Rombauer was a singularly intriguing character, this is truly our loss, but *Little Acorn* does contain gossipy vignettes nonetheless, including pages of glittering reviews well into the 1960s.

Irma Rombauer's entry in Radcliffe's *Notable Women* was penned by James Beard. To date, *Joy* has sold fifteen million copies and still makes the best-seller list during the holiday season. It is available in four formats: paperback, hardcover, a two-volume set, and comb-bound. Not bad for a family project that was virtually snubbed by the national media for almost a decade and yet became the most popular independently-produced American cookbook of the twentieth century.

Betty Crocker was thirty-two years old when she wrote *Betty Crocker's Picture Cookbook* in 1950. She was thirty-two years old when she revised it superbly in 1956 (my favorite old cookbook) and wrote more than one hundred additional cookbooks, and she is still thirty-two years old today. She is ageless in other ways, too. Not content with a common nip-and-tuck facelift like other women,

---

3. *Little Acorn* was published as a gift from Bobbs-Merrill to booksellers at their June 1966 convention in Washington, D.C.

Betty Crocker

Janette Kelley

Betty has taken her entire face off and put on another six times in seven decades. Yet in spite of her youthful appearance, bank roll, and culinary seductiveness, she remains single. Worse, she has no family to support her in her lavish cookbook endeavors—or so it would seem.

It all started in October of 1921, when Washburn Crosby, a milling company, ran a jigsaw puzzle advertisement in a national magazine, showing a street scene with people hauling home sacks of flour. As a prize to everyone who put the pieces together, the company offered pincushions resembling a miniature sack of flour. The company received more answers than it anticipated and appointed Sam Gale of the Advertising Department to deal with the incoming mail.[4]

The mill had already published a few cookbooks, including the effort by Maria Parloa. Two young home economists, Agnes White and Janette Kelley, were using a corner of a room to test recipes on a stove, compiling entries for the anonymous publications. White would fade into obscurity, but Kelley had two careers at General Mills separated by thirteen years at Lever Brothers, where she set up the first test kitchen. Born in Montana and a home economics graduate of Montana State College, Kelley wrote the first bread booklet for Washburn Crosby. She also made the first chocolate layer cake pictured in a Gold Medal advertisement, according to later public relations releases.

When the commotion in the Advertising Department began, the women's job descriptions suddenly expanded. The puzzle answers were accompanied by requests for food answers—Why doesn't my cake rise? How long do you knead bread dough?—and the male staff was stymied. White and Kelley were invited to stuff pincushions but, more significantly, at least in their eyes, to research whatever culinary advice was needed. It would be Sam Gale who signed the letters, however. At some point, someone (and the company is vague on who) decided that it wasn't right that a man (who couldn't even cook?) should be telling women how to shape their buns. But instead of turning to White or Kelley—genuine flesh-and-blood females—the men deigned to "personify" a woman, or in the later words of Harry Bullis, General Mills chairman of the board, "the personification of the idea that we ought to help women with their

4. As a result of the Betty Crocker promotion Gale became an advertising legend. He started his career by choosing the name "Jack Armstrong, the All-American Boy" for an early radio program that ran eighteen years with one sponsor—Wheaties.

cooking troubles." *Crocker* was chosen as her surname because retired director William G. Crocker had been popular, and *Betty* just seemed nice. A piece of paper was circulated in the office, and the women were all requested to write the name down. The most legible was chosen for Betty Crocker's signature, that of Florence Lindeberg.

By 1924 the Gold Medal Home Service Department was flourishing, with the "most modern equipment," including both gas and electric ranges surrounded by cozy furnishings in white and delft blue. Washburn Crosby's friendly fantasy was fast becoming a household authority in Minneapolis, and the letter answerers and cooking pamphlet writers were so stunningly successful that women all over the country continued to confide not only their cooking woes, but also personal joys and sorrows in Betty Crocker. Outside Minneapolis, however, the company abstained from emphasizing the fact that Betty was not a real woman.

In 1924, right before Washburn Crosby joined General Mills, Kelley left and Marjorie Child Husted joined, another home economics graduate, from the University of Minnesota.[5] It was Husted's congenial voice that introduced "Betty Crocker's Cooking School of the Air" on WCCO radio in Minneapolis, an outgrowth of a casual chat format inaugurated by another "Betty," Blanche Ingersoll. It was the first women's service program to go to a national network. By 1926, Husted was director of a staff of five in General Mills's Home Service Department, a position she held for twenty years. From the start, Betty Crocker was portrayed as a demure but capable homemaker who only stripped off her spotless apron to do an occasional lecture or radio show. The irony was that "she" was actually a team of highly motivated, polished female executives led by Husted, who also possessed superior domestic talent. As such, they would have been capable of inspiring even more women had industry wanted to encourage more women into the workplace. However, working women throughout America were not by any stretch of the imagination recognized—or paid—fairly.

Marjorie Child Husted
(1892–1986)

According to a remarkable and candid interview with Marjorie Child Husted "The Real Betty Crocker Is One Tough Cookie" by Carol Pine in the November 1978 *Twin Cities Reader*, it wasn't long before a competitor threatened to sue the company for misleading advertising, that is, pretending Betty was real. Apparently the only

---

5. None of the "Child" cookbook authors are related.

way out of the dilemma was to prove that there was such a person—
one person. The Legal Department sent Husted to a "well known"
attorney who heard her answer yes to such questions as, Do you do
the broadcasting? and Do you do the recipe testing? Husted added
that she watched over every phase of every endeavor. "Well," ex-
claimed the lawyer, "you *must* be Betty Crocker."

Originally, Husted was required to respond that she was merely
director of the Home Service Test Kitchens when women visited the
company and asked to meet the famous personality, but under President D. D. Davis she was given permission to state that she was indeed Betty Crocker, and for twenty years she did just that. She
appeared on the first commercially sponsored CBS color television
program, "The World Is Yours" on June 26, 1951; was introduced
as Betty Crocker; and, while perspiration dripped from her brow
under the hot lights, authoritatively whipped up a mouth-watering
apple roll.

From 1936 on, the public was treated to portraits of Betty
Crocker on cookbooks and General Mills products. The first was
commissioned from artist-illustrator Neysa McMein, who thought-
fully did what she said was a composite rendering of the women
who worked in the test kitchens. This strikingly attractive portrait,
meant to serve Betty forever, lasted for twenty years. Although the
company claims it is only a coincidence, at the same time Betty got
her first renovation, McMein's bohemian and all too human youth
had just come to light. It seems the artist's New York studio had
been a haven where friends played poker until all hours and—
during prohibition—drank gin from her bathroom still. Coincidence
or not, McMein's Betty was history. In 1955 the illustrator Hilda
Taylor created an almost perky face, and subsequent portraits de-
pict a woman who looks like a 1950s' Republican woman's club
president.[6]

After Kelley's return, General Mills went to great lengths to an-
nounce that Husted had been advanced to the new post of consultant to the officers and directors of General Mills; Kelley was made
assistant director of the Home Service Department. They both still
answered to Sam Gale.

---

6. To this day, consumers may receive photos of the seven Betty render-
ings just by asking; the flyer includes information about the artists. Sam Gale
and Bill Crocker are also immortalized, but nowhere in the flyer is there any
allusion to, or proud acknowledgment of, Marjorie Child Husted, or any of
the other women who supported her, as the true personification of Betty
Crocker.

In "Tough Cookie," Husted confided that she felt like an oddity in the board room, that the men did not feel comfortable with her, nor did they wish to try. "In those days, you couldn't be a militant feminist while working with a lot of men," she said, "you had to be subtle." She subtly invited her secretary to share an office with her rather than follow the executive-row tradition that jams secretaries into cubbyholes in a centralized, windowless room. And she noticed the discrepancies in salary between hers and those of the men with whom she shared a cooler and remained silent in order to keep her enviable position.

Meanwhile, both Gale and Husted were receiving honor and notoriety. Wooing Madison Avenue in the July 1947 issue of *Horizons*, Gale wrote an article titled "Our Advertising Must Be Truthful, Informative and Educational." The then–vice president of General Mills (photographed with his hands in his pockets) stated that studies indicated that Americans "discount advertising more today than they did ten years ago" and discussed the company's noble attempts to educate consumers away from such folly.

Among other recognition Husted received was the first Businesswoman of the Year Award from the Woman's National Press Club, presented by President Harry Truman; at that same ceremony Anna Mary (Grandma) Moses was honored for her art, and Eleanor Roosevelt for her work with the United Nations. But while Gale's star was rising nationally, unfortunately, publicity about any of the real women connected with General Mills seems to have been released almost exclusively on a local basis. In fact, a 1950 Associated Press news exclusive released by General Mills described Kelley as a "seldom-publicized food authority."

At that same time, the women had begun work compiling the greatest cookbook the company would ever produce, *Betty Crocker's Picture Cookbook* (1951). Highly organized by menu item (although heavy on yeast breads, quick breads, pies, and cakes), Husted and company's cookbook set a standard of excellence that could only have been achieved with massive corporate resources abetting their splendid talents, and vice-versa. The recipes were clear, producing no-fail, delectable results. There was just enough explanation to do it right the first time, along with a few sentences of encouragement, perhaps with an impudent exclamation point. Taking the best ideas from all previous best-sellers, including Rombauer's unmistakable rhythm, *Picture* was a unique, highly stylized presentation with multiple typefaces. It was absolutely consistent, and no recipe spilled over onto a page to be turned with a soiled hand. Black and white and irresistible color photographs inspired cooks and showed how to perform such complicated tasks as getting coconut meat out of the shell, mounding and filling cream puffs, and frenching green beans. Ingredients were listed in the order of usage in the recipe. Measurements were exact and double-specified when needed, for example, a number 2½ can tomatoes (3⅓ cups). Under Husted's perfectionist direction it wasn't enough to present a recipe for angel food cake. She demanded, and got, the best recipe. She supervised photographs from the top of a ladder and looked at the picture through the camera lens before the shot was taken.

Published jointly by McGraw-Hill and General Mills, *Betty Crocker's Picture Cookbook* was priced—irresistibly—just a bit lower than other best-sellers on the market, a shrewd policy that continues to this day. Sometimes erroneously referred to as *Betty Crocker's Cook Book* (as its descendant is known), the book in its multiple incarnations is acknowledged by book dealers and statisticians to be the top selling cookbook in American history. An estimated fifty-five million have been sold. (A completely unrecognizable version is currently available in three formats: ring-bound binder, paperback, and floppy disk.)

Although cooks have favorites among the more than 150 additional Betty Crocker titles the company has produced through the years, Ms. Crocker's enviable and lasting reputation was grounded in the 1951–56 achievement.[7]

Strangely and sadly, just when this incomparable cookbook was finding its way into more and more American kitchens, at the acme of her success Betty developed schizophrenia. General Mills released public relations material for Kelley that stated that she was "responsible for the widespread activities of Betty Crocker, probably influencing the cooking habits of the housewives more than any other person in the country"; at the same time, Husted's public relations averred that she "did most to shape the Betty Crocker personality until it was synonymous with 'service' to the homemakers of America." Why, suddenly, were there two Bettys? Was General Mills preparing for Husted's inevitable retirement, and if so, why not do it up right? Was Husted becoming uppity? Were they deliberately trying to cause friction? And if so, why?

---

7. In 1990, Donnelley's Marketing asked 2,500 households what celebrity endorsements would make them more likely to purchase a product. Betty Crocker came in first.

By 1954 General Mills boasted that Betty's propaganda had cost $50 million and that ninety-nine out of a hundred women recognized her name. The company now had five testing kitchens equipped with seventeen ovens hovered over by a staff of forty-five sedulous cooks, twenty-four of whom had home economics degrees. In a peculiarly defensive information flyer produced in 1954 that contradicted all previous news releases, there was an effort to affix multiple personality disorder to Betty's schizophrenia diagnosis, connecting no less than eleven women equally with her name.

In the mid 1950s, Husted resigned. Contrary to anything General Mills has released since—that is, pretending that Betty was only a myth—the ultimate proof of Marjorie Child Husted's singular contribution and irreplaceability was the fact that Betty Crocker was never the same. The void could not be filled. Eventually, the company shoved her "personification" aside to concentrate on publicity about the progress of Betty's physiognomy, and all reference to Husted et al. was obliterated in favor of a "sweet-talking" abstract.

Janette Kelley died in 1958, a single woman who had thoroughly enjoyed having what for the time was an extraordinary career. Marjorie Husted was ninety-four years old when she died in 1986 in her modest apartment near Lake Calhoun in Minnesota. Her beloved husband Wally, a Clark Gable look-alike, had died a decade earlier. In the 1978 interview Husted revealed that she had written that summer to General Mills (whether for money or acknowledgment or something else she does not say), stating that Sam Gale had often told her she "had done more for the sale of General Mills products than anyone else in the company." The interview does not reveal whether the letter was answered.

She was the real thing. Marjorie is as nice a name as Betty. The real woman was beautiful well into old age and never required a face lift. Her absence proved that Betty Crocker was not an inflatable toy that any woman could puff up and fly away with, that Betty Crocker was the pseudonym of a superbly accomplished executive who gave heart and soul to inspire and teach women just as perfect, and imperfect, as she. Husted was worth whatever salary any man in the company received. She spearheaded the creation and development of one of the greatest cookbooks in American history. Then, as now, Marjorie Child Husted deserved more than the on-again, off-again loyalty of a company that still profits by pretending it was all in a name.

"I didn't want to be a blue-stocking intellectual—or a businesswoman, really. I expected to marry and have children. When I pledged the sorority, a fortuneteller said I would make money late in life by my own efforts. I can remember thinking what a crazy idea that was. No girls I knew were making money by their own efforts."
—Marjorie Child Husted (1978)

Fiesta Tamale Pie
"Picturesque dish from Old Mexico"

Saute until onion is yellow. . . .

    1 small onion, minced

    1 clove garlic, minced

in

    3 tablespoons butter, 3 tablespoons olive oil

Add, and cook until brown. . . .

    1 pound ground beef

    ½ pound bulk pork sausage

Simmer 20 minutes. . . .

    no. 2½ can tomatoes (3½ cups)

    no. 2 can whole kernel corn (2½ cups)

    2 teaspoons salt, 2 teaspoons chili powder

Add to meat mixture and pour into 11 × 7-inch oblong baking dish.

Press into mixture. . . .

    20 to 24 pitted ripe olives

Spread over filling a mixture of. . . .

    1 cup corn meal, 1 cup milk, 2 eggs well beaten

Sprinkle with. . . .

    1½ cups grated American cheese

Bake. Temperature: 350 degrees (mod. oven)

Time: Bake 1 hour.

Amount: 8 to 10 servings.

—Betty Crocker's Picture Cook Book
(Minneapolis: General Mills, 1956;
reprinted with the permission of
General Mills, Inc.)

Greens

"Great grandmother never heard of vitamins, but she knew that greens were good for her family. So she gathered the wild greens and planted the seeds of many others. One to two pounds serves four."

Chicory	Radish
Collards	Romaine
Dandelion Greens	Spinach
Escarole	Swiss Chard
Kale	Tops of Beet
Kohlrabi	Turnip
Lettuce	Watercress
Mustard Greens	

Trim root ends and damaged ends. Wash well by lifting in and out of cool water about three times. Or use a salad basket for washing. Sand will sink to the bottom. Save tender young greens to add raw in salads! Cook covered, using only the water that clings to the leaves after washing, three to ten minutes, or just until tender. Older greens will take longer than younger ones. Kale will take longer than spinach.

IDEAS FOR SERVING

- Serve with butter, salt, pepper. Vary with dash of vinegar or lemon juice.
- Minced onion or garlic, grated nutmeg, prepared mustard, or horse-radish may be added during cooking, together with oil, butter, or bacon drippings.
- Add bacon or salt pork to dandelion and turnip greens. Just before serving, add a little brown sugar and vinegar and garnish with slices of hard-cooked eggs.
- To collard greens, add clove of garlic, celery salt, pepper, sugar, pod of red pepper during cooking time.
- Serve with wedges of lemon or slices of hard-cooked eggs.
- Serve as Cuban greens—cooked chopped greens seasoned with salt, pepper, onion juice, horseradish, served on toast squares and topped with crisp bacon and chopped dill pickle.

> —*Betty Crocker's Picture Cook Book*
> (Minneapolis: General Mills, 1956;
> reprinted with the permission of
> General Mills, Inc.)

Pineapple Upside-Down Cake
"Handsome dessert to serve at table."

First, prepare the pan: Melt ⅓ cup butter in heavy 10-inch skillet or baking dish. Sprinkle ½ cup brown sugar evenly over butter. Arrange slices of pineapple over butter-sugar coating, and garnish with maraschino cherries and pecan halves as shown in picture below.[8] Make the Cake Batter and pour it over fruit. Bake until wooden pick thrust into center of cake comes out clean. Immediately turn upside-down on serving plate. Do not remove pan for a few minutes. Brown sugar mixture will run down over cake instead of clinging to pan. Serve warm with plain or whipped cream.

CAKE BATTER

Beat until thick and lemon-colored (5 mins.)

    2 eggs

Gradually beat in. . . .

    ⅔ cup sugar

Beat in all at once. . . .

    6 tablespoons juice from fruit, 1 teaspoon vanilla

Sift together and beat in all at once . . .

    1 cup sifted Gold Medal Flour or Softasilk Cake Flour

    ⅓ teaspoon baking powder

    ¼ teaspoon salt

Temperature: 350 degrees (mod. oven).

Time: Bake 45 mins.

—*Betty Crocker's Picture Cook Book* (Minneapolis: General Mills, 1956; reprinted with the permission of General Mills, Inc.)

---

8. Pineapple slices in a circle, with one more in center; half a cherry, upside-down, in each pineapple hole; pecan halves, upside-down, between slices, as needed, facing center.

Linzer Torte

The following recipe is for a delicious German "company" cake. It looks like an open jam pie and, being rich, is usually served in thin wedges.

Sift:

1 cup sugar

Beat until soft:

⅞ cup butter

Add the sugar gradually. Blend these ingredients until they are very light and creamy. Add:

1 teaspoon grated lemon rind

Beat in one at a time:

2 eggs

Stir in gradually:

1 cup sifted bread flour

1 cup unblanched almonds, ground in a nut grinder

½ teaspoon cinnamon

¼ teaspoon cloves

1 tablespoon cocoa

The German recipe reads "stir for one hour," but of course no high-geared American has time for that. If the dough is very soft, chill it. Roll it to the thickness of ⅛ inch between sheets of waxed paper. Put it into a pyrex dish, giving it a good edge. Cover the bottom of the cake generously with a good quality:

Jam, preserves or apple butter

Roll the remaining dough into strips. Make a lattice over the preserves. (If the room is warm and the dough is temperamental, place the dough in a pastry tube and make the strips by forcing the dough through the bag.) Bake the cake in a hot oven, 400 degrees.

—*The Joy of Cooking*
by Irma S. Rombauer
(Indianapolis: Bobbs-Merrill, 1936
reprinted with permission of Macmillan Publishing Company from *The Joy of Cooking* by Irma S. Rombauer and Marion Rombauer Becker. Copyright 1931, 1936 by The Bobbs-Merrill Company, Inc., renewed © 1959, 1964 by Ethan Becker.)

8

Imported Influences: Great Chefs

There were among the Native Americans and the early (willing and unwilling) immigrants accomplished cooks who would merit a place in this chapter. Certainly Eliza Leslie, Elizabeth Goodfellow, Sarah Tyson Rorer, Maria Parloa, and Mary Randolph would also qualify. But women and Indians were not considered for the position of chef when hotels and restaurants began to open in the great cities, and black Americans hired in eateries were referred to simply as cooks, or uncle or aunt, and paid accordingly. Male white Americans rarely chose the profession because so many other less-stressful, better-paying possibilities were open to them. Thus, male Europeans, coming mainly from Northern and Western Europe before the 1880s, dominated the field. These imported experts often brought with them the staff they had worked with when enticed by the riches of the New World.

From New England down the Atlantic Coast, British settlers introduced various styles of cooking; the French contributed to the Creole cooking of Louisiana and helped form the cuisines in our major cities; the Spaniards influenced the Southwest and, to a certain extent, the deep South. All inaugurated what are now known as the hyphenated cuisines of America, for example, Franco-American, Italian-American, and Polish-American.

The traditional distinction between home cook and professional chef emigrated with these men, a distinction ineluctably based on financial backing. Having at his disposal the world's resources allowed a man to accomplish memorable feats of culinary wizardry to satiate the wildest expectations of the wealthy and elite. Having at her disposal only what was growing on the homestead or what she could afford to purchase at market formed another sort of wonder, a fairy godmother of the kitchen who could turn ordinary baked potato orts into delectable "skins" by incanting the word *frugality.* One must ponder who was the greater sorcerer.

There were other differences. The home cook was dedicated to nurturing and kept things fresh. She also kept them simple because she had to wash the dishes herself. On the other hand, the professional cared not one whit about the effects of conspicuous consumption on the health of his patrons and routinely worried a perfectly good natural resource through several nutrient-destroying cooking processes to erect a masterpiece. The wreckage was cleaned up by kitchen assistants. Dealing with the public also gave the chef confidence to achieve, and money to reinvest in his own talents, hard-to-come-by assets for the homemaker.

The homemaker took inspiration from the master chefs, to whom she humbly gave acknowledgment through newspaper, magazine, and cookbook participation. But it was the rare chef (most were often critical of, or condescending to, women) who admitted that his frequent sojourns in rural Europe and America were to sniff out what was going on in the pots and pans of local women. Although these travels incited his own competitive experimentation, a chef would never disclose the origin of a resulting Great Dish—unless it was his mother. Today's society continues to distinguish between everyday "cooks" and hired "chefs" as though the latter calling demands a greater vocation. Yet when the everyday cook is enthusiastic and talented, her magic is performed out of true love.

One sure route to national or regional acclaim would be through the pages of a cookbook, and ethnic cooks both in homes and restaurants were quick to write such efforts, in English or bilingually, or have them written or translated by others. Foreign cuisine was introduced to the masses in this way, and still is.

But not every treatise was snatched up by the public. Some cookbooks were confusing, unattractive, passé, or the recipes were incomplete. Asian cultures did not generally produce cookbooks, but rather depended on the spoken word to pass on formulas, so these food cultures remained mysterious well into the twentieth century. Cookbooks that survived as documentation of these early ethnic influences, mostly European, were praised at the time of writing for authenticity, originality, and for the author's unusual talent in imparting food knowledge from a foreign culture and "Americanizing" it (without completely corrupting it) using available resources. They had one other feature in common. Most authors also had a love for, and interest in, their fans, even if they did get paid for their trouble!

Delmonico's produced not only a good many chefs-turned-authors but also the weightiest cookbook produced in U.S. history. In 1827, brothers John and Peter Delmonico came from the vineyards of Switzerland to open a confectionery they called Del's, in New York City. As their families grew, so did the family enterprise, and soon nephew Lorenzo was summoned to help. Under his expert guidance the menu was enlarged to support an extraordinarily imaginative, representative Continental cuisine that was presented in an elegant decor surpassed by none. Several chefs were hired as the establishment became a mecca for gourmets, gourmands, and celebrities. During the next nine decades (the last original Delmonico's closed in 1923) every American and foreign visitor to New York who could afford to, including Abraham Lincoln, William Thackeray, and Charles Dickens, ate at one of the eight locations. While seated at his regular table at the 14th Street and Fifth Avenue site Sam Morse sent the first transatlantic telegram. Delmonico steak and Delmonico tomatoes (stuffed with sweetbreads), as well as scores of other "Delmonico" recipes mentioned in period cookbooks, originated here, while great chefs developed other "secret" formulas in restaurant kitchens all over the country.

Antoine's of New Orleans opened its doors in 1840 but released only a few of the recipes that made it famous (e.g., oysters Rockefeller) until Roy F. Guste, Jr., the fifth-generation proprietor, wrote *Antoine's Restaurant Cookbook* in 1980.[1] One of the largest, most popular of the "chef" cookbooks (906 pages, twenty-six of them index), *The Cookbook by "Oscar" of the Waldorf* (where Waldorf salad was invented) was published in 1896 and again in 1908. Oscar Tschirky was a maître d'hôtel of the Waldorf-Astoria, not a chef, who collected recipes from several New York chefs without ac-

Oscar Tschirky (1866–1950)

---

1. Also connected with New Orleans, the exotic author and world traveler Lafcadio Hearn was discovered to have written an anonymous work titled *La Cuisine Creole* (1885), now a valuable collector's item.

knowledging them in this impressive endeavor. He then considered it a "strange coincidence" that the public thought him to be a chef.[2] Tschirky admitted to his biographer Karl Scheissgiesser (*Oscar of the Waldorf*, 1943) that although he had "planned many feasts truly fit for the gods," his repertoire peaked at scrambled eggs.

Fanny Lemira Gillette and Hugo Ziemann, steward at the White House, paired to compile the *White House Cook Book*, "a selection of choice recipes original and selected during a period of 40 years' practical housekeeping." The recipes were Euro-American in nature. It was published in 1887 with full-page plates of the wives of four presidents, including the wife of the newly elected Benjamin Harrison.[3] Extremely popular around the country, it was published again and again—sometimes as poorly as the original was so that surviving copies are extremely fragile—as *The Presidents Cook Book* (1895), with full-page advertisements interspersed between pages, and coupons (e.g. "Bride's Coupon: This coupon presented at our creamery entitles the newly married housewife to a wedding present with her first purchase; The Medina County Creamery Company"); *The Capitol Cook Book* (1896); and *Mrs. Gillettes Cook Book: 50 Years of Practical Cooking* (1899), all published in Chicago and Cleveland.

Formerly of the Metropolis Monte Carlo and Cannes, the Café de Paris, and the Hotel Richelieu in Chicago, the irresistible Henrí Charpentier (a favorite of Irma Rombauer's) lit up his future by putting a match to the crêpes Suzette (which he had invented by obvious accident as a youth) that were being served flamboyantly in his own establishments called Henri's in Lynbrook, Long Island, and Rockefeller Center, New York. He wrote a couple of cookbooks as well as a charming autobiography titled *Life à la Henrí* (1934), complete with a few sensational recipes within the text. In *Food and Finesse; the Bride's Bible* (1945) each recipe in the twelve-month menu of meals is named after a famous American man except for desserts, usually soufflés and puddings, which are named after not necessarily puffy or sweet famous women.

Irrefutably, New York City attracted the most adventuresome diners between the mid 1800s and 1900, with Delmonico graduates exploiting their grand talents on paper. *French Dishes for American*

Henrí Charpentier
(1880-1961)

---

2. This is still going on. Many currently famous chefs credit him with inventing Waldorf salad.

3. Harrison may have been inspired by Gillette's success to spearhead *The Washington Cook Book* (1890) subtitled *The Most Complete and Valuable Cook Book in the World*. It wasn't.

Alessandro Filippini

Charles Ranhofer

Tables by Pierre Carron (1886) was translated from the French and edited by Mrs. Frederick Sherman for D. Appleton in New York. Carron was a former chef d'entrements [desserts]. Another more notable master was Italian Alessandro Filippini (not Phillipi), who published several cookbooks with Doubleday, Page & Company, including *The Table: How to Buy Food. . . .* (1889) and *The International Cookbook* (1911).

The most famous of the Delmonico artistes during the Gay Nineties was Charles Ranhofer, born in Alsace. He came to America in 1861 and served the family for thirty-four years, overseeing every facet of every restaurant. His contribution to cookbook history was aptly titled *The Epicurean* (1908), a self-published, massive 1,200-page 10-pound tome bound in keratol levant (faux leather) grain, with the title embossed in gold. He dedicated it to the memory of the Delmonicos, stating boldly in his preface that "the profession will acknowledge its indebtedness to [them] for the interest shown . . . in developing the gastronomic art in this country." Billed as an "all-around cookbook," it did not become a "tome-for-the-home"; rather, it invaded the hotel world as "The King of Cookbooks" at a pricey $7. Other chefs, such as Arnold Shircliffe of the Edgewater Beach Hotel in Chicago and Thomas J. Murrey of the Astor House in Washington, D.C., also prepared pocket-sized handbooks of approximately fifty pages to assist and impress their peers, priced at $2.

The numbers of categories in *The Epicurean*, and their completeness, was overwhelming. There were 248 pages of menus and meals and garden parties, dancing parties, and menu information. Full explanations were given of kitchen utensils, china, glass, and silver; as well as a table of supplies in English and French; a pep talk on the drudgery tasks that apprentices should appreciate doing; 134 pages of garnishings; 165 beef recipes, 218 fish, 100 egg, and 170 cake; and 44 pages of index, and so on. All with more than eight hundred fine illustrations.

Although the public outside the hotel trade knew little of its existence, *The Epicurean* was a significant contribution to that trade, the only one of its kind, a voluptuous volume combining genius with gluttony, sublime with ridiculous. The reader who might actually develop an interest in sculpting a preposterous sugar-candy chariot filled with miniature candy apples or shaving truffles into "thin slices a sixteenth of an inch thick" to form doilies under molded salads or mousselines might, however, balk at the likes of Figure 404, which pictures six cute, unsuspecting reed-bird fledglings nestled very snugly into single metal cups-on-a-kabob (although instructions do call for gutting them first), for roasting. More like medieval feasting than what we think of as American eating, *The Epicurean* presents a sobering slice of historical reality!

Inevitably, an upstart with a flair for publicity and a technique for delivering comparable quality at slightly lower prices came along to rival Delmonico's: George Rector. Rector's grandfather founded the Frontier House at Lewiston, New York, on the Niagara River in 1845. During the late 1890s and early 1900s Rector's and Delmonico's competing though completely different Continental cuisines vied for the patronage of celebrities, including legendary glutton "Diamond" Jim Brady, whom Rector described as "the best 25 customers we had."[4] Rector's gaudy, mirrored digs was satisfaction-guaranteed as "the national museum of habits, the börse of gossip, and the clearing house of rumors," where "who's who went to learn what's what." When the hotel heyday was severely hampered by the advent of prohibition, Rector propelled a *Saturday Evening Post* article (July 1926), "The Girl From Rector's," into a modest literary career featuring *The Rector Cookbook* (1928).[5] It was reprinted in 1949 by Doubleday as *Rector's Naughty 90's Cookbook*.

Throughout the twentieth century, a steady stream of chefs and outstanding cooks entered the picture, bringing with them, or exploiting, ethnic cuisines from world cultures. Each would have its proper era of faddishness with American cooks as its essence was absorbed into the mainstream diet. Leonard Jan Mitchell presented traditional German fare with celebrity preferences in *Lüchow's German Cookbook* (1952) from Lüchow's. In the memory of Luisa Leone, better known as the proprietor of Mama Leone's, her son Gene wrote down a thorough, entertaining, and appetizing record of another fine New York establishment, *Leone's Italian Cookbook* (1967). In Chicago in the 1960s and 1970s, the Bakery restaurant exhibited the talents of its founder Louis Szmathmary, who would go on to write introductions for, and haphazardly update, at least

> "My lady assistants all knew cooking and they loved it. This was the secret of keeping Mother's high standard of quality in the kitchen. I always felt that women were for cooking and men for lifting."
> —Gene Leone, (1967)

---

4. It was common knowledge that James Buchanan Brady (with his sometime-friend actress Lillian Russell) ate his days away, climaxing with a dinner of several dozen six-inch oysters, six lobsters, a couple of ducks or roasting chickens, a large steak (smothered, some said, in veal cutlets), selected sauced vegetables, a platter of pastries, two pound-boxes of chocolates, and two gallons of orange juice. He did not drink spirits. The last article that the incomparable Mary Frances Kennedy Fisher wrote for *Gourmet* (September 1992) recounts tales about this omnivore.

5. Although the "girl" existed only in the script of a naughty Parisian play on Broadway, Rector reports that "wifely indignation" caused many businessmen to move from that "terrible hotel where the Girl . . . made her habitat."

twenty classic American cookbooks for Arno Press, as well as a previously unpublished cookery manuscript written by Nelson Algren, *America Eats* (1992), published by the University of Iowa Press. Possibly purchased by patrons more for their sentimental value as souvenirs rather than a vested interest in cooking cacciatora or potato pancakes, thousands of these chef cookbooks were sold (between 1952 and 1970 *Lüchow's* was reprinted nineteen times), and many ended up on used bookstore shelves until they were ultimately seized and cherished by appreciative collectors—explorers with vision and insight.

Deviled Chestnuts

Peel the raw chestnuts and scald them to remove the inner skin; put them in a frying-pan with a little butter and toss them about a few moments; add a sprinkle of salt and a suspicion of cayenne.

Orange-Cocoanut Salad

Fruits served as a salad are most enjoyable; served with a crispy croûton or quantity of little cakes they are very acceptable. Peel and slice four Florida oranges. Cover the bottom of a compotier with slices of oranges, and strew over them a layer of fresh-grated cocoanut; add layers of sliced orange and cocoanut until the dish is full. Add powdered sugar, and over all pour a pint of champagne.

Croûtons

Cut sandwich-bread into slices one-quarter of an inch thick; cut each slice into four small triangles; dry them in the oven slowly until they assume a delicate brownish tint, then serve, either hot or cold. A nice way to serve them is to spread a paste of part butter and part rich, creamy cheese, to which may be added a very little minced parsley.

—*Puddings and Dainty Desserts*
by Thomas J. Murrey of the Astor
House in Washington, D.C., formerly
of the House of Representatives, and
the Continental Hotel in Philadelphia
(New York: White, Stokes & Allen,
1886)

Swiss Nuts Appetizer

[NOTE: Shircliffe was the author of many small, clothbound decorated handbooks (e.g., *The Salad Portfolio*, 1926). All, plus other books of interest to chefs, were advertised in each. He was also a cookbook collector himself.]

Grated Swiss cheese (two ounces); whipped or raw cream; shelled pecans (three ounces). Stir into 1½ ounces of the grated cheese, 2 tablespoons of whipped cream, or 1 tablespoon raw cream, and make cheese and cream into a paste. Take a little of the paste and stick 2 pecans together with it. After you have stuck all pecans together, roll them in the ½ ounce of dry grated cheese you have left and also sprinkle them with salt. This gives the nuts a very nice appearance. They are very delicious and something new. They are to be eaten out of hand as you would celery or olives. The 1½ ounces of Swiss cheese is enough for 90 medium sized pecans.

—*The Edgewater Beach Hotel
Sandwich Book*
by Arnold Shircliffe
(Chicago: Hotel Monthly Press, Merchandise Mart, 1930)

Oyster Brochettes with Truffles
(Hûitres en Brochettes aux Truffes)

Poach in their liquid three dozen large oysters; when they are cold, pare and season, run a small wooden skewer through their centers, alternating each oyster with a round slice of cooked truffle. Dip these brochettes into a well reduced allemande sauce, into which has been added chopped mushrooms and fine herbs. Range them at once on a baking sheet, and leave them in the ice-box until the sauce is thoroughly cold. Three hours later detach them from the sheet, remove the superfluous sauce, and shape them nicely, roll them in white-bread-crumbs, dip them in beaten eggs, and again in bread-crumbs, smooth the surfaces, and plunge the brochettes into very hot fat until they attain a golden color; then withdraw the skewers and dress them at once on a folded napkin. Garnish with fried parsley.

"Should the menu be intended for a dinner including ladies, it must be composed of light, fancy dishes with a pretty dessert; if on the contrary, it is intended for gentlemen alone, then it must be shorter and more substantial."
—Charles Ranhofer (1908)

Allemande sauce is made by reducing some velouté [butter, flour, chicken broth], incorporating a little good raw cream slowly into it. When the sauce is succulent and creamy thicken it with several raw egg yolks then boil the sauce for one minute to cook the eggs, pressing against the bottom of the pan with a spatula. Strain it through a tammy into a vessel. Stir it, then put this by until cold.

—*The Epicurean*
by Charles Ranhofer
(New York; C. Ranhofer, 1908)

Salad à L'Italienne

"The pleasures of the table are enjoyed by all who possess good health . . . and yet, of the immense number that enjoy the good cheer and luxuries of the table, how few, very few, there are who stop to consider the vexatious trouble our host undergoes when arranging the daily bill of fare."
—Alexander Filippini
(1889)

Pare a good-sized carrot and a good-sized turnip, cut them with a vegetable scoop, and cook them in separate salted waters; the carrot 15 minutes, and the turnip 10. Drain, let cool, then place them in a dome-shaped pile in a salad-bowl. Cut two good-sized truffles into julienne-shaped pieces; cut up six mushrooms the same way, also the breast of a cooked, medium-sized chicken. Cover the vegetables with a cluster of the truffles, the same of the mushrooms, and repeat with the chicken, keeping each article separate; form a small cavity in the centre of the dome, pour into it a teaspoon of anchovy sauce, a tablespoon of vinegar, one tablespoonful of sweet oil, a pinch of salt, and half a pinch of pepper. Cover the cavity with a piece of cooked cauliflower or Brussels sprouts, or in default of both, cooked asparagus–tops will answer the purpose. Send to the table, and mix well before serving it to the guests.

—*The Table; How to Buy Food, How to Cook It, and How to Serve It*
by Alexander Filippini
(New York: Webster, 1889)

Amber Soup

Ingredients: A large soup bone (say two pounds), a chicken, a small slice of ham, a soup bunch (or an onion, two sprigs of parsley, half a small carrot, half a small parsnip, half a stock of celery), three cloves, pepper, salt, a gallon of cold water, whites and shells of two eggs, and caramel for coloring.

Let the beef, chicken, and ham boil slowly for five hours; add the vegetables and cloves, to cook the last hour, having first fried the onion in a little hot fat, and then in it stuck the cloves. Strain the soup into an earthen bowl, and let it remain overnight. Next day remove the cake of fat on the top; take out the jelly, avoiding the settlings, and mix into it the beaten whites of eggs, and the shells. Boil quickly for half a minute; then, placing the kettle on the hearth, skim off carefully all the scum and whites of eggs from the top, not stirring the soup itself. Pass this through the jelly bag, when it should be quite clear. The soup may then be put aside, and reheated just before serving. Add then a large tablespoonful of caramel, as it gives richer color, and also a slight flavor. Of course the brightest and cleanest of kettles should be used. I once saw this transparent soup served in Paris, without color, but made quite thick with tapioca. It looked very clear, and was exceedingly nice. If this soup is to be served at a company dinner, it is more convenient to make the day before.

To Make Caramel, a Burned Sugar, for Coloring Broth

Put into a porcelain saucepan, say one-half pound of sugar, and a tablespoonful of water. Stir it constantly over the fire until it has a bright, dark-brown color, being very careful not to let it burn or blacken. Then add a teacupful of water and a little salt; let it boil a few moments longer; cool and strain it. Put it away in a close-corked bottle, and it is always ready for coloring soups.

"In serving a dinner a la Russe, the table is decorated by placing the dessert in a tasteful manner around a centerpiece of flowers. This furnishes a happy mode of gratifying other senses than that of taste; for while the appetite is being satisfied, the flowers exhale their fragrance, and give to the eye what never fails to please the refined and cultivated guest. . . . At a dinner party, place a little bouquet by the side of the plate of each lady, in a small glass or silver bouquet-holder. At the gentlemen's plates, put a little bunch of three or four flowers, called a boutonnière, in the folds of the napkin. As soon as the gentlemen are seated at table, they may attach them to the left lapel of the coat."

—Practical Cooking and
Dinner Giving
by Mrs. Mary [Foote] Henderson
(New York: Harper & Brothers,
1876)

Planked Whitefish, Rector

Clean and bone a whitefish weighing about four pounds. Season with salt and pepper and rub entire fish with soft butter. Place it on a buttered wooden plank, and cover empty space of plank with salt (this will keep plank from burning). Bake in moderate oven 30 minutes. Remove plank from oven, brush off all the salt and make a potato border around edge of plank by using a pastry bag and tube. Fill in the space between edge of fish and potato border with baked stuffed tomatoes, small mounds of string beans and small mounds of cauliflower. Place plank in hot oven to brown potato border. Remove from oven, garnish with parsley and lemon and serve from plank. Cover mounds of cauliflower with Hollandaise or cream sauce.

Stuffed Tomatoes

Select six firm tomatoes of uniform size. Core out the center with a sharp knife and prepare the stuffing as follows: Put into a large mixing bowl the pulp of the tomatoes which you have just removed, add ½ medium size onion, finely chopped, ⅛ teaspoon mixed herbs, 1 cup cold cooked meat, finely chopped (ham, tongue, chicken or veal) and 1 cup of stale bread crumbs. Moisten with melted butter and season with salt, pepper and paprika. Mix well and stuff the tomatoes with the mixture, place on a greased baking pan to cook in the oven 20 to 30 minutes (or with the fish).

—*The Rector Cook Book*
by George Rector
(Chicago: Rector Publishing, 1928)

Shrimp Bouchées

Remove the shells from three or four pints of fresh shrimps; bone and chop finely three anchovies, mix them with the chopped shrimps, and season to taste with pounded mace and cloves. Moisten the mixture with about one and one-half wineglassfuls of white wine. Prepare some puff paste, roll it to about one-half inch in thickness, cut the paste into rounds with a two-inch tin cutter, then with a one-inch cutter cut half way through the middle of each round of paste. Brush the rounds over with a paste-brush dipped in the beaten yolk of an egg, and bake them in a quick oven. While the pastries are baking, heat the shrimp mixture in a saucepan over the fire. When the pastries are cooked, cut off the piece marked with the cutter, scoop out the soft inside, fill them with the shrimp mixture, cover with the small rounds of paste. Arrange them on a hot dish over which has been spread a folded napkin, garnished with fried parsley, and serve.

—*The Cook Book by "Oscar" of the Waldorf*
by Oscar Tschirky
(Chicago: Werner, 1896)

Fillet of Shad, with Purée of Sorrel

After cleaning your shad, cut it in equal pieces, leaving the skin underneath. Put them on a plate, and sprinkle a little salt on them, add the juice of a lemon, and a few branches of parsley. A few moments before they are required to be served put them in a saucepan on a gentle fire for 15 minutes, with a glass of white wine and an ounce of butter. Pick and clean a quart of sorrel, which blanch in boiling water, drain, and press it through a sieve. Put an ounce of butter in a saucepan with half an ounce of flour, a little salt, pepper, and nutmeg, and, when beginning to color slightly, add your purée of sorrel and half a glass of cream. Simmer gently 10 minutes, then add the yolks of two eggs which you have mixed in a little milk. Boil five minutes longer, pour over your fish, and serve.

—*French Dishes for American Tables*
by Pierre Carron
translated and edited by
Mrs. Frederic Sherman
(New York: D. Appleton, 1903)

Spanish Style Quail
(Codornices a la Española)

[NOTE: Encarnación Pinedo's *El Cocinero Español* was the first American cookbook published in Spanish (San Francisco: E. C. Hughes, 1898). It was also the first to offer a significant number of Mexican and Latin recipes showing food preparation techniques used in California. In 1992, the book was edited and translated by Dan Strehl, senior librarian at the Los Angeles Public Library, who also wrote an exemplary annotated bibliography, *One Hundred Books on California Food & Wine*.]

After having feathered and gutted the quail, stuff them with the following: chopped cooked mushrooms, green onions, parsley and thyme. Mix all together with a good sized piece of butter, salt and the juice of a lemon. Fill them with this stuffing, and close the vent with a crust of bread. Coat them with lard or melted butter, and bread with finely ground crumbs. After this, coat them with beaten eggs, whites and yolks, seasoned well with salt and pepper; coat a second time with a generous helping of bread crumbs and place them in a baking pan with a little butter or lard, to bake in the oven. You can also roast the quail without breading by coating them well with butter, and adding a little water to keep them from burning, basting continuously so they will stay juicy.

—*The Spanish Cook; a Selection of Recipes from Encarnación Pinedo's El Cocinero Español*
edited and translated by Dan Strehl
(Pasadena: Weather Bird Press, 1992)

Turban of Chicken à la Cleveland

Select two very tender chickens, singe, draw, and wipe them well; bone them and cut them into quarters, then put them into a sautoire with one ounce of butter, a good pinch of salt and half a pinch of pepper; add half a glassful of Madeira wine, and let parboil very slowly for ten minutes. Take half a pint of chicken forcemeat, add to it one chopped truffle, three chopped mushrooms, and half an ounce of cooked minced tongue. Stir well together; put this forcemeat on a silver dish, lay the pieces of chicken on top, crown-shaped, and decorate with twelve whole mushrooms and two thinly sliced truffles. To the gravy in which the chickens were cooked add half a pint of Espagnole sauce [tomato, onion, green pepper, carrot], a teaspoonful of chopped chives, and a small pat of fresh butter. Pour this immediately over the chickens, put the dish in the oven, and let cook very slowly for ten minutes. Squeeze the juice of half a lemon over, and serve with six heart-shaped pieces of fried bread.

—*The Table: How to Buy Food, How to Cook It, and How to Serve It*
by Alessandro Filippini
(New York: Webster, 1889)

Lamb Chops Chicago

Trim and lightly flatten 6 lamb chops, mix in a deep plate 2 tablespoons of oil, a little salt, and white ground pepper; repeatedly roll the chops in this mixture. Peel and wash 6 large mushrooms and fry with 2 tablespoonfuls of melted butter, season with salt and pepper. Fry on both sides until tender and keep hot. Arrange 6 thin slices of broiled ham on a hot dish. Broil the chops for 5 minutes on each side; lay the chops over the slices of ham, arrange the mushrooms over the chops crown like, one overlapping another, add 2 tablespoonfuls of butter into the mushroom pan, squeeze the juice of ½ lemon into the boiling butter and a little chopped fresh parsley. Pour this over the crown of chops and serve.

Loin of Pork Nebraska

Blanch off in salt water a 4-pound piece of pork loin. Crush 1 teaspoonful of whole white pepper and rub this into the pork and place in a saute pan with a tablespoonful of lard and a sliced onion. Let cook for a while without coloring pork. Then add 1 cupful of white wine and 2 cupfuls of soup stock or broth. Peel 4 small white turnips and cut into ¼-inch slices, cut ½ small head of curly cabbage with a round cutter the size of a silver dollar, slice a good-sized leek, add soup stock until all is covered. Add a spice bag and salt to taste. Cover the pan and let simmer until half done, then add 6 small potatoes cut like the turnips and cook until done. Dish the vegetables on a service platter, slice the pork over same and sprinkle some chopped parsley over top. Time: 1½ hours.

Cigarettes à la Russe

Twelve extra thin-cut slices of bread spread with butter and caviar and rolled. Cover with white chaudfroid sauce [white sauce based on gelatin, with or without egg yolk], except the tip which is to be masked with a pink chaudfroid. When ready for serving place on a doily garnished with parsley and lemon.

—*The Palmer House Cook Book*
by Ernest E. Amiet, executive chef
(Chicago: Hotel Monthly Press, 1933)

[NOTE: The following is not from a cookbook, but from a disorganized yet sublime collection of Chef Charles Fellows's menus and hotel menu cards of the day. Fellows wrote several books such as this—great tools for recreating stylish and historical dinners of prominence. In 1919, Chef Victor Hirtzler produced a similar text for the Hotel Monthly, *Hotel St. Francis Book of Recipes and Model Menus.*]

Supper

**From the daily meals at the Cataract Hotel,
Sioux Falls, South Dakota.**

Essence of tomato en tasse
Cream of wheat   South Dakota comb honey
Stuffed olives   Pickled onions
Broiled fresh trout, maître d'hôtel
Potatoes à la Reitz
Sirloin or tenderloin steak, plain or with Spanish sauce
Armour's sugar cured ham   Pork chops
King Oscar imported sardines
Lobster salad, mayonnaise dressing
Eggs as ordered
Milk, dry or buttered toast   Chocolate eclairs
Griddle cakes, maple syrup
Assorted cake   Florida plums in syrup
Rye, graham or wheat bread
Tea   Cocoa   Iced Tea   Milk   Coffee

—*Fellows' Menu Maker*
by Charles Fellows
(Chicago: Hotel Monthly Press, 1910)

Toast St. Antoine

2 tablespoons butter
1 cup chopped green onions
½ cup white wine
2 cups crabmeat
½ cup Bechamel Sauce
2 tablespoons grated Swiss
cheese

2 tablespoons grated Romano
cheese
2 tablespoons grated
Mozzarella cheese
1½ cups breadcrumbs
salt and ground white pepper
to taste
6 toasts, trimmed of crusts

12 anchovy fillets

Saute the green onions in the butter until they become limp. Add the white wine and crabmeat and bring to a boil. Blend in the Bechamel Sauce, the grated cheeses, and ½ cup of the breadcrumbs. Season to taste with salt and pepper. Continue cooking until the mixture can hold its own shape. Cool slightly. Divide into six equal parts and shape into balls. Roll the balls in breadcrumbs and place them on the toasts. Cross 2 anchovy fillets over the top of each and bake in a 375 degree oven for 15 minutes. Serves 6.

—*Antoine's Restaurant Cookbook*
by Roy F. Guste, Jr.
(New York: W. W. Norton, 1980)

Pork and Apple Pie

Make the crust in the usual manner, spread it over a deep plate; cut nice fat salt pork very thin, and slice some apples; place a layer of apples, then a layer of pork; sprinkle with allspice, pepper, and sugar between each layer; have three or four layers, and let the last one be apples; sprinkle in sugar and spice; cover with a top crust, and bake an hour. This is a plain and wholesome dish; when the family is large and apples plentiful, it will be an economical way of giving the boys "apple pie."

—*La Cuisine Creole*
Anonymous [Lafcadio Hearn]
(New York: Coleman, 1885;
2d. ed. New Orleans: Hansell, 1885)

"Cooking is in a great measure a chemical process, and the ingredients of certain dishes should be as carefully weighed and tested as though emanating from the laboratory. Few female cooks think of this, but men with their superior instinctive reasoning power are more governed by law and abide more closely to rule; therefore, are better cooks, and command higher prices for services."
—Lafcadio Hearn (1885)

Green Tomato Pie

[NOTE: In 1964, Janet Halliday Ervin edited the original *White House Cook Book* (Chicago: Follett) and lovingly augmented the text with additional Victorian recipes, short biographies and portraits of First Ladies and other White House hostesses through Claudia Alta (Lady Bird) Johnson.]

Take medium-sized tomatoes, pare, and cut out the stem end. Having your pie pan lined with paste made as biscuit dough, slice the tomatoes very thin, filling the pan somewhat heaping, then grate over it a nutmeg and put in half a cup of butter and a medium cup of sugar, if the pan is rather deep. Sprinkle a small handful of flour over all, pouring in half a cup of vinegar before adding the top crust. Bake half an hour in a moderately hot oven, serving hot. Good. Try it.

—*The White House Cook Book*
by Mrs. F. L. Gillette and Hugo Ziemann
(Chicago: R. S. Peale, 1887)

Swan with Reeds and Rushes

"Among early European cookbooks, hardly any are written by homemakers . . . but from the beginning, the real hero of American cuisine has been 'Mrs. American Homemaker.'"
—Chef Louis Szmathmary in *American Gastronomy* (1974)

Have an oval bottom made of office paste[6] or wood, half an inch thick, fifteen inches long and eleven wide; glaze it with royal icing of a soft green color and place around an inch and a half from the border a band of pistachio nougat two and a half inches high. On top of this a platform of sugar cooked white to "crack," and the same size as the band; garnish the stand with reeds, rushes, etc. made of pulled sugar. Mold a swan with outstretched wings and neck in lemon virgin cream, the under part of the wings in coffee [cream] and the body in vanilla [cream]; pack it in ice and freeze for two hours. Unmold and lay the swan in the center of the platform, imitating the eyes with small dry currants. This dish can be garnished all around with flowers made of ice cream placed in small paper cases.

—*The Epicurean*
by Charles Ranhofer
(New York: C. Ranhofer, 1908)

6. Flour, sugar, whole eggs, and egg yolks.

Macédoine, or à la Washington

Make four omelets of four eggs each, one with apples, one with asparagus or sorrel (according to the season), a third with *fines herbs*, and the fourth *au naturel*. You serve them on the same dish, one lapping over the other. It makes a fine as well as a good dish. This omelet, or rather these omelets, were a favorite dish with the Father of his Country; they were very often served on his table, when he had a grand dinner.

—*Hand-Book of Practical Cookery*
by Pierre Blot
(New York: D. Appleton, 1867)

Cream Apple Pie

[NOTE: This is the first California cookbook published by an African-American author who describes her manual as being "a complete instructor, so that a child can understand it and learn the art of cooking."]

The best of apples to be used. To two pounds of apples use a gill of water; put on fire to steam till the apples will mash perfectly fine and soft; sweeten to taste and let them cool. Season with powdered cinnamon—one-half teaspoonful of the best. Have one crust of pastry only, and that at the bottom of plate; fill plate with the fruit, then bake quickly in a hot oven. Take one pint of fresh cream sweetened to taste; beat the white of five eggs light, and add to the (whipped) cream; flavor with vanilla.

—*What Mrs. Fisher Knows about Old Southern Cooking*
by Mrs. Abby Fisher
(diploma awarded at Sacramento State Fair, 1879; San Francisco: Women's Co-Operative Printing Office, 1881)

"We think the following friendly recommendations will not be out of place here. They are in the interest of both the house-keeper and the cook:

Make use of every thing good.

Waste nothing, however little it may be.

Have no prejudices.

Be careful, clean, and punctual.

Always bear in mind that routine is the greatest enemy of progress, and that you have agreed to faithfully perform your daily duties for a certain consideration."

—Pierre Blot (1867)

How to Compile a Best-Selling Homemade Cookbook

The homemade cookbook is not a basic cookbook. Readers must already know how to cook to enjoy a homemade cookbook. On the other hand, it is usually not an exhibition of food fantasy, either—with only a basic understanding of the craft, a reader can follow what's written down. If the book contains a remarkable collection of regional or ethnic-neighborhood recipes, whether there is one author or many, it is historically more valuable than any other type of cookbook because it signifies exactly what the natives were cooking—and how—in a certain place at a specific time.

For this reason, charitable cookbooks play a major role in American publishing history, more so than anywhere else in the world. Through the years, women who produced fund-raising cookbooks aided individuals in dire straits, from the Great Southern Relief Association to California victims of earthquake and fire and all causes in between, including recent cookbooks that support fine arts and disease research. Preliminary study reveals that Methodist and Jewish organizations were the most prolific sources of cookbooks after the turn of the century, perhaps influenced by Chautauqua and the Settlement in Milwaukee. Currently the field seems to be dominated by Catholic churches, which bring in ethnic traditions, and the Junior League, but statistics on true numbers of books and sales records of all groups have yet to be computed. Some claims are astonishing, as will be seen.

Resisting the redundant inclusion of too-familiar cooking school recipes in the 1950s, groups influenced by gourmet publications began imitating and creating recipes that were "easy" versions of international favorites, for example, beef Strogonoff, chicken Tetrazzini, and lasagna. In the 1960s, appetizers hit the forefront as a meal of sorts for luncheons, showers, and cocktail and recreation room parties, gaining a place in our culinary development as important as the *tapa* was to Spain. Currently, the microwave reigns as the appliance to be contended with, and nutrition continues to be a subject of grave dispute.

The *good* homemade cookbook is unparalleled as a gift and souvenir and cherished by discerning collectors. But not all homemade cookbooks are produced for charity; for some of us, creating a cookbook in our own kitchens is an irresistible challenge. In either case, there is no reason whatsoever not to meet this challenge splendidly.

First, writing a cookbook as an individual is quite different than a group effort, but much of this advice applies to both. Whether you decide to have the book printed yourself (and the probability of a very decent product is excellent), pay to have it published by a subsidy press, or try to attract a commercial publisher, the first step is to select an audience. If the book is solely a family affair, it should be both personal and intimate in the choice of recipes as well as the inclusion of any pertinent historical or genealogical information. On the other hand, if you wish a larger audience, the text and recipes must be interesting and informative, something that readers would not find elsewhere.

You must be self-motivated. The group project will gain a momentum of its own and probably sell whether its contents are spectacular, mediocre, or even paltry so long as the committee sees that the book is publicized and remains on bookstore shelves. The entrepreneur will have the same onerous responsibility with a privately published effort. It isn't publishing that is the bread and butter of a literary effort, it's distribution. Equally dismaying for the entrepreneur is finding that radio, television, and newspaper reporters will cooperate with publicity for charitable causes on a frequent basis while you will be welcomed only when your book is hot off the press. Bookshops are fair to both, however, and you can autograph your book right in the cookbook department while you subtly talk customers out of buying anything but yours. Even the professionally marketed cookbook benefits from an author's constant promotion, a discouraging task when the individual author realizes that the competition is a crowd of enthusiastic clubwomen who take turns.

In the business of home-grown cookbooks, the charitable cause directly rivals the gifted regional cook for that small slot in aisle seven, and the charitable causes rival each other. The same construction advice applies to all, however, because there is no reason why one cook or a clutch of cooks can't produce a masterpiece. Too often, however, the theme of the book is unfocused, and the so-called motivating instruction is simply, Send in your best recipes. The result is a hodge-podge, repetitive and unimaginative. There is a glut of this type assemblage out there. In the past, some editors have succeeded in noteworthy efforts in spite of this vague directive by accidently producing remarkable collections of tasty regional treats; spice-laden international favorites; original, secret canapés or hors d'oeuvres recipes released only in the name of Charity. Sometimes the book takes on a singular quality all its own, for example, military women's clubs often feature an array of shocking punch and cookie recipes for adult entertaining. Food fashions change quickly, however, and regional specialties don't stay regional very long. The common advice begins by advocating a strong, sensuous theme and adopting the pluck of young Mickey and Judy, who might have said, "Let's write our *very own* cookbook!!"

If it's to be regional or historical recipes, do your homework and plan to make a real contribution to posterity. Ferret out old cookbooks and manuscripts from libraries, historical societies, and private collections and have a lot of fun doing it. Perhaps reissuing a cookbook already in public domain would be your best route, adding an overview and historical addendum to names of contributors long gone. If the book is small, combine it with another or add timely recipes from manuscripts, or oral history. Bringing a cookbook up to date—very carefully—is another idea, but sometimes recipes are like coins, more valuable left as is. For the new book, choose genuinely engaging recipes that feature regional or ethnic foods, focusing your research on menus, famous family meals, letters discussing meals or menus, diaries, newspaper accounts of significant dinners, appropriate quotes, and good photographs.

Copyrights shouldn't be a problem. Anything in the public domain (including many older cookbooks) may be used freely. For works under copyright protection, a brief excerpt is considered "fair use," but you must give proper acknowledgment. *Fair use* is a legal term; to print two lines of a four-line poem would not be fair use because you have taken 50 percent of the poem. Recipes are like poems; however if a cookbook author won't allow reproduction of a recipe, you might be able to select a short passage from the accompanying text. It is easiest to acquire recipes from books in the public domain, uncopyrighted material, and living authors (write to the publisher but don't expect a prompt answer). Recipes from books owned by estates and publishers may be available at between $50 and $300 for a recipe of perhaps a hundred words or fewer, unfashionable recipes to boot, from chefs who are no longer household words. Not surprisingly, clubwomen, churchwomen, and women's publishing houses are usually not only willing to allow permission, they're proud to do it. When permission must be gotten, ask for world rights and, once procured, keep the permission in a safe place.

Once you have focused your book, be clear about what you are offering. It should be a book about a subject you love. Other bestsellers have zeroed in on modern recipes, but on one type in particular, for example, recipes for boating or camping, all desserts, all savories, vegetarian recipes, all tomato, all berry, all bread, backyard barbeque, international (specific or regional), holiday, recipes for pets, patriotic recipes, all breakfasts, and what all. Knox Gelatin was an avid homemade cookbook sponsor in years past, with Mrs. Knox herself submitting special recipes to some collections. You might wish to consider featuring local products on the time-honored chance of a hefty donation or the acquisition of an industrial backer.[1]

If you're working on a family cookbook, compiled for family or for the world, you will want to include stories about how holidays were spent, who loved what recipe, perhaps extra material about games, how the table was set, the meals prepared, when gifts were exchanged, and also include family photos. Secrecy holds no charm for the personal cookbook; the rule of thumb is, Tell it all.

Whether talking to your editor at the publishing house you've

---

1. The Walter Baker Cocoa and Chocolate Company placed advertisements in many charitable cookbooks, usually stating "Established 1780, 'X' Years of Successful Manufacture." Thus, collectors with undated cookbooks or cookbooks missing frontmatter can successfully estimate the publication date by adding the "X" years to 1780 if this advertisement is present (Longone's *American Cook Books and Wine Books*, p. 32).

contracted with or friends and collaborators, be sure the feedback you receive comes from practiced cooks familiar with a whole range of cookbook types. Don't let misguided criticism deter your enthusiasm. When testing recipes, write down every ingredient, every step in the instructions, then retest the formula and edit what's written. All recipes should be tested at least twice unless they are obviously historical and are included for that reason (then it's a good idea to highlight them in some way to set them apart). You may even want to add a note in the Preface about where, when, how, and by whom this process was accomplished. You're probably not writing a how-to cookbook, but you will want to study the method of recipe writing you most admire and use, then follow it throughout, being consistent with abbreviations and style. Styles differ. Julia Child's is completely different from Irma Rombauer's, which is completely different from James Beard's, and they all bear no resemblance to Mollie Katzen's hand-lettered and illustrated masterwork.

Ingredients should be listed, whether in a column or within the instructions, in the order in which they are used in the recipe. Instructions should be checked for modern technique and current nutrition theory to some extent. Could that carrot cake be whipped up in the blender to eliminate the time-consuming job of grating carrots? Can the vegetables and herbs be sautéed together in one step instead of two? Can the mushrooms be cooked in a little broth rather than butter?

Once you have decided on content and who will help test and taste the recipes, the next challenge is designing the format. Although a handwritten or hand-printed manuscript may be more homey and treasured, it does take a considerable amount of time, space, and effort. However, if you have artistic talents, don't pass up this opportunity to share them. Otherwise, desk-top publishing possibilities are almost limitless. Invest in a user-friendly computer or visit your nearest copy center to discuss your ideas with the experts. Binding processes are also extensive, but don't make snap decisions. Think over each step of the publishing process for at least a few weeks.

Remember to leave a margin for binding. Try not to spill recipes onto a second page which requires that the cook turn the page with a sticky hand. Double-space every page if you're sending the manuscript to a publisher; one recipe per page. Accuracy cannot be overstressed. Recipes must be proofread every time they are transcribed, not just in the final phase of production. Once an error enters a recipe, that error will travel forward in time unless your editor is gifted in your type of cuisine. Cover material should be soil-resistant or washable. The book should lie flat on the table.

There is no quicker way to turn your exciting project into a mundane affair—or worse, one that looks mundane—than using mass-produced tables, clip art, charts, and generic sayings interspersed between the recipes. Choose a subsidy press carefully if you must do so at all.

Title your masterpiece anything except *Tried and True* or *Choice Recipes*, titles that have had their day, and most were fibbing anyway. You will automatically decide on chapter titles by the submissions sent in or the theme of your original idea. Be sure they are realistic; don't end up with more recipes in the miscellaneous chapter than anywhere else. Number pages consecutively at the final manuscript stage, even if you have to handwrite the numbers on printed or typed pages. Compose the Index when page numbers are finalized; each item should be listed at least three times: (1) under the name of the recipe itself; (2) under the category of recipe or chapter heading (e.g., entrees, desserts); and (3) under the main ingredient of the recipe (e.g., blackberries, beets, bologna). If there is a reason why people might look for a certain recipe under some other category, list that also. A bibliography would be very responsible.

If the book is a compilation of historical recipes, or recipes have been solicited from hither and yon, it is only fair that Hither and Yon be acknowledged. Some choose to list donors in the back of the book, but remember that without these generous people there would be no cookbook, and it seems proper to salute them at the end of their contributions.

When, at last, you are ready to reproduce the manuscript, add a title page and a copyright page. Keep librarians in mind when you choose the title, the subtitle, and the "author" in the case of fundraisers, for this small page is not the place to start a separate literary effort. If you are reprinting an old cookbook, leave at least the first words of the book the same so that inquiring minds can find it. For instance, it is not easy to locate the latest edition of *The House Servant's Directory*, retitled *Robert's Guide for Butlers and Household Staff*. Officially copyright the whole if you so desire, although in the case of family cookbooks it won't be necessary unless you produce one that is very popular outside the family. Practice your autographing skills.

Whether group-produced, professionally published, or desktop done, some day you may find that your homemade, regional paperback has been so appreciated by the local library that they have hardbound a copy or three for posterity. Nothing, in my opinion, so eloquently speaks of success.

> "The first fund-raising "receipt books" were compiled and sold in the United States during the Civil War at the Sanitary Fairs held to raise money for military casualties and their families.[2] After the war was over, the ladies' aid societies formed during the war turned to local charities, and published their recipe collections to benefit hospitals, homes for the friendless, schools, and churches in every part of the country.
>
> "Though the recipes in early locally-published cookery books are often amateurish, they reflect the cooking fashions of the period in various parts of the United States more accurately than the standard works by professional authors. Through this early period (1861–1915) these books chronicle the transition from wood-burning stoves to gas and electric appliances, and the development of refrigeration and commercially canned or pre-packaged foods. Roast snipe and woodcock, quail and pheasant, pickled wild mushrooms, potted prairie hens and pigeons, barbequed suckling pigs, suet and whortleberry puddings, calf's head soup and calf's foot gelatin, rabbit and squirrel pies, brandied peaches and homemade wines: all have a place in the cook books published in the small towns of America before the first World War.
>
> "The great fascination of these early regional cookery books for collectors and local historians is their elusiveness. Seldom copyrighted—sold locally, usually to acquaintances of the ladies whose recipes appear—they have generally not been considered library fare. Although more than 2,500 libraries and private collectors were approached for titles, three-fourths of the books listed in this bibliography are unique copies, located in only one collection. Those that survive are nostalgic reminders of a time when philan-

---

2. The first charity cookbook is believed to have been *Camp Cookery and Hospital Diet, For the Use of U.S. Volunteers, Now in Service*, published in New York City (1861).

thropy was perhaps less mechanized and a good cause was the de-light of the charitable ladies who were also such good cooks.''

—*America's Charitable Cooks; a
Bibliography of Fund-raising Cook
Books Published in the United States
1861–1915*
by Margaret Cook
(Kent, Ohio, 1971)[3]

Tomato Soup

Boil soup-bone four or five hours; remove meat and strain; add one small onion, chopped fine, three potatoes, one tablespoon of rice, one can tomatoes; season with salt and pepper, and boil one hour.

Beef Soup
(Contributed by Mrs. M. E. Warren)

Boil soup-bone two and one-half hours; after boiling one-half time add one tablespoon fine-cut cabbage, one medium size onion cut fine, two Irish potatoes cut fine; salt and pepper to taste; one teaspoon of flour made into a thin batter; add the latter when done, stir and cook a few minutes longer.

Crab Gumbo
(Mrs. T. C. Armstrong, Galveston)

Take one dozen crabs, boil thoroughly and pick out; two and a half quarts okra, chopped, and one large onion, also chopped; fry two-thirds of the okra with the onion. Have a gallon of water in a pot, take two slices of ham, all the okra and two tablespoonfuls of

---

3. Margaret Cook collected a vast quantity of fund-raising cookbooks that were auctioned in California and claimed by the Blagg-Huey Library, Texas Woman's University, Denton, for their outstanding collection. However, the library regrets that it did not obtain biographical data about the stouthearted Margaret Cook, and no information was found in any institution contacted in Kent, Ohio. It is hoped she will lose her enigmatic status presently.

rice, put into the water and boil down to a thick gumbo; this will take two or three hours; season to taste, and about an hour before ready to serve put in the crabs.

To make beef gumbo, use beef instead of crabs, and add a few tomatoes.

To make chicken gumbo, fry a chicken brown and pick off from the bones, and use in place of crabs or beef, adding tomatoes as before.

> —*The Texas Cook Book, a Thorough Treatise on the Art of Cookery*
> by the Ladies' Association of the First Presbyterian Church
> (Houston, 1883); facsimile titled *The First Texas Cookbook*, Austin: Eakin-Sunbelt Press, 1986)

Dedication

> *"O ye tired and weary house-wives*
> *O ye never-tiring house-wives*
> *Here's a solving, solving, solving,*
> *Of the daily eating problem.*
> *Here's an answer, answer, answer*
> *To the oft-repeated question*
> *To the quite perplexing question*
> *That confronts us, that annoys us.*
> *What shall we eat? What shall we eat?*
> *Here's a book of tested cooking,*
> *Here's a book of tried proportions*
> *Kindly given by our women,*
> *Thank we them for their donation*
> *Thank them for this little cook book.*
> *Dedicate it to these women*
> *To these helpful, trusty women.*
> *Take it to your friends and neighbors,*
> *May it prove a blessing—to you."*

> —Mrs. Bertha L. Turner (1910)

Breakfast, Dinner and Supper Menu

(Contributed by Kate Mann Baker)

Fruit
Oatmeal and Cream
Panned Bacon   Corn Muffins
Coffee

Cream of Corn Soup
Boston Steak
Rice   String Beans
Beet Salad
American Ice Cream   Wafers

Cold Sliced Beef   Potato Salad
Sandwiches
Tea

Cream of Corn Soup

Drain the liquor from 2 cans of corn (or use 12 green ears) and chop the kernels fine. Put them over the fire with a pint of water and simmer for 15 minutes. Strain through a fine strainer and return to the fire. Season with salt, pepper and a heaping teaspoon of sugar. Cook together two tablespoons each of butter and flour and when they are blended, pour upon them 3 cups of milk and a cup of cream to which a generous pinch of baking soda has been added. Stir until smooth and thick, add the corn puree, and as soon as the mixture is scalding hot, take from the fire and pour in gradually, beating all the time, the beaten yolks of 2 eggs. Serve immediately.

—*The Federation Cook Book; a Collection of Tested Recipes Contributed by the Colored Women of the State of California* by Mrs. Bertha L. Turner, state superintendent, Domestic Science (Pasadena, ca. 1910)

Devilled Turkey
(Contributed by Mrs. S. T.)

Place the legs and wings (jointed) on a gridiron. Broil slowly. Have ready a sauce made of:

1 tablespoon pepper vinegar
1 tablespoon made mustard
1 tablespoon celery sauce
1 tablespoon acid fruit jelly
A little salt and pepper

Lay the broiled turkey on a hot dish. Pour the dressing and sift pounded cracker over it.

—*Housekeeping in Old Virginia*
by Marion Cabell Tyree
(Louisville: Morton, 1879)

Printers Four Hour Stew
(Contributed by Allie Thompson, *Mid-County Times*, Pardeeville)

2 pounds stewing beef or round steak cut to 48-60 point cubes
6 carrots cut into pieces approximately 10 picas long
2 medium onions or two small bunches 60 picas long
4 stalks celery, cut into 7 to 8 pica lengths
1 tablespoon sugar
2 tablespoons salt
4 tablespoons minute tapioca

Pour medium size can V-8 juice over all. Place in 300 degree oven for 4 hours, covered with foil. (Do not brown meat.)

—*Feasting with Wisconsin's Fourth Estate*
(Madison: Wisconsin Newspaper
Association, 1976)

To Stuff Peppers
(Contributed by Mrs. J. G. Downrey)

Take a dozen large peppers, remove the seeds; then throw them upon a bed of live coals and turn continually until they are light brown. When taking them up, throw them immediately into a bowl of cold water and remove the skins. Put a tablespoonful of lard or butter into a saucepan and when hot add an onion, finely chopped; fry slightly; add a large tomato, or two if small, half a teacupful of grated corn; pepper and salt to taste. Let it simmer fifteen minutes, stir occasionally to prevent scorching; then remove from the fire. Add a heaped teacupful of finely chopped meat or chicken (a small piece of ham or bacon greatly improves the flavor); mix well, and stuff the peppers; dip into batter and fry to a nice brown.

SAUCE FOR THE PEPPERS

Put a spoonful of butter into a saucepan; add a spoonful of flour, one onion, one tomato, one green pepper, cut small; two apples sliced, a few raisins if liked, and olives. Add enough water to make a sauce, and let it boil until the apples are done. Before serving the peppers, put them into the gravy and let it simmer just a moment; then serve.

—*Los Angeles Cookery*
by the Ladies' Aid Society
(Fort Street Methodist Church, 1881)

Hunt's End Chicken Gumbo

[NOTE: Made with home-grown ingredients, this gumbo became a favorite at hunt teas beginning in the 1930s.]

Cut into 4 or 5 pieces:	1 frying chicken
Brown in:	Bacon or chicken fat

Bake in covered casserole until tender, about 30 minutes. Cool. Remove skin and bones and coarsely chop the meat.

Slice:	2-3 large onions
Brown in:	Chicken fat
Add:	2 cups sliced okra, fresh or frozen

Cook until okra is tender.

Drain and add, reserving juice:	4 cups tomatoes
Add:	2 cups fresh corn

Add all ingredients to casserole. Bake at 325 degrees until heated through and flavors blend. Thin with tomato juice, if necessary. Season to taste with salt and pepper, and chopped parsley. Serve over brown rice, toast, or English muffins.

Christmas Dinner for Horses and Ponies
A Treat for a Frosty Night

Heat to boiling:	1 cup apple cider
Mix with:	1 cup corn oil
	2 ounces glycerine
Pour over:	2 pounds crimped oats
	5 pounds flaked corn

Stir thoroughly. Let this blend stand for 5 minutes before serving to your faithful friend.

—*Treasured Recipes From Camargo to Indian Hill*
compiled by Virginia S. White and the Cookbook Committee of the Indian Hill Historical Society
(Cincinnati, 1987)

"Almost all cookbooks, especially the endearing paper-bound volumes edited around the turn of the century by farflung Ladies' Guilds and other churchly societies, contain many [good] recipes. They should be read with one canny eye on the cooking time, since fuel is an increasing expense and time itself is not a thing to be thrown about lightly. Another point about which to be wary in the usually dependable recipes given in most such collections is the seasoning; it is, to put it mildly, a challenge to your inventive palate, since it either says, "Salt, pepper," or "Salt." Apparently any other condiments were considered foreign and perhaps even sacriligeous by members of the Saint James' Sewing Circle in

*1902. Otherwise, recipes in such books are dependable, if you
like salty things."*

—M. F. K. Fisher in
How to Cook a Wolf
(Cleveland: World, 1944)[4]

Pollos de la Bella Mulata
(Chicken à la the Beautiful Mulatto)

[NOTE: The Landmarks Club was incorporated to conserve the
missions and other historic landmarks of Southern California; Lummis was its president when the book was written.]

For four small chickens, brown in lard half a pound of fresh
pork, quarter of a pound of almonds, a piece of bread, four ripe
tomatoes. Grind all in a mortar or metate. Fry onions chopped fine,
with a little parsley (a bit of garlic if desired). Add the chickens,
with the broth in which they have been fully cooked, with pepper,
salt, ground clove and cinnamon. Let come to a boil, add a cup of
sherry, and serve.

—*The Landmarks Club Cook Book; A
California Collection of the Choicest
Recipes from Everywhere*
by Charles F. Lummis
(Los Angeles: The Out West
Company, 1903)

Baked Tomatoes and Eggs

Tomatoes, Salt, Eggs, Butter. Select smooth, good-sized tomatoes. Cut a slice off the top. Scoop out part of the meat of the tomatoes, being careful not to break the skin. Sprinkle with salt, break an
egg into the tomato cup, add a lump of butter, put into a buttered

---

4. Produced during the war, when the "wolf" was at the door. All five of
Fisher's early works, *Serve It Forth, Consider the Oyster, How to Cook a Wolf, The
Gastronomical Me,* and *An Alphabet for Gourmets* are contained in *The Art of
Eating* (Macmillan, 1954, 1971).

pan with just enough water to keep from scorching, and bake at 400 degrees for 15-20 minutes or until eggs are done.

—*The Brown County Cookbook*
by Nancy C. Ralston and
Marynor Jordan
(Bloomington: Indiana University
Press, 1983)

Maple Sandwiches

"Vermont school children like these in their lunch boxes."

1 cup soft maple sugar
1 cup chopped nut meats
3 tablespoons cream

Blend together and use as filling in whole wheat sandwiches.

—*Vermont Maple Recipes*
by Mary Pearl
(Burlington: Lane, 1952)

Parker House Rolls

[NOTE: A nationally popular recipe from the Boston Hotel (now Omni-Parker House) that introduced "à la carte" to the American menu.]

Scald a little more than a pint of milk, let it stand till cold; two quarts of flour, rub a tablespoon of lard into the flour, make a hole in the flour and pour in the milk; having mixed with the milk one large spoon of sugar, a little salt, and a half cup of yeast; sift a little flour over the hole and let it stand till risen; then knead it well, let it rise again, roll out and cut with a pint-pail cover, and cup over like a turn-over; let them rise again, and bake 20 minutes. Splendid; never fail if the directions are followed.

Lemon Tarts

Grated rind of two lemons, juice of one lemon, piece of butter size of an egg, one egg, sugar to taste; simmer all together till thick; bake puffs, and fill while hot. Makes 30 tarts.

—*California Recipe Book*
by the Ladies of California
(San Francisco, 1875)

Cabbage Pickle

(Contributed by Mrs. Patsey Edwards)

[NOTE: The first charitable cookbook published in Kentucky, *Housekeeping in the Blue Grass*, has undergone at least nine reprintings. More than twenty thousand copies were sold.]

For a two gallon jar take cabbage enough quartered to fill it, then pour on the hot brine; let the brine remain on them four days. Squeeze them of the brine and pour weak vinegar over them, letting it remain several days. Take strong vinegar, put into it two ounces of cinnamon bark, essence of cloves to suit the taste, two ounces of turmuric; put this over the cabbage and tie closely. This has taken the premium at the Bourbon Fair several times.

—*Housekeeping in the Blue Grass*
by the Ladies of the Presbyterian
Church
(Paris, Ky., 1875)

"Usually I speak to a possible beginner, assuming the accomplished cook will graciously skip the more elementary instructions. I also tend to add tidbits of detail that experienced people might find interesting, even if a new cook might find it superfluous. I do start with a baseline assumption that the person using the book is at least halfway intelligent, knows what a spoon is, and is cooking by choice and with interest."

—Mollie Katzen, in "Katzen's
Cookbooks: Tips for Writing a
Cookbook"
(*Writer's Digest*, November 1987)

Best Roasted Corn-on-the-Cob
(Contributed by Uncle Pete Maxwell)

Fresh corn-on-the-cob, unshucked
Butter, salt and pepper to taste

Plunge the corn into a bucket of cold water and let it sit while you play tennis. While the coals are heating, shuck the corn almost to the bottom of the cob and remove as much of the silk as possible. Rub with butter and sprinkle with salt and pepper. Pull the shucks back up and tie at the top with a piece of shuck or string. Place the corn on an outdoor grill and cover them with a wet, wrung-out gunny sack to keep in the steam. Roast 15 to 20 minutes, turning frequently, or until the corn is cooked through and smells irresistible.

Ohio River Baked Chicken
(Contributed by Uncle "Dutch" Maxwell)

Borrow a chicken. Take it down to the riverbank and build a good fire. Chop off the head, feet and remove innards. Do not remove feathers. While the fire takes hold and turns into burning embers, cover the chicken, feathers and all, with a thick coating of mud. Sit the chicken directly upon the embers. Turn frequently with the hands, being careful not to get burned. After an hour or two the chicken will be baked. Remove the baked mud along with the feathers. Sit down on a comfortable log and enjoy your meal. Potatoes and onions can be added to the coals in the same way, or without the mud if you're careful not to let them burn.

—Cincinnati Recipe Treasury: The Queen City's Culinary Heritage
by Mary Anna DuSablon
(Athens: Ohio University Press, 1988)

"The belief that the Hawaiians emigrated from the islands of the Southern Pacific region is strengthened when their foods are studied, for these bear a close resemblance to those of the Tahitians, Samoans, and other South Sea Islanders. Women, apparently, never took much part in food preparation. It was the man of the household who prepared the taro root, made poi, wrapped taro leaves around the fish he caught and cooked, grated the coconut meat. He dug the underground oven or imu. History does

not record that he washed the dishes for the simple reason that banana leaves or ti leaves served as plates, and hollowed coconuts as poi bowls and drinking cups . . . when there was a pig to be roasted he took hot stones from the depth of the imu, put them in the abdominal cavity of the pig, lowered the pig into the heated pit, covered the pig with banana or ti leaves, spread a mat over the pit and covered the whole thing with earth. Three or four hours later he returned; dug out the, by now, well-done pig, the bananas, breadfruit, and sweet potatoes he had buried with the meat. Everything would be done to a turn."

—*Hawaiian and Pacific Foods*
by Katherine Bazore, associate
professor of home economics,
University of Hawaii
(New York: Barrows, 1947)

Norwegian Dribble Toast
(Contributed by Louise Hanson)

Butter slices of white bread (at least one day old) generously. Place in ungreased pan and dribble about one tablespoon milk on each slice so it is moist but not wet. Place under broiler until milk is absorbed and bread is toasted.

Italian Cannoli Cake
(Contributed by Mrs. H. F. Costello)

One pound Italian cottage cheese
One pound confectioners sugar

Blend at high speed until light and fluffy. Add cherries and chopped nuts. Mix well and add one teaspoon vanilla. Chill in refrigerator for three hours. Spread between layers of cake and cover with whipped cream and chill over night. Half of this recipe is plenty for three layers.

Swedish Pepparkakar

(Contributed by Mrs. Helen Johnson)

½ cup water
¼ cup dark syrup
1½ cups brown sugar
½ cup butter
1 teaspoon baking soda

½ teaspoon each cinnamon, cloves
 and ginger
1 teaspoon grated orange peel
3½ cups flour

Mix brown sugar, water and syrup together and let come to a boil. Remove from fire and add butter, cinnamon, cloves, ginger, baking soda and orange peel. When cold, add flour. Roll and cut. Bake in oven at 275 degrees.

—*Parish Pantry*
by Ladies Aid, Edison Park Lutheran
Church
(Chicago, 1952)

Jeff Davis Pudding

(Contributed by Mrs. Nancy Cabell Naret)

1 cup suet, chopped
1 cup molasses
1 teaspoon soda
1 cup sour milk

3 cups flour
1 cup currants
1 cup raisins
½ cup citron

1 teaspoon each, cinnamon, cloves, and spice

Steam from 2 to 3 hours. Serve with sauce.

—*Tried and True Recipes*
by Elizabeth Burford Bashinsky,
Alabama Division, United Daughters
of the Confederacy
(Troy, 1926)

Ribbon Cake

Two and one half cups of sugar, one cup of butter, one of sweet milk, one teaspoon of cream tartar, one half teaspoon of soda, four cups of flour, four eggs. Reserve a third of this mixture, and bake the other in two tins. To the reserved third add one cup raisins, one of currants, one half cup of chopped figs, two tablespoons of molasses, teaspoon each of all kinds of spices; bake in tin same size as the other. Put together with icing or currant jelly, placing fruit layer in center.

> —*K. K. K. Cook Book*
> by the "Kute Kooking Klub,"
> Honey Grove, Texas
> (Cincinnati: Robert Clarke, 1894)

Egg Nog
(Contributed by Colonel H. E. Sheppard)

30 eggs, beaten separately (very light)
2 lbs. powdered sugar
3 pints brandy
1 quart Jamaica Rum
3 pints cream

Beat sugar and yolks together; add the liquor a little at a time; add the beaten whites, and lastly add the cream. Grate a little nutmeg on top as served.

> —*The Bragg-About Cookbook*
> by the Ft. Bragg, North Carolina
> Woman's Club (1961)

Army and Navy Punch
(Contributed by Admiral Timothy J. Keleher)

1 gallon French brandy, 1 quart Jamaica rum, 1 quart peach brandy, 1 pint curacao, juice of 2 dozen lemons, 1¼ pounds fine granulated sugar. Dress with small slices of orange and lemon. When ready to serve put in a lump of ice. Will serve 25 people. Strong but good.

Army and Navy Punch
Devilled Maryland Ham   **Crabmeat Balls**
Tiny Maryland Biscuits
Hot Chicken Mousse   **Crabtown Deviled Crabs**
Mattie's Baked Rice
Oven Creamed Mushrooms
Spiced Beef   **Lobster Salad Bowl**
Mixed Green Salad   **Jubilee Rolls**
Strawberry Ice Mould   **Lemon Sherbet**
Seven Seas Cake   **Coffee**

Seven Seas Cake

(Contributed by Mrs. Paul Heineman)

2 eggs, 1 cup sugar, 1 cup flour, 1 teaspoon baking powder, ½ cup milk, 1 tablespoon butter, 1 teaspoon vanilla.

Beat the eggs until thick and lemon-colored. Add sugar, very little at a time, beating constantly. Gradually add flour, sifted with baking powder. Then, slowly add milk and butter, which have been heated just to the boiling point; add vanilla. Bake at 350 degrees for 30 to 35 minutes in an ungreased pan.

ICING

3 tablespoons butter, 2 tablespoons cream, 5 tablespoons brown sugar, ½ cup cocoanut. Make these measurements generous.

Heat butter, cream and sugar just until sugar is melted. Add cocoanut, mix well; spread on hot cake as it comes from the oven. Put under broiler until it bubbles and is brown. This cake freezes wonderfully. It also keeps fresh for days on end. Use fresh or prepared cocoanut.

—*Maryland's Way*
by the Hammond-Harwood House
Association
(Annapolis, 1963)

Angel Food Charlotte Russe
(Contributed by Mrs. Howard L. Baldwin)

[NOTE: The Sarah Daft Home is the oldest continually operating residential care facility for the elderly in Utah, financed by Sarah Ann Daft, an early stockholder in the Independent Telephone Company and well-known philanthropist.]

CAKE PART

Whites of 9 to 11 eggs	1½ cups sugar (sifted)
1 level teaspoon cream of tartar	1 cup cake flour
¼ teaspoon salt	½ teaspoon vanilla

Beat eggs partly, add cream of tartar and beat until stiff. Gradually add sugar. Fold in flour, salt and vanilla. Bake in slow oven 45 minutes. When cold, cut off top of cake, remove center, leaving 2-inch wall, and make filling as follows: 1 tablespoon gelatine, 6 stale macaroons, rolled fine, 12 marshmallows cut in small pieces, 2 tablespoons chopped candied cherries, ¼ pound chopped almonds, 1 cup sifted sugar, 1 pint whipping cream and vanilla. Dissolve gelatine in ¼ cup cold water then add ¼ cup boiling water, add sugar. When mixture is cold, add cream whipped stiff, and other ingredients; fill the cake, place lid on top and sprinkle with powdered sugar.

—*Sarah Daft Home Cook Book*
by Mrs. Glen Miller
(Kaysville, Utah, 1923)

Peach Leather

"Everybody has the right to think whose food is the most gorgeous,/And I nominate Georgia's."
—Ogden Nash, from the Introduction poem (1933)

One peck of peaches peeled and mashed through collander. To each gallon of peach pulp, add three-quarters pound of sugar, and let come to a boil. Remove from fire and spread on tin pie plates, and put in the sun to dry. Old receipts say it should stay in the sun three or four days, being brought in at night. When dry enough to peel away from the plate, it is done. Sprinkle the top with sugar, cut in strips and roll into wafer-like pieces, of any length preferred. It will keep indefinitely in tin.

—*The Savannah Cook Book: A Collection of Old Fashioned Receipts from Colonial Kitchens* by Harriet Ross Colquitt (New York, 1933)

Guava Chiffon Pie

1 pint shelled guavas

½ cup sugar plus 1 tablespoon for egg whites

1 envelope gelatin

¼ cup cold water

3 eggs, separated

¼ teaspoon salt

½ cup milk

small box of vanilla wafers (roll wafers into crumbs and put loosely into pie pan for shell)

½ pint heavy cream, whipped and sweetened to taste with sugar and flavored with sherry

Cook guavas, put through sieve, add 1 cup sugar, yolks of eggs, salt and milk. Mix and taste for sweetness, add more sugar if necesary. Cook over low heat, stirring constantly until thick. Dissolve gelatin in cold water and add to above, stir until dissolved. When cool, fold in 3 beaten egg whites with sugar added. Pour into pie shell and when ready to serve, cover with the whipped sweetened cream flavored with sherry.

—*St. Augustine Cookery; A Collection of Recipes Handed Down by Spanish, French, English and American Settlers of the Nation's Oldest City* by the Flagler Hospital Auxiliary (St. Augustine, Florida, 1965)

10

Celebrity Cooks

Why celebrity cooks? Why not celebrity landscaping or celebrity plumbing? The terrible truth about celebrity cookbooks is that although a star may shine brilliantly in other artistic heavens it doesn't necessarily follow that this radiance can fire up the stove.

Movie stars, musicians, artists, athletes, Democrats, Republicans, and, yes, writers who can't cook, won't cook, or cook forgettably usually choose to keep it to themselves. But a few will sacrifice any detail of their private lives for further fame, or royalties, and are easily convinced by derelict publishers that the world is waiting to sample their most meager offerings. The collector purchases the cookbook not because she has studied the recipes and stories and found them satisfying, but because she is curious about what the star does with a rump roast in the privacy of his home, or how the star defers to the ubiquitous mushroom, artichoke, or avocado. When she realizes ten years later that she has never used the book, she has no one to blame but herself. Stars are stars, however, and as long as the bulb doesn't flicker out completely, the book will hold some value. Somewhere.

Rare volumes worth collecting—put forth by luminaries who not only possess a unique ability to cook and serve but also an ability to write clearly and entertainingly—are worthwhile investments. These talents are separate altogether from whatever original talents got them into the limelight and should not be underrated in comparison. The ultimate test for a celebrity cookbook is determining whether the venture would have a chance of standing on its own as a cookbook, or literary effort, had the celebrity sent it to the publisher under an unknown name. Some do qualify, superbly.

> "Cookbooks have always intrigued and seduced me. When I was still a dilettante in the kitchen they held my attention, even the dull ones, from cover to cover, the way crime and murder stories did Gertrude Stein. When we first began reading Dashiell Hammett, Gertrude Stein remarked that it was his modern note to have disposed of his victims before the story commenced. Goodness knows how many were required to follow as the result of the first crime. And so it is in the kitchen. Murder and sudden death seem as unnatural there as they should be anywhere else . . . all the same . . . before any story of cooking begins, crime is inevitable . . . [My] first victim was a lively carp brought to the kitchen in a covered basket from which nothing could escape."
>
> —The Alice B. Toklas Cook Book
> (New York: Harper & Brothers, 1954)

Of course any, say, Dashiell Hammett fan, would also be familiar with the sixty murder mysteries recorded verbatim by the sleuth Archie Goodwin and solved by his boss, detective-gourmet extraordinaire Nero Wolfe, who weighs more than an "eighth of a ton." Wolfe's massive appetite is daily satiated by chef-in-residence Fritz Brenner. This fictional trio got together in 1973 with the author Rex Stout and the editors at Viking Press to publish *The Nero Wolfe Cookbook*, actual recipes based on mouth-watering descriptions of meals taken as plots unfold. Descriptions interlarded, however, between gunshots, poisonings, visits to the orchid chamber, and the obligatory roundup of suspects in Wolfe's perforated office environs.

> "When I went to the kitchen to tell Fritz that lunch would be at one o'clock sharp[1] because we were leaving at two for an appointment, he had a question. For Wolfe he was going to make a special omelet, which he had just invented in his head, and would that do for me or should he broil some ham? I asked what would be in the omelet, and he said four eggs, salt, pepper, one tablespoon tarragon butter, two tablespoons cream, two tablespoons

---

1. Readers are aware that luncheon is customarily served in the dining room at one-fifteen.

dry white wine, one-half teaspoon minced shallots, one-third cup whole almonds, and twenty fresh mushrooms. I thought that would do for two but he said my God, no; that would be for Mr. Wolfe and did I want one like it? I did. He warned me that he might decide at the last minute to fold some apricot jam in, and I said I would risk it."

—*Plot It Yourself*
by Rex Stout
(New York: Viking, 1959)

Of the many Hollywood cooks, the best-known cookbook author is the late actress Dinah Shore, who serenaded her way into the hearts of millions during the 1940s ("Buttons and Bows," "Stars Fell on Alabama"). From 1951 to 1961 she hosted a television variety show for Chevrolet, sending her famous loud, lip-smacking kiss to fans across the nation. But it was "Dinah's Place," debuting on NBC in August of 1970 and featuring a set that duplicated her home in Beverly Hills, that showcased her culinary talents. The program was not a hit with feminists during the tumultuous decade, as Shore's warm slightly addlepated style of interviewing often disguised the fact that the show provided a rare opportunity to see famous people as human beings, as houseguests rather than nervous or overconfident interviewees. Martha Mitchell, wife of the then-attorney general, said that she wished her son was in Canada rather than in Vietnam; Hubert Humphrey burned himself on a hot pot, cried out "Oh my God!" and then groaned, "Well, I just blew the Bible belt!" "Cliff Robertson made a linguine. Leslie Uggams made sweet potato pie. Burt Lancaster made a perfect Italian spaghetti sauce. Senator Muskie hypnotized a lobster. Frank Sinatra showed up to cook spaghetti and to sing."[2] After the first season, Dinah put the tried recipes into a small cookbook, *Someone's in the Kitchen with Dinah* (1971), published it with Doubleday, and received a "first-rate" review from Craig Claiborne in the *New York Times*.

Many cookbooks would follow, but one preceded, a ninety-three-page compilation of outstanding recipes collected on behalf of Women For, a volunteer, nonpartisan political organization in Hollywood, titled *The Celebrity Cookbook* and published in Los Angeles by Price, Stern and Sloan in 1966. Bette Davis, Natalie Wood, Edward G. Robinson, Phyllis Diller, and other notables sent in recipes

---

2. Bruce Cassidy, *Dinah!* (New York: Franklin Watts, 1979).

on their own stationery, and in most cases in their own handwriting. A delightfully original assemblage, the book was a celebrity collector's dream come true.

The author of an earlier Hollywood cookbook was an entrepreneur who prepared special meals for movie stars at home and in his restaurant, then sold them their favorite recipes for $50 each. In *Servants and Stars*, Chef Gene W. Milliers shared his feelings about the "duties" of each, then exposed the culinary preferences of Bazil [*sic*] Rathbone, Charlie Chaplin, Gloria Swanson, Marion Davies, Will Rogers, Norma Shearer, Greta Garbo, and gave a physically demanding entry that was Joan Crawford's favorite:

Surprise

Line the bottom of a serving dish with thin slices of cake ¼-inch, no thicker. Place a flat mold of very hard vanilla ice cream on top of cake. Beat six eggs separately, then beat them together. Pour over the vanilla ice and bake (have the oven hot) for a few minutes, the time necessary to make an omelette soufle. The eggs rise and brown ever so slightly and the ice does not melt. Serve immediately, with hot plates. Serve cookies or petits fours.

—Servants and Stars
by Gene W. Milliers (n.d.)

A smart-aleck little cookbook from 1936, *The American Association of Gourmets Presents the Epicurean Delights of Those Who Really Like to Know What to Eat, in the Hope that the Tea Room, the Quick Lunch Counter and the Hamburger Stand Will Take Their Place Along With the Vanishing American and the Forgotten Man* by Herbert Cerwin of the Hotel Del Monte in California, produced some real treats contributed by Zane Grey and Sinclair Lewis, as well as John Steinbeck's recipe for "Tortilla Flat." Lynn Fontaine and Alfred Lunt, who "cook and act together," submitted the following:

Fit for Man or Shrew

One and one half pounds of beef, no fat, ground four or five times. Beat into this four or five egg yolks, one cup cream, salt and pepper, two tablespoons finely chopped onions, two tablespoons finely chopped pickled beets, three cups finely chopped *boiled potatoes (or bread crumbs that have been previously soaked in milk). Form into balls three or four inches in diameter and pretty thick. Fry quickly in very hot butter. They should be very rare in the center. Serve with fried potatoes and brown butter.*

In *Pearl's Kitchen: An Extraordinary Cookbook* (New York: Harcourt Brace Jovanovich, 1973), Bailey observed, "Cooking is not drudgery for me, *any time*. During the festive seasons, I love to keep my house full of good smells. I like to spread the finest table that my pocketbook will allow. It gets back to my feeling about the kitchen and food as a way of sharing and giving. . . . My feast comes in the preparation; my gift, in the anticipation of everyone's enjoyment. I like to have that holiday seasonal music playing on the radio and smell the mixture of delicious aromas. I like to conjure in my imagination the quality of the meals I want to serve. Then I like to give the task my full attention. I get my brain going in three or four channels at once. I turn on all the burners and hold nothing back."

To assemble *The All-American Cook Book*, Gertrude Frelove Brebnor wrote more than two thousand letters to famous military and political personages and men of celebrity. Remarkably, many responded, including John Philip Sousa, William Jennings Bryan, Thomas A. Edison (whose wife contributed to another collection), Herbert Hoover, Army General Leonard Wood, and Marine Commandant John Archer Lejune. It was published by the Judy[3] Publishing Company in Chicago as a fund-raiser for needy veterans of World War I and their families.

Rolled Chops with Truffle Sauce
(Contributed by William Howard Taft, Chief Justice of the Supreme Court, and former President of the United States)

Rolled Chops

Cut eggplant into rounds, roll them in egg and bread crumbs, and fry. Take loin chops, cut thick, and roll them in rounds, putting a toothpick into them. Broil them and put them on the eggplant and pour truffle sauce over them.

---

3. Will Judy was an avid dog lover and author of several self-published books on their care.

Truffle Sauce

Rub together one tablespoon of butter and two tablespoons of flour. Put two cups of brown stock on the stove, season, and when it is boiling, put in the flour and butter. Chop up the truffles very fine and put them in the sauce.

—*The All-American Cook Book*
by Gertrude Frelove Brebnor
(Chicago: Judy Publishing, 1922)

The original *Congressional Club Cook Book; Favorite National and International Recipes* was put together in 1925 with a rather dull introduction by the otherwise-spunky Lou Henry (Mrs. Herbert) Hoover. The book was reprinted in 1927 and revised in 1933 with the word *Club* omitted from the title forevermore. It is currently in its eleventh edition. Membership in the club automatically comes with the husband's election to Congress. It is the only women's organization ever chartered by the Congress of the United States. All editions of the book are historically interesting, containing recipes from wives of congressmen, governors, justices, cabinet members, and internationals; as well as from Senate and House of Representative restaurants and nearby hotel eateries. The older editions contain an explanation of invitational and dining protocol and extensive indexing.

Kedgeree
(Contributed by Mrs. Franklin D. Roosevelt, wife of the
President of the United States)

1 cupful white fish, boiled and flaked
1 cupful rice, boiled
2 eggs, hard boiled
seasoning to taste, salt, pepper, curry powder

Mix fish with ingredients; add milk or cream, if one likes the mixture a little moist; put in the oven to brown; serve hot with rice.

—*The Congressional Cook Book*
(1933)

Finally, from the collection *Famous Recipes of Famous Women* (New York: Harper & Brothers, 1925), comes a sassy sampling:

Cheese Soufflé in Ramekins
(Contributed by Mrs. Thomas A. Edison, Wife of Electrical Genius)

4 rounded tablespoonfuls of cheese, cut up
1 heaping cupful of fine bread crumbs
Full half-cupful of milk
2 rounded tablespoonfuls of butter
1/3 teaspoonful of dry mustard and salt
Sprinkle of cayenne
2 eggs, separated

Boil the bread crumbs in the milk, and then add the cheese, then the butter, already seasoned with the salt, mustard and cayenne; then the well-beaten yolks, then the whites beaten to a stiff froth. Bake in a buttered dish for twenty minutes in a moderate oven.

Breakfast
(Contributed by Mrs. F. Scott Fitzgerald, Wife of author of *The Beautiful and Damned*, *The Jazz Age*, etc.)

See if there is any bacon, and if there is ask the cook which pan to fry it in. Then ask if there are any eggs, and if so try and persuade the cook to poach two of them. It is better not to attempt toast, as it burns very easily. Also in the case of bacon do not turn the fire too high, or you will have to get out of the house for a week. Serve preferably on china plates, though gold or wood will do if handy.

How to Mix a Salad
(Contributed by Miss Ida M. Tarbell, Writer)

Pinch of salt.
Sprinkle of pepper.
Niggard with the vinegar.
Spendthrift with the oil, and
Devil of a stir.

"There are those, I know, who believe any interest in eating
betokens an inferior order of beings. They eat only to live, they
say. I have little patience with them. They are limited souls, like
the people who can't stand music or hate poetry, for a really good
life means a wide enjoyment of good living, and cooking is no less
art because its tools are familiar to every household. Breaking
bread together is still a symbol of something far beyond swallow-
ing enough food to keep soul and body together. And when the
family and friends gather around the table, life is suddenly warmer
and more pleasant."

—*Stillmeadow Kitchen*
by Gladys Taber
(Philadelphia: Macrae-Smith,
1947)

11  The Big, Beautiful Cookbook

It is difficult to imagine pondering a meal without access to a big, beautiful hardbound cookbook, lavish and inspiring, with provocative indoor and outdoor photographs interspersed throughout pages of novelistically described cooking experiences. Slick and generous to the touch, such books are almost satisfying enough to curb the appetite just by looking.

But there was a beginning, a first effort, in fact a downright roguish presentation of books with a secret agenda not to end up in an untidy kitchen at all. The time was 1966, and it was Time-Life Books that would develop the brilliantly futuristic Foods of the World series and plan to market it in a time-honored fashion—by mail order. Editor Richard L. Williams, who oversaw the entire twenty-seven-volume culinary-cum-travelog project, had in his grasp a concept that would be new and unique for two distinctive reasons. First, a big, beautiful, irresistible coffee-table text would be supplemented by a second, smaller text, a spiral recipe "workbook" to suffice in the messy kitchen. Thus, lofty vision merged with practical application—an attitude that permeated the entire series.

But the major decisions concerned how the series' photography should reflect the world's foods. It started with ingredients, dishes, and meals, like other cookbooks, but exploded into realistic news-quality color scenes depicting where resources for these menus were grown, caught, marketed and processed. Readers met the cooks in their own settings, learned about their daily fare and special meals, and how traditional foods were prepared and when. Celebrations were given rapt attention as cameras captured the very essence of the costumes, history, exotic food, and ritual—all of this in the faces, hands, and active bodies of people many Americans had never had the opportunity to observe before.

The text mingled the writers' personal descriptions with an acknowledgment of the tourist's curiosity, and even in cases where the overall product was not smooth or consistent, authenticity rang true. It was like traveling abroad. It was like learning a foreign language and picking up on customs with an accomplished guide. It was savoir-faire in the rec room.

Acknowledging the "food field" to be the most temperament-ridden of all arts, Williams decided to confront this challenge by choosing established authors, consultants, and photographers who not only were opinionated and had a distinct style, but who also had the ultimate ability to express these talents and feelings admirably on paper and film. The New York cooking teacher and child prodigy pianist Michael Field was enlisted as consulting editor throughout most of the series until his untimely death of a heart attack. He commanded, with his wife, Frances, one of the last books, A *Quintet of Cuisines* (1970). Richard Meek, Mark Kauffman, Milton Greene, Fred Lyon, and Richard Jeffery were the big time photographers involved who shot on location or in studio close-ups. Chef John Clancy eventually headed the test kitchen personnel. Various food authors were approached as authorities on specific countries, including M. F. K. Fisher, James Beard, Waverley Root, Jonathan Norton Leonard, and Dale Brown; other noteworthy editors throughout most of the series were Gerry Shremp and Lyn Stallworth. Choosing from such talents, a team was selected for each book, four leaders who would work with assistants at home and stringers abroad to achieve their lavish goal. At some point the team was sent to visit the country and hobnob with native experts.

Time-Life had a policy that any reporter was expected to work any story assigned, but in this case an exception was made so that no one working on any one food discipline be uncomfortable or uninterested. A reporter who did not like Italian food, for instance, could ask for a transfer, and permission was given, much to the relief of the Italian-food lovers involved. The method of final production was the same throughout. For each selected recipe a cook was delegated, often an amateur, who would whip up the dish in the test kitchen while a researcher wrote down all he or she saw. The recipe was typed up then retested until the result was satisfactory.

At the start, Foods of the World did not aspire to include twenty-seven volumes. Although the original number of books planned has faded in time, editors agree that the whole American regional segment was an afterthought, done in 1970 and 1971 in response to the success of the first sixteen volumes.

Books were sold individually, and some were far more popular than others, the fact being that some books were simply better than others. *Spain and Portugal* and *China* went into multiple printings, with *Japan* and *Italy* being highly popular personal favorites. M. F. K. Fisher's *Provincial France*, with Julia Child as consultant, was considered a classic, whereas Craig Claiborne and Pierre Franey's *Classic French Cooking* was not overwhelmingly received. Food reviewers, many of whom were not familiar with the foreign cuisines, were picayune with their criticism about one recipe or another without observing that the bulk of the material would challenge a staff of ten, let alone one timid homemaker! But accidentally or on purpose the series would ultimately become a superb reference work rather than a humble cookery effort. Homage was paid at the onset, but reviewers eventually fell into the maddening "ho-hum, another masterpiece: if you liked the others you'll like this one too" mode. *The Cooking of Vienna's Empire*, with pastry clouds on the front cover, sold well but another outstanding book, *The Cooking of Scandinavia*, did not. Editors suspected in hindsight the reason to be the jar of pickled herring and carrots on the cover. Praises such as "exceptional color photographs," "beautifully printed," and "fascinating narration, tantalizing recipes" were the norm; *Best Seller* recommended that "the large book can serve also as a resource study for students in grades 8 and above" (September 1, 1969).

The series sold an average two million copies during each of the five years of work. It opened the door for subsequent oversize cookbooks, big-budget artifacts for such authors as Lee Bailey and Martha Stewart.

Every used book store in America that features cookbooks reserves a spot on its shelves for these volumes, however they arrive: sets broken up, spiral workbooks separated from their handsome partners, or the two volumes without the retail protective sleeve. Some sell better than others from region to region, while overall the Asian and European sell better than the American regionals. The Foods of the Worlds volumes were big-budget productions, and they looked it—they still do.

The 27 Time-Life Foods of the World Volumes

The Cooking of Provincial France	M. F. K. Fisher	1968
The Cooking of Italy	Waverley Root	1968
The Cooking of Scandinavia	Dale Brown	1968
The Cooking of Vienna's Empire	Joseph Wechsberg	1968
Latin American Cooking	Jonathan Norton Leonard	1968
American Cooking	Dale Brown	1968
The Cooking of China	Emily Hahn	1968
Wine and Spirits	Alex Waugh	1968
Russian Cooking	Helen and George Papashivly	1969
The Cooking of the British Isles	Adrian Bailey	1969
Middle Eastern Cooking	Harry G. Nickles	1969
The Cooking of Japan	Rafael Steinberg	1969
The Cooking of Germany	Nika Standen Hazelton	1969
The Cooking of Spain and Portugal	Peter S. Feibleman	1969
The Cooking of India	Santha Rama Rau	1969
Pacific and Southeast Asian Cooking	Rafael Steinberg	1970
The Cooking of the Caribbean Islands	Linda Wolfe	1970
Classic French Cooking	Craig Claiborne, Pierre Franey	1970
African Cooking	Laurens Van der Post	1970
A Quintet of Cuisines (Switzerland, Belgium, Luxembourg, Netherlands, Poland, Bulgaria, Romania, Tunisia, Algeria, Morocco)	Michael and Frances Field	1970
American Cooking: The Northwest	Dale Brown	1970
American Cooking: New England	Jonathan Norton Leonard	1970
American Cooking: Creole and Acadian	Peter S. Feibleman	1971
American Cooking: Southern Style	Eugene Walter	1971
American Cooking: The Great West	Jonathan Norton Leonard	1971
American Cooking: The Eastern Heartland (New York, Ohio, New Jersey, Michigan, Indiana, Illinois, Pennsylvania)	José Wilson	1971
American Cooking: The Melting Pot	James P. Shenton	1971
Menu Guide and Recipe Index to the Time-Life Books	(spiral only)	1971
Kitchen Guide		1968

Shireen Polo

(Iranian—Persian—steamed rice with chicken, nuts, orange peel, and carrots)

Peel of 2 oranges, cut into strips 1 inch long and ⅛ inch wide

8 tablespoons (1 quarter-pound stick) butter

3 medium-sized carrots, cut into strips about 1 inch long and
    ⅛ inch wide

1 cup slivered blanched almonds

2 cups sugar

1 teaspoon ground saffron (or 1 teaspoon saffron threads, pul-
    verized with a mortar and pestle or with the back of a spoon)
    dissolved in 1 tablespoon warm water

¼ cup plus 2 tablespoons finely chopped unsalted pistachios

2 cups imported Iranian rice or other uncooked long-grain rice,
    soaked and drained

¼ cup olive oil

2½ to 3-pound chicken, cut into 8 serving pieces

1 teaspoon salt

5 cups water

1 large onion, quartered

4 tablespoons melted butter combined with 1 tablespoon water

Blanch the orange peel by dropping it into a small pan of cold
water, bringing it to a boil, then draining it immediately and running
cold water over it. In a heavy 10- to 12-inch skillet, melt the butter
over moderate heat. When the foam subsides, add the carrots and,
stirring frequently, cook for 10 minutes, or until they are soft but
not brown. Add the orange peel, almonds, sugar and saffron, and
reduce the heat to low. Stir constantly until the sugar dissolves, then
cover tightly and simmer for 30 minutes. Stir in the ¼ cup of pistachios and cook for 2 or 3 minutes longer. Set aside.

Meanwhile, bring 6 cups of water to a boil in a heavy 3- to 4-
quart casserole with a tightly fitting lid. Pour in the rice in a slow,
thin stream. Stir once or twice, boil briskly for 5 minutes, then
drain in a sieve. In a heavy 12-inch skillet, heat the olive oil until a
light haze forms above it. Pat the chicken dry with paper towels and
brown it in the oil, a few pieces at a time, turning it with tongs and
regulating the heat so that they color richly and evenly without
burning. As they brown, transfer the pieces to a plate. Pour off and

discard the fat remaining in the skillet and replace the chicken in the pan. Sprinkle the pieces with the salt and scatter the onion quarters on top. Pour in the 5 cups of water, bring to a boil over high heat, cover and simmer over low heat for 30 minutes, or until the chicken is tender.

While the chicken is simmering, pour the melted butter and water mixture into the casserole and spread half of the rice evenly over it. Add 2 cups of the carrot mixture, smooth it to the edges, cover with the remaining rice and spread the rest of the carrot mixture on top. Cover tightly and steam for 20 minutes, or until the rice is tender. To serve, remove the bones from the chicken breasts and thighs. Spread half the rice on a heated platter and arrange the chicken over it. Mound the rest of the rice on top and sprinkle it with the remaining pistachios.

—*Foods of the World:*
Middle Eastern Cooking
by Harry G. Nickles and the Editors of
TIME-LIFE BOOKS
Photographed by David Lees and
Richard Jeffery
(New York: Time-Life Books Inc.,
1969)

12

Guru versus Gourmet:
A Media Battleground

By 1962, an estimated 850 cookbooks were in print in the United States. By 1984, the estimate was closer to six thousand, with an average two cookbooks a day being published. Statistics such as these are bound to confuse the serious cookbook collector who must pause to consider what cookbooks will be collectible in the future? Which ones already are?

Once a chef has an outstanding national reputation, cookbooks with his or her name, even first editions, will be published in the tens, perhaps thousands.[1] Collectors in the cookbook game return to the same playing field as other collectors. They look for early first editions issued before the chef was known, obscure publications, pristine copies, and unusual inscriptions. Limited editions of unknown authors who produced outstanding cookbooks are another source of interest, the investment being more in anticipation of the book reaching the desirable status for one reason or another. Every cookbook published before 1960 is of some interest, perhaps a lot, to someone, somewhere. The older the publication date, the greater the possibility of the book having a value of more than $100.

---

1. Because the works of authors cited in this chapter are readily available in new and used bookstores and libraries, only exemplary recipes of my "wholesome gourmet" theory will be cited.

While the history of American cookbooks evolves as an organic, visible, changing pattern, there is a central motif that has not changed. There were, from the beginning, food authors who cared more about taste and presentation than nutrition, and those of the opposite school of thought who cared more about nutrition than how the food looked on the plate or how it appeased the palate. Examples of both types have been cited throughout this book. These authors played a critical part in the recent climax of our culinary history by submitting articles to newspapers and magazines, which, in turn, developed their own cooking staff and food editors. For the most part, these Wednesday food-page writers were the experts responsible for translating the efforts of both guru and gourmet into recipes that average homemakers could sample within the limits of their own kitchen resources.

Born in Oregon on May 5, 1903, James Andrews Beard learned to cook from his mother, who had operated a hotel and a specialty foods shop in Portland. He trained as an actor and opera singer but eventually made a living as a New York caterer. His first publication, *Hors d'oeuvre and Canapés* (1940), was a pioneer effort in that it concentrated solely on presenting foods best served with particular liquors, a venture wholly influenced by that era's ubiquitous cocktail party. Beard's easy but lavish style caught the attention of *Herald Tribune* columnists Lucius Beebe and Clementine Paddleford, who directed him toward an association with *House & Garden* magazine, where he inaugurated "Corkscrew," a column about spirits. Although he disdained the use of the word *gourmet*, epicurean entertaining would be the mainstay of Beard's activities for the rest of his life and probably added a few of the many pounds to his six-foot frame (he enjoyed referring to himself as a "butter boy").

In the small town of Lizton, about twenty miles northwest of Indianapolis, Adelle Davis was born on February 24, 1904. Beard and Davis, born in the same decade, couldn't have had more opposite life-styles; the two authors symbolized the two genres of food philosophy that had been so diverse but were now about to crash head-on. Davis was not a member of a religious cult and did not ascribe to any political cause concerning her nutritive theories. This made her accessible to a greater segment of the public, and when her book *Let's Cook It Right* appeared in 1947, it caught the nation's interest. By its first paperback edition in 1970, the sixth printing, it was lauded by the *New York Times*: "No cook can help taking a greater interest in each dish she prepares after reading [this book] . . . Guidance toward the best in cooking is given through friendly, firm, often amusing advice." The book carried an impressive disclaimer of sorts, "Owing to her extremely heavy writing schedule, Adelle Davis regrets that she cannot answer mail from individuals."

Although he was reportedly petty, selfish, even ruthless at times, and certainly was not above taking credit for someone else's achievement, Jim Beard was a personable, disconcertingly charming, bow-tied homosexual who was at his best hosting a party in his New York brownstone. Davis was a mother—not at all charismatic, but rather studious, bossy, and stern with an odd sense of humor. What these two had in common was that they inspired a multitude of disciples. They, in turn, influenced others who began for the first time in our history exchanging theories and listening to each other on the subjects of taste, presentation, and nutrition.

Beard's followers were legion. He realized early in his career that he had clout, and he used it. Among his first protégés was another six-footer, Julia Carolyn (McWilliams) Child, who exuded confidence and class. When she and coauthors Louisette Berthold and Simone (Simca) Beck wrote volume I of *Mastering the Art of French Cooking* (1961) as "nobodies from nowhere," it was James Beard who kindly opened doors throughout New York City. This was particularly significant because Child, although America's first woman chef, was not considered a "real" chef by some because, however *Cordon Bleu* her credentials, she did not own or preside over a restaurant.[2] Child would go on to surpass her mentor in popularity, however, influencing America's attitude toward international cooking more than any other person in the twentieth century. It was not her recipes or her cookbooks that did the trick, but the sheer dynamics of her (lovingly satirized) television persona as seen on Boston's WGBH.

Among the many other nationally known authors who frankly admitted indebtedness to Beard's patronship were Jacques Pepin, Richard Olney, Marion Cunningham, and Barbara Kafka. By 1972, when Beard wrote his dissertation on the subject he was most noted for promoting, *James Beard's American Cookery*, he had more than fifteen titles to his credit as well as a legend in the making.

Adelle Davis inspired Frances Moore Lappé to write *Diet for a Small Planet* (1971), which in turn had a tremendous effect upon *Laurel's Kitchen* (1976) authors Laurel Robertson, Carol Flinders,

---

2. Child's correspondence with Simone Beck, James Beard, Louisette Bertholle, and M. F. K. Fisher, as well as manuscripts and television scripts and photographs, are held in the Arthur and Elizabeth Schlesinger Library on the History of Women at Radcliffe College.

and Bronwen Godfrey, as well as on the multitalented Mollie Katzen, who sold the first precious hand-lettered and illustrated, self-published copies of *The Moosewood Cookbook* (1977) to bookstores personally, out of the back of a 1972 Datsun stationwagon. It is interesting to note that these women have much in common with our foremothers who planted the seeds of America's culinary garden in that they continue to bear the responsibility of the nation's women and children and are involved in facets of society other than those that are food-oriented, as their essays exhibit. Indeed, in Katzen's art, kitchen items, long called "women's thing's," are beautifully honored. The books were written during the radical Renaissance decades of the sixties and seventies, when the market clamored for "back to the earth" recipes that were delicious and wholesome. (Some formulas came in with a positively decadent bent and used the entire planet's spices, herbs, and grains.) In spite of the tofu backlash and professional chefs who called a halt on the use of yogurt in place of sour cream, families were discovering once and for all that good-for-you food could taste good. The movement didn't even experience a setback when *Prevention* magazine's J. I. Rodale died of a heart attack on camera during a Dick Cavett interview in 1971.

Throughout these latter decades, high-profile individuals began receiving attention from the food sections of influential newspapers, in the glossy pages of national magazines, and eventually on television. This new adulation was coveted by all cooks and chefs because the food world had never been known for its high salaries in spite of the fact that no other artistic endeavor involves all of the senses as well as the intelligence on multiple levels of consciousness. Now, with the help of the national media, they began cashing in.

Opportunistic journalists got into the act by producing their own cookbooks, thus newspapers and magazines continued to wield their own influence over the minds and hearts of homemakers. Next to the *Betty Crocker* output, the most popular picture-cookbooks in American history were published in Des Moines, Iowa by Meredith, who was famous for *Better Homes & Gardens*. The first, issued in 1930 under the title *My Better Homes & Gardens Cookbook*, was written by Josephine Wylie. The third edition in 1931 carried a more comprehensive title: *My Better Homes & Garden Lifetime Cook Book*; updated, specialized cookbooks bearing BH&G titles and reputation have continued to appear since 1930. However, magazine publishing companies, just like General Mills, did not intend to share the spotlight with budding superstar authors, and the casts of characters who organized the cookbooks remained almost as anonymous as actors in theme park productions.

Another magazine cookbook with historic roots commenced as *The Good Housekeeping Home Cook Book*, arranged by the prolific cookbook author Isabel Gordon Curtis, editor of that magazine for many years. Genevieve A. Callahan put together the first Menlo Park, California, cookbook, *Sunset All-Western Cookbook* in 1933. *Sunset Magazine* was an outgrowth of the Southern Pacific Railroad Company's small booklet for train travelers until Larry Lane began traveling west for *Better Homes and Gardens* and decided that eastern magazines weren't showcasing the culture west of the Rockies to its fullest potential. Lane bought out *Sunset* in 1928 to start his own empire; his wife Ruth (Bell) Lane eventually took over the culinary leadership of both magazine and subsequent cookbooks; over forty titles are still in print.

There was hardly a newspaper in the country that did not produce a cookbook at some time, some of them achieving great success, such as those produced by the *New York Times*. The food critic Craig Claiborne found that it wasn't as easy to write a cookbook as it was to write restaurant critiques and wasted no time hooking up with the French chef Pierre Franey, to the enhancement of both careers. Another good example of the best-selling cookbook-from-newspaper genre, recently revised, is *The Picayune's Creole Cook Book . . . from the lips of the old Creole Negro Cooks* (New Orleans, 1901).

The guru versus gourmet battle continues as established publishers bow in acknowledgment to the country's growing commitment to nutrition while the alternative presses learn attractive ways to educate consumers. Chefs who embody both persuasions are on the cutting edge, but few have brought forth cookbooks that succeed as well in this respect as *The Victory Garden Cookbook* (1982), a winning collaboration between Marian Morash, Jane Doerfer and the WGBH Educational Foundation in Boston. In the book, both meatless and meatful meals originate in the produce drawer rather than the meat freezer; contents are actually alphabetized by vegetable rather than meal category; and Morash's cooking talent and gardening heritage shines. Daily and artful cookery is offered to genuinely and nutritiously excite gourmet palates via flavors of pure, fresh food with enhancements that range from subtle to fiercely foreign.

Morash and Katzen also exemplify the new standard of excellence in cookbooks that gives equal time to midwestern and northern (root) vegetables rather than concentrating on California or tropical vegetables to the former's exclusion. They encourage experimentation by offering a treasure trove of variations on basic formulas, yet delivered in totally different personal styles. The ultimate lesson being that whether a recipe is simple or confusing, its aim to enlighten or control, the cost of the cookbook $7 or $70—America's culinary heritage is still in the making.

The James Beard Foundation

In 1985, two months after James Beard died, Julia Child began inquiries about what was to happen to his brownstone, the New York home on West 12th Street that had so generously welcomed guests from all over the world. This was a moment of inspiration, not uncharacteristic of the woman who had always labored to establish gastronomy as a respected art and bona fide discipline. The movement needed momentum, and the name that could propel it forward at this strategic time in history was that of James Beard.

In spite of the fact that the property came with a legacy of eccentricities—a fourth floor tenant with a nine-year lease, a third floor tenant with a lifetime lease (Jim's gift to a friend who had rented from him for years), a huge kitchen, no bedrooms at all, and a bathroom shower on the glass-enclosed balcony—the price was $1,500,000. Acknowledging the dedicated interest of the Beard enthusiasts the estate finally cut the price in half with the stipulation that a $250,000 down payment be raised in 30 days. In response, chefs, cooking teachers and friends held benefits in their restaurants, schools and homes to raise the money, and quite a hoopla at the same time. They were successful, and The James Beard Foundation was established as a charitable foundation in 1986 to foster "the appreciation and development of gastronomy by preserving and promulgating our culinary heritage, and by recognizing and promoting excellence in all aspects of the culinary arts." It is our first and only culinary center.

When the group moved in, they found that the only room left almost as Beard had had it was the kitchen, primarily because so much of it was "built in." However, while the space comfortably accommodated Jim and 12 students, it was a nightmare for a chef preparing a meal for 70 diners anticipating miracles. So the renovation of the kitchen, and the reacquisition of many of the pots, pans and utensils that were sold at auction, became highest priority. Today, to old friends who knew it when, the kitchen appears the way it did when Beard first built it up, complete with the world map wallpaper. Artfully, it also contains the modern equipment that enables chefs to perform at their best.

Beard's library was always a working writer's collection, as he had convenient access to the vast collection of food and wine volumes at the Corner Book Store on 4th Street, and the friendship of its proprietor bibliographer Eleanor Lowenstein. Again, his personal collection of books was sought after to restock the shelves, and new treasures were acquired with a concentration on "Beardiana." Also housed here is the nation's Cookbook Hall of Fame; one part of the extensive James Beard Awards and Scholarships, which honors outstanding books continuously in print for ten years or more.

Each week, chefs from America's finest restaurants and hotels entertain in Jim's famous kitchen, presenting their work to gatherings of members, friends and the press. The facility also provides a meeting place for non-profit culinary organizations such as the International Association of Cooking Professionals, The New York Culinary Historians, The New York Association of Cooking Teachers, and the New York Women's Culinary Alliance. Membership fees ranging from Associate Non-Resident ($50) to Corporate ($500) allow participation in various activities and subscription to "News From the Beard House," a monthly calendar of events.

—Lifted in part from The James
Beard Foundation
167 West 12th Street
New York, N.Y. 10011

"As I see it, a cookbook should not merely teach a beginner how to prepare foods or list proportions of ingredients any housewife may easily forget. One of its chief purposes is to aid in menu planning, bringing to mind, as one flips its pages, foods enjoyed yet infrequently served. Variety lends interest to meals. A woman should be able to prepare thirty or more different entrees without repeating a menu if she wishes to do so; once she has used a recipe it is hers for a lifetime."

—Let's Cook It Right
by Adelle Davis
(New York: Signet, 1970)

Gado-Gado
(An Indonesian dish with spicy peanut sauce)

The sauce:

1 cup chopped onion

2 medium cloves crushed garlic

1 cup good, pure peanut butter

1 tablespoon honey

¼ teaspoon cayenne pepper

juice of 1 lemon

1 bay leaf

1-2 teaspoons freshly grated
  ginger root

1 tablespoon cider vinegar

3 cups water

½-1 teaspoons salt

dash tamari

2 tablespoons butter for frying

In a saucepan, cook the onions, garlic, bay leaf and ginger in butter, lightly salted. When onion becomes translucent add remaining ingredients. Mix thoroughly. Simmer on lowest possible heat 30 minutes, stirring occasionally.

Underneath the Sauce: The sauce goes over an artful arrangement of combined cooked and raw vegetables. Extra protein comes from garnishes of tofu chunks and hard-cooked egg slices. Base your arrangement on a bed of fresh spinach (or rice, or both).

shredded cabbage, steamed or
  raw

celery slices, steamed or raw

broccoli spears, steamed

carrot slices, steamed or raw

fresh, whole green beans,
  steamed

fresh, raw mung bean sprouts

tofu chunks, either raw or sautéed in oil with sesame seeds

Garnish with: apples, lemons, oranges, raisins, toasted seeds and nuts, a drizzle of sesame oil, pieces of hard-cooked egg.

—*The Moosewood Cookbook*
Compiled, Edited, Illustrated, and
Hand-Lettered by Mollie Katzen
(Berkeley: Ten Speed Press, 1977)

Sweet Potato-Chocolate Nut Cake

The natural sweet potato orange color looks beautiful swirled together with chocolate, while the flavors complement each other. Sprinkle this cake with confectioners' sugar or drizzle it with the sugar glaze that follows recipe.

4 ounces semisweet chocolate

1 teaspoon vanilla extract

3 cups flour

1½ cups sugar

2 teaspoons baking powder

2 teaspoons baking soda

2 teaspoons cinnamon

½ teaspoon ground ginger

¼ teaspoon ground cloves

¼ teaspoon nutmeg

1 teaspoon salt

2 cups mashed cooked sweet potatoes

1½ cups vegetable oil

4 eggs

1 cup chopped nuts

Butter and lightly flour a 10-inch tube pan. Place chocolate and vanilla in a small saucepan and set, covered, in a larger pan that you've just filled with boiling water.

Sift together all dry ingredients and set aside. In a large bowl, beat the sweet potatoes and oil together, then beat in the eggs one by one until well blended. Slowly add dry ingredients and mix well; stir in nuts. Put one-third of the mixture in another bowl and stir in the chocolate, which should be melted smooth by now. Alternate the batters in a tube pan, as you would with a marble cake. With a knife, cut through the two batters to slightly swirl together. Bake in a preheated 350 degree oven for 1¼ hours or until the sides have shrunk away from the pan, the top is springy, and tester comes out dry. Let cool 10 minutes and then remove from the pan and cool on a rack.

Sugar Glaze: 2-3 tablespoons boiling water, 1½ cups confectioners' sugar. Beat water gradually into sugar until mixture has the consistency of a thick cream sauce; drizzle over cake.

—*The Victory Garden Cookbook*
by Marian Morash
(New York: Knopf, 1982)

What Cookbooks Do Americans Collect?

Regional, souvenir cookbooks from every state in the union.
Cookbooks from certain states only.
Ethnic cookbooks: some prefer translations of foreign cookbooks,
   others prefer American publications.
Books for investment, old and new.
Cookbooks with Christmas motifs to display during the holdiays.
Cookbooks bound in certain colors to match kitchen decor.
Military cookbooks, wartime, military post or base wives' clubs,
   even MRE (Meals-Ready-to-Eat) cookbooks.
Meatless cookbooks, or various types of vegetable–grain oriented
   volumes.
Genuine African-American or Native-American cookbooks.
Restaurant or chef cookbooks.
Autographed cookbooks, particularly celebrity.
Cookbooks containing recipe names of animals or birds.
Cookbooks containing red, white, and blue recipes (e.g.,
   blueberry muffins, red cole slaw, Baltimore white cake).
Cookbooks related to each of the chapter headings in this
   book, cooking schools gaining in popularity.
Regional souvenir cookbooks from foreign countries visited.
Tomes by personal favorite authors, usually American.
Spiral-bound only (or no spiral-bound).
Old ones, the older the better, from all over the world.
Junior League cookbooks.

"For a long time now we have been given a heavy dose of
propaganda from the food industry that the working woman
(and, of course, man) hasn't got time to cook anymore. But what
are we saving all the time for?"

—Marion Cunningham in
The Fannie Farmer Cookbook (1990)

Glossary of Old and Unusual
North American
Cooking Terms

Addled: Rotten or spoiled.

Alligator pear: Avocado.

Almonds: Sweet almonds are the ones commonly eaten; bitter almonds are used to make almond extract but can be toxic if used improperly.

Amber gum or **ambergris:** Waxlike secretion from sperm whales used to enhance or "fix" seasonings in cooking or fragrances in pomanders.

Angelica: Herb used in folklore cooking, decorating, and for medicinal purposes almost worldwide.

Antiquarian book: Book traded because it is nationally important (or in demand) and scarce, that is, only a dozen or so come onto the market in a year's time.

Arrowroot: The starchy roots of this plant are dried, ground, and used as a thickener in gravy and sauces and in cooking for babies and invalids.

Asafetida: A bitter, onion-flavored gum resin used in Asia as a condiment.

Ash bread: Cornbreads, usually wrapped in cabbage leaves, baked in the ashes of the fireplace (e.g., corn pone); "hoe" cake was placed on the hoe to bake in the fire or fireplace.

Aumlet: Omelette.

Avocate: Avocado.

Bain marie: A double-boiler saucepan.

Baked flour: (*See* brown or baked flour).

Bannocks: Scottish cakes made of barley or oatmeal, cooked on a griddle.

Bards or **bardes:** Slices of pork fat, salt pork, or bacon laid on game or meat terrines to baste them while roasting.

Barley sugar: Confection made by heating white sugar to the melting point when it forms small grains resembling barley.

Bee sweetnin': Honey.

Beef olives: (*See* recipe, page 104).

Bennie: That which is called sesame seed in the North, bennie seed in the South.

Bladder and **liver:** Animal membranes tied over jars and crocks (used before paraffin) to preserve contents.

Boil to a height: Boiling to the point of candying or crystallizing.

Borecole: Variety of kale that grows six feet or more in height; also called "palm-tree cabbage."

Bouchées: Small pastry shells filled with creamed meat.

Brandy papers: Parchment or writing paper soaked in brandy and tied down over jars and crocks (used before paraffin) to preserve contents.

Broom straws: Fresh, clean straw used to make brooms, or the topmost, clean pieces of a broom broken off and (1) used to separate two pie crusts baked in the same pan before filling is added; and (2) used to test cakes and quickbreads for doneness.

Brown or **baked flour:** White flour baked to a brownish color on a cookie sheet in the oven, or "bubbled" with fat before the liquid is added when making gravy, to take away the "raw" taste.

Bullace: Wild plum.

Burgoo: (1) Thick stew (Kentucky) served at outdoor gatherings; (2) oatmeal gruel; (3) hardtack and molasses cooked together.

Butter the size of a walnut: About two tablespoons of butter.

Butter the size of an egg: About ¼ cup of butter.

Cabinet pudding: Although versions of this dessert are made with items from the kitchen cabinet, (e.g., dried rather than fresh fruit), the English origin refers to the political connotation.

Calapash and **calipee:** The meat adjoining the upper and lower turtle shells, respectively.

Capsicum: Chili pepper pod, but used irregularly to mean various peppers.

Caramel coloring: (See recipe, page 129).

Carolina rice: Rice (first planted in the Carolinas).

Caruwaie: Caraway.

Cassava: Sweet cassava root is a staple in tropical America and Africa that is cooked and eaten as a vegetable. Dried and ground it is used in breads and as a basis for tapioca.

Caster or **castor** (as in sugar): Small vessel with a perforated top for shaking condiments on foods at the table.

Catsup, ketchup, catchup: Liquid or puree extracted from tomatoes, walnuts, mushrooms, for example, and used as a sauce.

Caul: Lacy membrane heavily laden with fat, used to wrap sausage meat to hold or keep from drying out.

Cauled: Heated to just below the boiling point, when scum forms.

Chayote: A pear-shaped delicate-tasting tropical squash, light, dark, or jade green in color, from Mexico.

Chile: Usually chili peppers (e.g., cayenne or jalapeno). El Paso and New Mexico use the word *chile* to describe chili (con carne) while the rest of the non-Hispanic population of Texas and elsewhere spell it *chili*.

Chine: (1) Backbone; (2) cut of meat including all or part of the backbone.

Chitterlings (pronounced chit-lins): The small intestine of swine, soaked and simmered by African Americans into a tasty pot dish served with vinegar and hot sauce, and by Creoles to stuff Andouilette sausage. Term used as early as 1533 in England (*chytterlynges*).

Civet: (1) Game stew; (2) another fixative, from the glands of the African civet cat (*see* Amber gum and Musk).

Clinkers: Biscuits, sometimes stale, for dunking.

Cochineal: A brilliant red dye made from dry female wood louse bodies (New Orleans). Currently, red food coloring is used instead.

Cockerel: Young male domestic fowl.

Coffeecupful: In measuring, about one cup of liquid or dry ingredients.

Coffin: (1) Pie crust; (2) the dish or mold in which a pie is baked.

Colander seed (from Simmon's *American Cookery*): Coriander? Sugar-coated seeds left to dry on a colander?

Colewort: (1) Originally, the generic name for any plant of the cabbage family; (2) cabbage.

Collops: Slices or small pieces of meat.

Come: (1) As in butter, to thicken; (2) as in fried foods, to stick to the pan.

Compotier: Dish used at dessert for holding fruit enough for all diners.

Cooter: Terrapin, that is, a land turtle not a sea turtle.

Coquina, donax, periwinkle: Tiny clamlike mollusks.

Corn: (1) Green corn is sweet corn; (2) mature or dry whole corn is popcorn.

Cracklins': (1) The delectable, crisp, nutty-flavored residue left from making homemade lard from hog fat; (2) any fresh uncooked pork fat scraps fried until rendered crisp.

Cree: To boil any variety of grains into a porridge.

Cullender: Collander.

Cutting and folding: Cutting vertically through the mixture and turning over and over with the spoon at the same time; most frequently used to combine beaten egg whites with batter.

Cymling: Summer squash with a scalloped edge.

Desiccated: Dried.

Dessertspoon: In measuring, about 1½ teaspoons.

Digester: Apparatus for softening bones, by high heat or chemical process, to make gelatin or tallow.

Donax: (*See* Coquina).

Doughspur: Scalloped wheel with a handle, used for decorating pastry.

Dram or **drachm:** ¾ teaspoon; an apothecary weight equaling ⅛ ounce.

Dresser: (1) Sideboard or table in the kitchen used for dressing foods; (2) side table used for serving food.

Dunghill fowl: Barnyard poultry, as opposed to wild or game birds.

Eggs: Use medium eggs in old recipes: extra-large ones did not exist (*see* Pound of eggs).

Elderblow: Elderberry.

Emptins or **emptings:** Yeast, made from beer dregs (*see* recipe page 7).

Eringo-root: Root of the sea holly plant.

Estragon: Tarragon.

Facsimile (in publishing): (1) An exact copy including binding; (2) photocopy of book pages, possibly with additional pages, and modern in binding. Although many cookbook reproductions are said to be facsimiles, they resemble the latter, not adhering to the true definition.

Fair water: Fresh water.

Farce, farcied: (*See* Forcemeat).

Filé: Powdered sassafras leaves added to gumbo or other southern dishes to thicken and flavor.

Fine herbs or **fines herbes:** Bouquet of fresh herb sprigs used to flavor a dish: (e.g., parsley, sage, rosemary, thyme, chives, and celery).

Firkin: (1) Small wooden vessel used to hold butter or cheese; (2) in Britain, ¼ of a barrel.

Five-cent jar: Usually an eight- to twelve-ounce jar (e.g., jam, marmalade).

Floating island: Dessert made of thin custard with "islands" of whipped cream, meringue, or another combination of these ingredients.

Flummery: Jellied dessert often flavored with rosewater or orange-flower water.

Forcemeat: Chopped meat, poultry, or fish seasoned with herbs and used for stuffing or forming meatballs.

French vinegar: In old cookbooks, usually tarragon vinegar.

Freshening: Rinsing salt-preserved butter (or other items) in several changes of water to make it palatable.

Frizzle: Cooking an item in butter or fat, such as dried beef, until it curls or crisps.

Frost grape: Native American variety, also called chicken grape.

Frowy: Stale or musty.

Frumenty: Hulled wheat cooked in milk and sweetened.

Gallipot: Small, glazed ceramic pot.

Gammon: English word for side of bacon, in current use.

Garth: (*See* Hoop).

Gem: Muffin or cupcake.

Giam: Jam.

Gill: ½ cup of liquid.

Ginny pepper: Peppers soaked in gin?

Glassful: As in shot glass, a full measure, about ¼ cup (frequently mentioned in Creole cooking).

Goetta: (Cincinnati-Northern Kentucky) pudding of pin-oats, pork scraps, sausage, and herbs, usually molded, sliced and fried (*see* Scrapple).

Graham flour: (*See* chapter 3, Sylvester Graham).

Green pepper: Usually a sweet green bell-shaped pepper (*see* Mango), but in the Southwest it can mean the poblano pepper, used for stuffing.

Grits or groats: (1) Whole or coarsely ground grain; (2) southern breakfast cereal or "vegetable" dish (*see* Hominy).

Groundnut: Peanut.

Guinea squash: Eggplant.
Gumbo filé: (*See* Filé).

Handful: In measuring, about one ounce.
Hardtack: (*See* Sailor's biscuit).
Heartslet: Heart and liver of animal.
Hoe cakes: (*See* Ash cakes).
Hominy: Puffed kernels of corn, white or yellow, that have been soaked in lye solution or boiled in water or milk to remove hulls.
Hoop: Deep ring used to form large cakes, first made of wood, later made of iron.
Hot closet: Warming oven.
Hot oven: 400 to 450 degrees Fahrenheit.
Hyson tea: Green tea from China.

Indian meal: Cornmeal.
Injun or **injun flour:** Cornmeal.
Isinglass: Gelatin made from the air bladder of a sturgeon and dried into sheets (leaves); also used as a clarifying agent.

Jelly bag: Cheesecloth used for straining fruit pulp for jelly (or soup bone residue for aspic).
Jelly cake tin: Shallow, rectangular pan similar to a cookie sheet, used for baking a thin cake, to roll, while warm, with jelly.
Jill: (*See* Gill).

Kohlrabi: Completely edible cabbage with a turnip-shaped stem, popular in Germany and midwestern and northern states.

Lamb's quarters: Edible wild green, mild tasting.
Laurel leaves: Bay leaves from the laurel tree (not the bush, which is reportedly poisonous).
Leverat: A young hare.
Lively emptins: (*See* Emptins).
Loaf sugar: Refined, crystallized sugar moistened and compressed into hard cones called *loaves*; pieces were broken off for table use, to be picked up with sugar tongs, or grated.
Loquat: Chinese fruit, not unlike a plum, that grows on trees.
Love apples: tomatoes.
Lump: In measuring, about two tablespoons (usually of butter).

Macaroni: (*See* Paste).
Macédoine: Mixture of vegetables or fruit used in a salad, sauce, for decoration, or in a jellied dessert.
Made mustard: As opposed to dry mustard or mustard seeds, mustard in a jar as we now know it.

Mango: (1) Word casually attributed to any vegetable or fruit (e.g., melon, squash, green pepper) that can be stuffed and pickled; in the Midwest the words *mango* and *green pepper* are synonymous; (2) roundish tropical fruit, edible and sweet when rose-yellow.

Mango pickle: Young melons, squash, cucumbers, green peppers cut in chunks or stuffed with cabbage and pickled.

Marrow: English word for summer or winter squash, in current use.

Marrow fat: The soft tissue occupying bone cavities, prized by gourmets.

Martynia: Also called *devil's claw* and *unicorn plant*, the young green pods of this smelly and aptly nicknamed plant are used to make pickles (Mexico, Texas).

Mead: Wine made with honey instead of sugar.

Medallion: Small round shape, as in fillets.

Mele: Meal.

Metate: Flat, rectangular tripod made of basalt and used for grinding corn, chilies or dry seasonings.

Moderate oven: About 350 degrees Fahrenheit.

Molasses: (*See* Treacle).

Muffin-rings: Small rings, usually of tinned iron, used to make muffins such as English muffins (small cat food cans, cleaned and opened on both ends will suffice).

Mush: (1) Cornmeal pudding or porridge (called hasty pudding in England, polenta in Italy); (2) this same pudding formed into a loaf, molded, sliced, and fried.

Musk: (1) Various plants and fruits producing a musky odor (theoretically), for example, musk apple, cherry, pear, grape; (2) a "fixative" from the glands of the male deer used to enhance seasonings in cooking or fragrances in pomanders.

Mutton: Sheep meat, as opposed to lamb.

Neet or **neat:** Ox or bullock, cow, or heifer.

Neufchâtel: Soft rennet cheese, cottage- or cream-type, originally from France but eventually made in the United States (Philadelphia).

Noir: Black.

Nonpareil: Small flat disk of chocolate covered with tiny hard sugar pellets; literally, "unequaled."

Nun's toast: French toast.

Ochra: Okra.

Orleans sugar: Brown sugar or molasses.

Oyster cracker or **biscuit:** Small, round, slightly hard crackers eaten with oyster stew.

Oyster plant: (*See* Salsify).

Palm-tree cabbage: (*See* Borecole).

Pannikin: Small metal vessel, usually for drinking.

Parts: Pounds (e.g., "Take 3 parts of beef").

Paste: (1) Pastry; (2) pasta (in Midwest various pasta is called *spaghetti*; in San Francisco and elsewhere, *macaroni*).

Paste-board baking pan: Sort of an early disposable cake-baking pan or bread board, homemade of cardboard covered with parchment paper.

Peach kernels: Yes, it's the peach pit.

Pear: Used as a verb, it means *pare* or peel.

Pearl ash: Grey-colored leavener made from wood ash that was used as a rudimentary baking powder (with sour milk); potassium carbonate, commonly called *potash* (*see* Saleratus).

Penny's worth: One unit, or one package (of yeast, for example).

Periwinkle: (*See* Coquina).

Persian apple: Apple probably grown in, or from seeds generating from, Southern Europe.

Pickle: Anything preserved in vinegar or a vinegar-sugar-water mixture, usually with herbs, seeds, or spices.

Pigeonberry: (*See* Poke).

Pimento: (1) Usually, a red pepper; (2) allspice.

Pint-pail cover: Metal rimmed lid of a pint-sized pail, sometimes used as a cookie, biscuit, or roll cutter.

Pippin: (For our purposes) the word given any apple from a tree raised from seed.

Plum, plumb: Raisin or other sweetmeat (unless used as the fruit itself).

Pocketbook rolls: (*See* recipe for parkerhouse rolls, page 153).

Poke, pokeweed: Wild green, edible when young but developing toxic properties as it matures.

Porringer or **poringer:** Small vessel or dish for porridge or soup.

Potage: Soup.

Pouder, powder: To season or preserve food with salt or spices.

Pound of eggs: About twelve small eggs. (Even today eggs are classified by weight rather than "size" or quality, as some people think.)

Pound of flour: Varies greatly, depending on the type of flour used, usually from 3 to 4½ cups.

Prauline: Praline.

Prickly pear: Pear-shaped, reddish-centered cactus with a juicy, acid pulp, grown in the Southwest.

Pudding mold: (1) Thick, glazed ceramic dish; (2) shaped-metal mold with tight-fitting lid.

Pulverized: Powdered, or finely ground.

Pumpion or **pomkin:** Pumpkin.

Purslane: Edible, succulent green herb popular in Europe but not America, where it is often mistaken for a weed.

Quahog or **quahaug:** Round clam of the Atlantic Coast.

Quaking plum or **pudding:** Custard, with or without sweetmeats.

Quick bread: Bread leavened with baking powder, eggs, or steam rather than yeast.

Quire: Little book.

Race: Root, as in one of the roots of raw ginger.

Ragoo, ragou, ragout: Highly seasoned meat and vegetable combination in a thick sauce.

Rattle: Shank or brisket.

Redware: (1) The first American pottery, made from red clay in the Northeast and extensively used; (2) unglazed earthenware.

Reed bird: (1) Bobolink; (2) any small bird meandering in the high grasses and reeds near freshwater ponds, lakes, and rivers.

Rissoles: Puff pastry turnovers filled with creamed meat.

Rocambole: Leek.

Rolled oats: Oak kernels that have been husked, cleaned, sterilized, steamed slightly, and flattened by heated rollers.

Rose-water: (*See* recipe, page 36).

Roux: Thickening agent made by combining browned flour and butter or fat.

Sack: (1) Sweet sherry wine; (2) dry wine; (3) white wine originally imported to England from Spain and the Canaries in the sixteenth and seventeenth centuries. You're on your own.

Sago: (1) Tree pith from which starch is prepared; (2) starch itself used as a thickener similar to arrowroot or cornstarch.

Sailor's biscuit, sea biscuit, or **hardtack:** Large, coarse, hard unleavened bread traditionally supplied to sailors and soldiers because of its keeping potential.

Salamander: Circular iron plate that is heated over a fire and placed on top of a dish of food to brown it.

Saleratus: Bicarbonate of potash; rudimentary baking powder that replaced pearl ash. Equal amounts of baking soda may be substituted.

Salpicon: (1) To pickle (*sal* = *salt*); (2) a finely chopped mixture of meats, vegetables, and herbs bound with white sauce or gravy, used for stuffing veal breast or other prepared cavities.

Salsify: Long, fleshy root of this plant, when cooked, tastes a little like an oyster.

Salt cellar: (*See* Saltspoonful).

Saltpetre, saltpeter: Potassium nitrate, added to the brine in which beef was preserved to give it redness.

Saltspoonful: About ¼ teaspoon (from a small spoon used to ladle salt from a "cellar"—small dish—before shakers were introduced to the table.

Samp: (*See* Hominy).

Sapolio: Cleaning substance.

Scrapple: Pennsylvania-Dutch pudding of sausage meat scraps or pork, buckwheat meal, and seasonings, usually molded, sliced, and fried (*see* Goetta).

Scruple: Apothecary's weight, about ¼ teaspoon.

Scum: (1) Foam that rises to the surface right before boiling; (2) to skim.

Scuppernong: Grape used as a relish in North Carolina, named for the Scuppernong River Basin.

Searce (from search): To sieve; to remove lumps from pounded loaf sugar or impurities from flour.

Seed-pepper: Cayenne pepper pod, usually.

Send it up: To bring food to the dining table from the kitchen, whether up stairs or not.

Shaddock: Large orangish citrus fruit, pear-shaped, found in Jamaica and Barbados; the smaller, rounder variety is the grapefruit.

Shepherd's pie: Meat pie topped with mashed potatoes instead of crust.

Singe and draw: To scorch off excess feathers and gut, removing intestines.

Sipet or **sippet:** Small piece of toasted or fried bread served in soup or used to sop up gravy; often cut in triangles or "fingers."

Slow oven: 300 to 325 degrees Fahrenheit.

Sop, sops, soppet: (*See* Sipet).

Sorghum or **sorgum:** Type of molasses made from grain such as Indian millet or Guinea-corn. Traditionally served with pumpkin pie in Georgia and Alabama.

Souse: Sour pork in aspic, currently sold commercially as luncheon meat, sliced.

Soy bean curd or **soy bean cheese:** Tofu.

Spider: Cast-iron frying pan with a long handle and three legs that stands over a bed of coals on the hearth.

Steep: Process of extracting flavor from teas or herbs by adding boiling water and allowing the mixture to stand without reboiling.

Still: (1) Distillation chamber; (2) distillation apparatus.

Stive: To pack tightly, boil lightly, submerge in liquid, or stew, depending on usage.

String beans: All green beans, before the "string" along the edge was bred out of some varieties.

Succory: Chicory.

Sugar melon: Cantaloupe.

Swamp cabbage: Hearts of palm; the white core of a young palm tree.

Sweet almond paste: Marzipan.

Sweet oil: Olive oil.

Sweetbreads: (1) The two-part thymus gland of the calf; (2) the pancreas of same (less desirable).

Syllabub: Beaten dessert, usually made with sweetened milk or cream and fortified wine, such as sherry.

Tamis or tammy: Sieve.

Tansy: (1) Strong-flavored herb popular as tea; (2) omelet flavored with tansy.

Tea-cupful: In measure, about ¾ cup.

Thoroughwort: Boneset; herb used to remedy "breakbone" fevers and cure stomach ache.

Timbale or **timbal:** Kettledrum-shaped custards, baked in molds, made of dessert, vegetable, meat, or fish ingredients.

Tin: (1) Can; (2) pan, such as muffin tin or cookie tin.

Tin kitchen: Type of reflector oven.

Tomato figs: Pear or plum tomatoes, sun-dried for preserving.

Tomato sauce, basic: From around 1900 to 1920, this was a homemade condiment, clove-seasoned and thickened with butter and flour.

Treacle (pronounced *trick-el* or *tree-k'l*): Uncrystallized syrup produced in the process of refining sugar cane, as opposed to "molasses," the uncrystallized sap that drains from raw sugar cane. Currently used interchangeably.

Treadles: The two opaque threads of a raw egg, once thought to be rooster sperm (the word *tredd* at one time meant copulation).

Tree sweetnin': Maple syrup.

Trencher: Serving dish, usually square.

Tripe: Stomach or intestines of beef or oxen. Ruminants possess two stomachs; the first is the rumen that provides plain tripe, the second is the reticulum, providing honeycomb tripe, generally the more preferred.

Truffle: (1) Delectable black or white subterranean cluster fungus; (2) currently, a chocolate candy.

Try, try out, or **tryed:** Render fat.

Tumbler full: About two cups.

Turnip-cabbage: (*See* Kohlrabi).

Unbolted wheat flour or **unbolted cornmeal:** Coarsely ground grain with bran, unsifted.

Vegetable pear: (*See* Chayote).

Viands: Food resources, especially meat.

Virgin cream: Mixture of cream, sugar and egg whites (no yolks).

Wafer iron: Cast-iron device heated on the hearth and brought to the table to cook batter into thin wafers (about two per trip).

Wassail: From the old English *waes hael* ("be whole" or "be well"); (1) used as a toast; (2) the bowl from which the toast is drawn.

Water cracker: (*See* Oyster cracker).

White bacon: Salt pork, in Florida and elsewhere in the South.

White loaf sugar, or **white sugar:** (*See* Loaf sugar).

Whortleberry: Type of blueberry.

Wineglassful: About ¼ cup.

Yellow sauce: White sauce colored yellow by the addition of egg yolks.
Yeast: Use one package granular yeast for each yeast cake.
Yelk: Yolk.

Zest: Rind or peel of citrus fruit, usually grated.

Selected Bibliography

(Every cookbook cited in *America's Collectible Cookbooks* is listed in the index under title, author and publisher.)

Collections, Bibliographies, and Annotated Sources

American Antiquarian Society, 185 Salisbury Street, Worcester, MA 01609. Archives house more cookbooks published before 1860 than any other library in America; primarily the Waldo Lincoln collection.

Ash, Lee. *Subject Collections; a Guide to Special Book Collections and Subject Emphases as Reported by University, College, Public, and Special Libraries and Museums in the United States and Canada.* New York: R. R. Bowker, 1985; revised irregularly. See "Cookery and Cook Books" for state-by-state listings, descriptions of collections, and numbers of books held.

Axford, Lavonna Brady, ed. *English Language Cookbooks, 1600–1973.* Detroit: Gale Research, 1976. Bibliography based on previous works of Bitting, Lowenstein, Brown and Brown, Pennell, and McGee—and expanded.

Beard, James. *Delights & Prejudices: The Autobiographical Journal of America's Most Noted Food Authority with 150 Favorite Recipes.* New York: Simon and Schuster, 1964.

Beck, Leonard N. *Two "Loaf-Givers"; or, a Tour Through the Gastronomic Libraries of Katherine Golden Bitting and Elizabeth Robins Pennell.* Washington, D.C., Library of Congress, 1984. Former curator of these collections, housed in the Library of Congress Rare Book and Special Collections Division, discusses certain selections, primarily European. No index.

Becker, Marion Rombauer. *Little Acorn: The Story Behind The Joy of Cooking 1931–1966.* New York: Bobbs-Merrill, 1966. Gift to booksellers at their annual meeting in Washington, D.C.; biographical and autobiographical information; reviews; no page numbers.

Bitting, Katherine Golden. *Gastronomic Bibliography.* San Francisco, 1939. Ann Arbor: Gryphon Books, 1971. Concerning the 4,450 books on food and cookery, not all of them cookbooks, that she, a food chemist, and her husband, Dr. A. W. Bitting, donated to the Library of Congress. Alphabetized by author, American and foreign. The Bitting Collection is housed in the Rare Book and Special Collections Division, Thomas Jefferson Building.

Brown, Eleanor, and Bob Brown. *Culinary Americana, 100 Years of Cookbooks Published in the United States from 1860–1960.* New York: Roving Eye Press, 1961.

Cassidy, Bruce. *Dinah!* New York: Franklin Watts, 1979.

Charpentier, Henrí, and Boyden Sparkes. *Life à la Henrí: Being the Memoirs of Henrí Charpentier.* New York: Simon and Schuster, 1934.

Claiborne, Craig. *Craig Claiborne's* The New York Times *Food Encyclopedia.* New York: New York Times, 1985. A personal conglomeration of terms and phrases having to do with cookery.

Cook, Margaret. *America's Charitable Cooks: A Bibliography of Fund-raising Cookbooks Published in the United States, 1861–1915.* Kent, Ohio, 1971. Cook's collection of cookbooks is now housed in the Blagg-Huey Library at Texas Woman's University in Denton.

Cook Book Collectors Club, P.O. Box 56, St. James, MO 65559. Newsletter edited by Bob Allen.

Cookbooks to Detective Fiction. The Encyclopedia of Collectibles, vol. 5. Alexandria, VA: Time-Life Books, 1978.

Coyle, L. Patrick, Jr. *Cooks' Books; An Affectionate Guide to the Literature of Food and Cooking.* New York: Facts on File, 1985. Mostly American.

Department of Food Economics and Nutrition. *A Dictionary of Culinary and Related Terms.* Division of Home Economics, Kansas State College of Agriculture and Applied Science. Manhattan, 1933.

Dickinson, Linda J. *Price Guide to Cookbooks and Recipe Leaflets.* Paducah: Collector Books, 1990.

DuSablon, Mary Anna. *Cincinnati Recipe Treasury: The Queen City's Culinary Heritage.* Athens: Ohio University Press, 1990. Includes bibliography.

Gourley, James E. *Regional American Cookery 1884–1934.* New York: New York Public Library, 1936. Listed by state and area; 36 pages.

Harrison, Harry P. *Culture under Canvas: The Story of Tent Chautauqua.* New York: Hastings House, 1958.

Herman, Judith, and Marguerite Shallett Herman. *The Cornucopia: Being a Kitchen Entertainment and Cookbook Containing Good Reading and Good Cookery from More than 500 Years of Recipes, Food Lore . . . 1390–1899.* New York: Harper & Row, 1973. Includes bibliography.

Hess, John, and Karen Hess. *The Taste of America.* New York: Grossman, 1977. Critique; includes bibliography.

Hines, Mary Anne, Gordon Marshall, and William Woys Weaver. *The Larder Invaded: Reflections on Three Centuries of Philadelphia Food and Drink.* Philadelphia: The Library Company of Philadelphia and The Historical Society of Pennsylvania, 1987. Guidebook, with illustrations, of a joint exhibition held from November 1986 to April 1987. Multiple editions and copyright papers for many early American cookbooks and manuscripts are held in these archives.

Hurlbut, Jesse Lyman. *The Story of Chautauqua.* New York: G. P. Putnam's Sons, 1921.

James, Edward J., Janet Wilson James, and Paul S. Boyer, eds. *Notable American Women 1607–1950: A Biographical Dictionary.* 3 vols. Cambridge: Belknap Press of Harvard University, 1971. Prepared under the auspices of Radcliffe College, this classified biographical dictionary lists sources, and is an invaluable and inspiring tool. Those sources used are not repeated in this bibliography.

Jones, Evan. *Epicurean Delight: The Life and Times of James Beard.* New York: Alfred A. Knopf, 1990.

Katzen, Mollie. *Moosewood Cookbook: Revised Edition.* Berkeley: Ten Speed Press, 1992.

Lane, L. W., Jr. *The Sunset Story.* New York: Newcomer Society, 1973.

Lincoln, Waldo. *Bibliography of American Cookery Books 1742-1860.* Worcester: American Antiquarian Society, 1929. Very active in the society, Lincoln donated to them his impressive collection of books and pamphlets printed in America before 1876, and itemized the 490 cookery books in this bibliography. (This is the origin of the 1860 cut-off date cited in other cookbook bibliographies.) Lincoln was an 1870 graduate of Harvard, which might account for his peculiar fondness for "Hasty Pudding" pamphlets. (See Lowenstein, Eleanor, revisor.)

Longone, Janice Bluestein, and Daniel T. Longone. *American Cookbooks and Wine Books, 1797-1950 . . . a Selection of the Significant Works by the Influential 19th Century Reformers, Teachers and Culinary Authorities . . .* Ann Arbor, 1984 (68 pages). Misleading on OCLC, this guide to the authors' exhibition of collected cookbooks at the University of Michigan, William L. Clements Library of American History in 1984 is full of valuable annotated bibliographic and biographic information. Author, title, city, and year, but no publishers cited.

Lowenstein, Eleanor. *Bibliography of American Cookery Books 1742-1860.* Worcester: American Antiquarian Society, 1954; 3d rev., 1971. A diligent and responsible editing and expansion of Waldo Lincoln's original, more than eight hundred entries.

Mann, Thomas. *A Guide to Library Research Methods.* New York: Oxford University, 1987. Valuable aid to gaining perspective when contemplating any library research.

McGee, John. *South African Cookery Bibliography,* 1951. (Mentioned in Axford's bibliography, but I was unable to locate.)

McGrath, Daniel F., ed. *Bookman's Price Index.* Detroit: Gale Research, 1985-92. Published biannually. A responsible and thoroughly entertaining reference tool for used-book enthusiasts.

Money, John. *The Destroying Angel: Sex, Fitness and Food in the Legacy of Degeneracy Theory, Graham Crackers, Kellogg's Corn Flakes and American Health.* Buffalo: Prometheus Books, 1985. Includes bibliography.

Ohio State University. *Catalog of the Home Economics Library.* 3 vols. Boston: G. K. Hall, 1976. *One Hundred and Fifty Years of Publishing, 1837-1987.* Boston: Little, Brown, and Company, 1987. A record of a distinguished publishing house.

Patten, Marguerite. *Books for Cooks: A Bibliography of Cookery.* New York: R. R. Bowker, 1975.

Pennell, Elizabeth Robins. *My Cookery Books.* Boston: Houghton-Mifflin, 1903. Concerning the 732 titles she, a prolific author, and her husband, Joseph, an artist, donated to the Library of Congress. First published in the *Atlantic* (June 1901, August and November 1902); three hundred copies of the subsequent book were printed by Riverside Press, Columbus, Mass. in 1903; scarce. The Pennell Collection is housed in the Rare Book and Special Collections Division, Thomas Jefferson Building.

Rudolph, G. A. *The Kansas State University Receipt Book and Household Manual.* Manhattan: Kansas State University Press, 1968. Pre-1900 chronological bibliography of holdings.

Rutledge, Anna Wells. *The Carolina Housewife* facsimile. Columbia: University of South Carolina Press, 1979. Contains bibliography of South Carolina cookbooks published before 1935.

Rugoff, Milton. *The Beechers: An American Family in the 19th Century.* New York: Harper & Row, 1981.

Samudio, Josephine, ed. *Book Review Digest.* New York: H. W. Wilson, 1970 and 1971.

Schremp, Gerry. *Kitchen Culture: Fifty Years of Food Fads.* New York: Pharos Books, 1991.

Schriftgiesser, Karl. *Oscar of the Waldorf.* New York: E. P. Dutton, 1943.

Shannon, Ellen. *American Dictionary of Culinary Terms.* New York: Barnes, 1962.

Shapiro, Laura. *Perfection Salad; Women and Cooking at the Turn of the Century.* New York: Farrar, 1986. Critique; includes bibliography.

Sicherman, Barbara et al., eds. *Notable American Women: The Modern Period.* Cambridge: Belknap Press of Harvard University, 1980.

Sklar, Kathryn Kish. *Catharine Beecher: A Study in American Domesticity.* New Haven: Yale University Press, 1993.

Smithsonian Institution, Washington, D.C., National Museum of American History (advertising); Product Cookbook Collection donated by Ellen Wells, not fully processed. (See Bitting and Pennell.)

Solkoff, Joel. *The Politics of Food.* San Francisco: Sierra Club Books, 1985.

Stark, Lewis M. *The Whitney Cookery Collection.* New York: New York Public Library, 1946.

Strehl, Dan, ed. *One Hundred Books on California Food & Wine.* Los Angeles: Book Collectors, 1990. Excellent reference tool for California cookbook bibliographers.

Szathmary, Louis S. *American Gastronomy; An Illustrated Portfolio of Recipes and Culinary History.* Chicago: H. Regnery, 1974. Contains chapter on converting old recipes for today's use; incomplete bibliography. The former chef and owner of The Bakery restaurant in Chicago donated ten thousand cookbooks to Johnson & Wales University in Providence, R.I., and twenty thousand to the University of Iowa in Iowa City.

Vincent, John Heyl. *The Chautauqua Movement*. Boston: Chautauqua Press, 1886.

Wheaton, Barbara Ketcham, and Patricia Kelly. *Bibliography of Culinary History; Food Resources in Eastern Massachusetts*. Boston: G. K. Hall, 1988. Data up to 1920.

Willan, Anne. *Great Cooks and Their Recipes from Taillevent to Escoffier*. New York: McGraw-Hill, 1977. Excellent text and illustrations; unfortunately, the only Americans covered are Simmons and Farmer. Contains bibliography.

Wise Encyclopedia of Cookery. New York: William H. Wise, 1948. Explanations of mostly "recent" cookery terms and procedures.

Periodicals

"Betty Crocker Gets a Facelift and Comes Out of the Kitchen." *New York Times*, November 6, 1980, 11.

Block, Joan Libman. "The Secret Life of Betty Crocker." *Woman's Home Companion*, December 1954, 22.

Braham, James. "Betty Crocker Gets a Face-Lift." *Industry Week*, May 26, 1986, 28.

Brown, Martha C. "Of Pearl Ash, Emptins and Tree Sweetnin'; America's First Native Cookbook." *American Heritage*, August-September 1981, 104-7.

Carlisle, Norman. "The Amazing Lady Who Ran Away with a Company." *Coronet*, December 1956, 143-46 (Betty Crocker).

Dailey, Pat. "Fannie Farmer Holds Court in America's Home Kitchens." *Chicago Tribune*, October 22, 1992, 7:1.

Diamant, Anita. "Cookbook Archive: Measuring History in Tablespoons." *Ms.*, February 1986, 38 (Arthur and Elizabeth Schlesinger Library at Radcliffe College).

DuSablon, Mary Anna. "Cincinnati's Collectible Cookbooks." *Cincinnati Post*, February 28, 1990, 1D.

Fisher, M. F. K. "The Fabled Days of Diamond Jim." *Gourmet*, September 1992, 108.

"Food & Drink in Cincinnati." Public Library of Cincinnati and Hamilton County, 1988. Bibliography booklet of holdings.

Gale, Sam. "Our Advertising Must Be 'Truthful, Informative and Educational.'" *Horizons*, July 1947, 2-3.

General Mills, Inc. "Bulletin: Betty Crocker . . . 1921-1954." Minneapolis, ca. 1954.

———. "Betty Crocker's Cookbooks." Booklet A35365. Minneapolis, 1992.

———. "The Story of Betty Crocker." Booklet A49346A. Minneaplis, 1992.

Hayes, Joanne L. "What Every Colonial Cook Knew: A Guide to the Terms and Measurements Found in Early American 'Receipt' Books." *Country Living,* March 1990, 154.

Ingrassia, Laurence. "The Face That Launched Millions of Sales Is Being Overhauled Again." *Wall Street Journal,* October 27, 1980, 22.

Lamalle, Cecile. "Library Szathmary: The Culinary Riches of the Past Are Well Represented at Johnson & Wales' Culinary Archives and Museum." *Restaurant Hospitality,* September 1990, 114–17.

McCray, Florine Thayer. "Marion Harland at Home." *Ladies Home Journal,* August 1887, 3.

Mendelson, Anne. "Reviews: Marginal Success; Two Regional Cookbooks Fall Short of Ambitious Goals." *Eating Well,* March-April 1992, 96.

Miller, Brian, and Anne De Ravel. "The 1796 Cookbook." *Hartford Courant,* April 25, 1984, 23.

Nickerson, Jane. "They Wanted to Cook Like Mother." *New York Times,* August 12, 1951, 6 (Irma S. Rombauer).

"Obituary: Waldo Lincoln." *American Antiquarian Society Proceedings,* April 1933, 25–32.

Pine, Carol. "The Real Betty Crocker Is One Tough Cookie." *Twin Cities,* November 1978, 46–50.

Rector, George. "The Girl From Rector's." *Saturday Evening Post,* July 24, 1926, 3–5.

Rorer, Mrs. S. T. "How I Cured My Own Ill-Health." *Ladies' Home Journal,* June 1905, 38.

"Samuel Gale of General Mills Dies." *Minneapolis Star,* February 7, 1961, 33.

Sass, Lorna J. "Book Reviews: Old Cookbooks in New Covers." *Americana,* May-June 1985, 76.

————. "What's Cooking in Cookbooks?" *Publishers Weekly,* September 20, 1985, 41–58.

Schlosberg, Jeremy. "Katzen's Cookbooks." *Writer's Digest,* November 1987, 30–33.

"Shop Talk: Betty Crocker's Voice of Experience." *McCall's Food Service Bulletin,* April-May 1956, 2.

Spedalle, Susan. "Beard: Legacy of an All-American Culinarian." *Restaurant News,* February 4, 1985, 4.

Strona, Proserfina, and Emily Cardin. "Ethnic Culinary Art in Hawaii: A Bibliography." Hawaii and Pacific Section, State Library, N.d.

Taylor, Mary K. "America's First Cookbook." *Early American Life,* February 1991, 41–43.

Warth, Terry. "What's Cooking in Special Collections." *Kentucky Review,* 3, no. 3 (1982): 74–84.

Index

Abell, Mrs. L. G., 36
Acton, Eliza, 20
Advertising, cookbooks used as, 61, 93-96, 179
African cookery (see Black cookery)
Alabama: Birmingham, 68; Troy, 157
Alcott, Louisa May, 21
Alcott, William Andrus, 21, 24, 31
Algren, Nelson, 126
Alice B. Toklas Cook Book, The, 163
All-American Cook Book, The, 166-67
Allen, Ida C. Bailey, 87, 88
Allen, Lucy A., 64
Allied Cookery, 105
Almond Cake, 37
Alsop, Richard, 4
Amber Soup, 128
America's Charitable Cooks, 145-46
American Antiquarian Society, 5
American Antique Cookbooks, 68
American Association of Gourmets Presents, The, 165
American Cook Book, The, 79
American Cook Books and Wine Books, 51, 52, 142
American Cookery, 1-8
American Domestic Cookery, 4
American Frugal Housewife, The, 22, 27, 33-34
American Gastronomy, 136
American Ladies Magazine, 20
American Woman's Cook Book, The, 90-92
American Woman's Home, The, 42
Amiet, Ernest E., 133
Angel Food Charlotte Russe, 160
Anonymous cookbooks (see Lady)
Anonymous to Pseudonym, 48-49

Antoine's Restaurant Cookbook, 122, 135
Appeal for That Class, An, 22
Apple Sauce, 26
Apple Snow, 77
Appledore Cookbook, The, 62, 77
Appraising cookbooks, 2, 176, 185
Arlington National Cemetery, 16, 17
Army and Navy Punch, 158
Art of Cookery, The, 72, 86
Art of Cookery Made Plain, The, 3
Artichoke Fricassee, 50
Asparagus Biscuit, 49
"Aunt Babette's" Cookbook, 56-57
Aunt Sammy's Radio Recipes Revised, 99

Bailey, Lee, 172
Baked Tomatoes and Eggs, 152-53
Ball Blue Book, 101
Barnum, H. L., 54
Barrows, Anne, 64
Barue, Sulpice, 18
Bashinsky, Elizabeth Burford, 157
Bazore, Katherine, 156
Beard, James, 18, 61, 76, 171, 177-78, 181-82
Beck, Leonard, 4
Beck, Simone, 178
Beckwith, Annie E., 11
Beebe, Lucius, 177
Beecher, Catharine Esther, 21, 39-44, 51, 70
Beef a la Mode, 28
Beef Olives, 104
Beef Tournedos, 48
Becker, Marion Rombauer, 106-109
Benson, Evelyn Abraham, 10
Bentley, Mildred Maddocks, 90-92

Berolzheimer, Ruth, 90-92
Berthold, Louisette, 178
Best Roasted Corn-on-the-Cob, 155
Best Seller, 172
Better Homes & Gardens Cookbook,
 (My), 179
Betty Crocker, 65, 93, 109-18, 179
Betty Crocker's Picture Cookbook,
 109-118;
Beverages: Army and Navy Punch,
 158; Beer, Table, 100; Bishop, 52;
 Blackberry Cordial, 33; Egg Lemon-
 ade, 56; Egg Nog, 158; Tea and Cof-
 fee, serving, 32
Bird, Mrs. W. S., 53
Bishop, 52
Bitting, Katherine Golden, 54
Black American cookery, 17, 19, 120,
 137, 148, 166, 173, 180
Black Americans, 17, 19, 22, 56, 120,
 137, 147, 148, 166
Blackberry Cordial, 33
Blot, Pierre, 68, 137, 138
"Booke of Cookery, A," 12
"Booke of Sweetmeats, A," 12
Boston Athanaeum, 22
Boston Cook Book, The, 62
Boston Cooking School, 61-65
Boston Cooking-School Cook Book, The,
 62-65, 73-76
Boston Cooking-School Magazine Com-
 pany, The, 64, 71, 72, 78, 79
Boston School Kitchen Text-Book, The,
 76
Bradley, Alice, 64, 100
Brady, James Buchanan ("Diamond"),
 125
Bragg-About Cookbook, The, 158
Breads: Biscuits, 7, 14; Bread Making,
 Short Process for, 97; Coffee Cakes,
 105; Dribble Toast, Norwegian,
 156; French Bread, 11; Fritters,
 12-13; Graham Bread, 31-32;
 Parker House Rolls, 153; Rye Drop
 Cakes, 35-36; Yeast, Home Made,
 104-105
Breakfast, by Mrs. F. Scott Fitzgerald,
 168
Breakfasts, Luncheons and Dinners, 78
Brebnor, Gertrude Frelove, 166-67

Briggs, Richard, 4
Broiled Pompano with Cucumber
 Sauce, 86-87
Brown County Cookbook, The, 152-53
Brown, Dale, 171, 173
Bryan, Mrs. Lettice, 47-48
Buckeye Cookbook, The, 46-47
Burr, Hattie A., 104-105
Butter Biscuit, 7
Butter Curls, 88-89
Butterick Cook Book, The, 90-91

Cabbage Pickle, 154
Cake Baker, The, 55-56
"Calendar of Dinners," A, 98-99
California: Berkeley, 183; Los Angeles,
 29, 131-32, 150, 165; Menlo Park,
 180; Oakland, 69: Pasadena, 132,
 148; Sacramento, 137; San Fran-
 cisco, 50, 52, 131-32, 137, 153-54
California Recipe Book, 153-54
Callahan, Genevieve A., 180
Camp Cookery, 62
Camp Cookery and Hospital Diet, 145
Canadian Cookery, 28, 72, 105
Capitol Cook Book, The, 123
Caramel Coloring, 129
Carolina Housewife, The, 13, 30
Carron, Pierre, 124, 131
Carrot Pudding, 13
Carrying Tea and Coffee Around, 32
Carter, Susannah, 1, 3, 22
Casserole of Rice and Meat, 83
Catering for Special Occasions, 64
Celebrity Cook, The, 164-65
Centennial Buckeye Cook Book, The, 46
Cerwin, Herbert, 165
Chafing Dish Possibilities, 64
Chambers, Mary D., 64, 78
Charitable cookbooks (see Fund-
 raising cookbooks)
Charlotte Polonaise, 79-80
Charpentier, Henrí, 123
Chatauqua movement (Chatauqua
 School of Cookery), 71-72, 86,
 107, 139
Cheese Soufflé in Ramekins, 168
Chicago Training School of Cookery,
 72
Chicken Tamales, 53

Child, Julia, 172, 178, 181
Child, Lydia Maria, 21-22, 27, 33-34
Chiles Rellenos de Queso, 53
Christian, Eugene and Mollie Griswold, 102-103
Christianity in the Kitchen, 104
Christmas Dinner for Horses and Ponies, 151
Cigarettes á la Rusee, 133
Cincinnati Historical Society, 12
Cincinnati Recipe Treasury, 155
Claiborne, Craig, 164, 172-73, 180
Clam Pancakes, 26
Clancy, John, 171
Clayton, H. J., 52
Clayton's Quaker Cook Book, 52
Club-House Sandwich, 97
Codfish Cakes, 26
Coffee Cakes, 105
Collins, Anna Maria, 45
Colonial Plantation Cookbook, A, 13
Colonial Recipes, 71
Colorado: Denver, 55
Colquitt, Harriet Ross, 161
Common Sense in the Household, 48
Compendious Repository, 4
Compleat Housewife, The, 3
Confederate Receipt Book, 100
Congressional Club, The, 29
Congressional Club Cook Book, The, 29, 96, 167
Connecticut: Chester, 34; Groton Heights, 11; Hartford, 1, 15, 40; Newhaven, 15; New London, 11; Saybrook, 13; West Suffield, 22; Westport, 5; Windham, 5
Conservation Cutlets, 98
Cook Book by "Oscar" of the Waldorf, The, 122-23, 130-31
Cook, Margaret, 145-46
Cook Not Mad, or Rational Cookery, The, 28
Cookbook Hall of Fame, 182
Cookbook of the Northwest, 57
Cookery As It Should Be, 69, 79-80
Cooking in Old Créole Days, 45
Cooking Manual, 69
Cooking on a Ration, 100
Cooking Schools, 59-72, 101
Cooper, Lenna Frances, 93, 101

Copyright law, 16, 141-42
Cookies, 8
Cornelius, Mrs. Mary Hooker, 36
Cornell University, 90
Corson, Juliet, 68-69, 70, 86-87
Cottage Kitchen, The, 49
Crab Gumbo, 146-47
Cracker or Matzos Balls, 82
Cramton, Laura Kay, 29
Crawford, Mrs., 55-56
Cream Apple Pie, 137
Cream of Corn Soup, 148
Creole cookery, 71, 120, 122, 173, 180
Crocker, Betty (see Betty Crocker)
Croûtons, 126
Crowen, Mrs. T. J., 61
Crystallized Flowers, 87
Culinary Arts Institute, 90-91
Cunningham, Marion, 75-76, 178, 185
Curtis, Isabel Gordon, 180
Custis, George Washington Parke, 16, 17
Cutlet Surprises, 50

Davis, Adele, 177-78, 182
Delineator Cook Book, The, 90-92
Delmonico's, 121, 123, 124, 125
Desserts: Angel Food Charlotte Russe, 160; Apple Pie, Cream, 137; Apple Sauce, 26; Apple Snow, 77; Cannoli Cake, 156-57; Carrot Pudding, 13; Cookies, butter, 8; Devils Food Cake, 98-99; Fritters, 12-13; Fruit Cake, Wedding, 56; Green Tomato Pie, 136; Guava Chiffon Pie, 161; Hen's Nest, 57; Honey Apple Candy, 100; Ice Cream à la Mexicana, 79; Ice Creams: Peach, Coffee, Oyster, 35; Indian Pudding (Corn Pudding), 7; Jeff Davis Pudding, 157; JELL-O with Fruit, 96-97; LaFayette Cake, 55-56; Lemon Tarts, 154; Linzer Torte, 119; Marble Cake, 54-55; Orange Pudding, 54; Peach Leather, 160-61; Pepparkakar, 157; Pineapple Upside-Down Cake, 118; Prunes in Ambush, 56; Pumpkin Pie, 7; Quaking Plum

Pudding with Sauce, 33–34; Rocky Mountain Cake, 54; Ribbon Cake, 158; Seven Seas Cake, 159: Sorbet, 75; Sugar Cakes, 14; Sultana Roll with Claret Sauce, 75; Swan with Reeds and Rushes, 136; Sweet Potato-Chocolate Nut Cake, 184; Tipsy Parson, 77; Toll House Cookies, original, 89; Whipped Cream, 8; Yum-Yums, 57

Deviled Chestnuts, 126

Devilled Turkey, 149

Devils Food Cake, 98–99

Diet for a Small Planet, 178

Directions for Cookery, 18

Doerfer, Jane, 180

Domestic Cookery, 27, 32

Domestic French Cookery, 18

Donnelley, Naomi A., 48

Drop Biscuits, 14

Duling, Mrs. Nellie, 97

DuSablon, Mary Anna, 155

Dutch cookery, 8, 173

Edgewater Beach Hotel Sandwich Book, 127

Egg Lemonade, 56

Egg Nog, 158

El Coinero Español, 131–32

El Paso Cookbook, 53

Emptins, 7

Encyclopedic Cook Book, The, 91

English cookery, 1–5, 9–14, 16, 42, 90–91, 173

Epicurean, The, 124, 127–28, 136

Ervin, Janet Halliday, 136

Eustis, Celestine, 45

Ewing, Emma P., 72, 86

Family Nurse, The, 22

Famous Recipes of Famous Women, 168

Family Receipts, 54

Fannie Farmer Cookbook, The, 185

Farmer, Fannie Merritt, 61–65, 70, 73–76, 108, 185

Farmer's School of Cookery, Miss, 64, 100

Favorite Old Recipes, 48

Feasting with Wisconsin's Fourth Estate, 149

Federation Cook Book, The, 148

Fellows, Charles, 134

Fellows' Menu Maker, 134

Female Obstructions, 57–58

Field, Michael and Frances, 171, 173

Fiesta Tamale Pie, 116

"Fifteen-Cent Dinners," 69

Filippini, Alessandro, 124, 128, 132

Fillet of Shad, with Purée of Sorrel, 131

Flinders, Carol, 178

First Principles of Household Management, 62

First Texas Cookbook, The, 147

Firsts: American cookbook, 1–5; American cookbook published in Spanish, 131–32; American cookbook translated into French, Spanish, and Japanese, 64; American cooking school, 18, 69–70; American periodical for children, 21; Book published by black American, 19; Businesswoman of the Year Award, 113; California cookbook published by African-American, 137; Canada's first cookbook, 28; Charitable cookbook, 145; Chocolate chip cookie, 89; Coffeetable cookbooks, 171–75; Commercially sponsored TV show, 112; Cookbook rap (poem), 147; Cookbook to tabulate ingredients, 63: French cookbook published in U.S., 51; German cookbook published in U.S., 51; Household encyclopedia (English), 4; Kentucky fund-raising cookbook, 154; Measuring cup, 43; Midwest cookbook, 54; Militant domestic scientist, 42–43; Spanish cookbook published in U.S., 51; Texas cookbook, 147; West of Indiana cookbook, 55–56

Fisher, Mary Frances Kennedy, 125, 151–52, 171–73

Fisher, Mrs. Abby, 137

Fit for Man or Shrew, 165–66

Fitzgerald, Mrs. F. Scott, 168

Florida: Mandarin, 62; St. Augustine, 161

Food and Cookery for the Sick, 64

Food and Finesse, 123
Foods of the World (see Time-Life)
Foreign-language Cookbooks in U.S., 51–52
Franey, Pierre, 172–73, 180
French Cook, The, 4
French cookery, 4, 17, 18, 51, 90–91, 120, 123–24, 127–28, 131, 172–73
French Dishes for American Tables, 123–24, 131
Fried Parsley, 85
Frugal Housekeeper, The, 3
Frugal Housewife, The, 22, 33
Fund-raising cookbooks, 96, 100, 103, 104–105, 107, 139–54, 156–61, 164–65

Gado-Gado, 183
Gale, Sam, 110, 112–13
Georgia: Atlanta, 46; Savannah, 161
German cookery, 4, 51, 66, 125
Gilette, Fanny Lemira, 123, 136
Girardey, Dr. G., 51, 52
"Girl From Rector's, The," 125
Glasse, Hannah, 3
Godfrey, Bronwen, 177
Gold Medal Flour Cook Book, 93
Good Cooking by Mrs. S. T. Rorer, 71, 80–81
Good Housekeeper, The, 20
Good Housekeeping, 71
Good Housekeeping Home Cook Book, The, 180
Goodfellow's Cooking School, Mrs. Elizabeth, 69–70, 79–80, 120
Gourmet, 125
Graham Bread, 31–32
Graham, Sylvester, 22–24, 93
Grahamites, 22–24, 31–32, 93, 96
Grant, Marion Hepburn, 13
Green Tomato Pie, 136
Greene, Milton, 171
Greens, 31, 116–17
Grilled Shoulder of Lamb, 50
Ground-nut Soup, 30
Guava Chiffon Pie, 161
Guste Jr., Roy F., 122, 135

Hale, Sarah Josepha, 20–21, 28
Halibut á la Poulette, 74–75

Ham Baked in Cider, 80–81
Hampton Plantation, 13
Hand-Book of Practical Cookery, 137
Handy Cookbook, The, 42
Harland, Marion (pseudonym), 48–49, 61
Harrison, Mrs. Benjamin, 123
Hart, Elizabeth, 13, 14
Hayes, Mrs. W. T. (Emma Allen), 56
Hawaiian and Pacific Foods, 155–56
Hearn, Lafcadio, 122, 135
Henderson, Mrs. Mary Foote, 128–29
Herald Tribune, 177
Hess, Karen, 12, 63
High Living, 50
Hill, Janet McKenzie, 64, 79, 98
Hirtzler, Victor, 134
Historical Society of Pennsylvania at Philadelphia, 10, 12
Hochst Nuzliches Handbuch uber Kock-hunst, 51
Home Made Yeast, 104–105
Homespun, Priscilla (pseudonym), 4
Honey Apple Candy, 100
Hooker, Richard J., 13
Horry, Harriot Pinckney, 13
Hors d'oeuvre and Canapés, 177
Hotel St. Francis Book of Recipes, 134
Household News, 71
Housekeeper Cook Book, The, 46
Housekeeping and Dinner Giving, 52–53
Housekeeping in Old Virginia, 149
Housekeeping in the Blue Grass, 154
House & Garden, 177
House and Home Papers, 42
House Book, The, 18
House Servant's Directory, The, 19, 32, 144
How to Cook a Wolf, 152
How to Cook Vegetables, 71, 81–82
How to Make Good Sandwiches, 85–86
How to Mix a Salad, 169
Howland, Mrs. Esther Allen, 36
Hunt's End Chicken Gumbo, 150–51
Hunter's Delight, The, 45
Husted, Marjorie Child, 111–15

Ice Cream à la Mexicana, 79
Ice Creams: Peach, Coffee, Oyster, 35

Illinois: Chicago, 48, 50, 55-56, 72, 90-92, 123, 124, 125, 127, 130, 133, 134, 136, 156-57; Quincy, 41, 43

Improved Housewife, The, 26

Indian Hill (Ohio) Historical Society, 151

Indian Meal Cook Book, 18

Indiana: Bloomington, 153; Muncie, 101; New Albany, 45

Ingersoll, Blanche, 111

Intelligence offices, 67-68

International Cookbook, The, 124

Iowa: Des Moines, 179; Dubuque, 41, 43; Keokuk, 57

Irish cookery, 18, 173

Italian Cannoli Cake, 156-57

Italian cookery, 5, 120, 124, 125, 128, 156, 171, 173

James Beard's American Cookery, 61, 178

Jeff Davis Pudding, 157

"Jefferson Cook Book, The," 29

Jefferson, Thomas, 16-17, 18, 25, 29

Jeffery, Richard, 171, 173, 175

JELL-O with Fruit, 96-97

Jewish Community Center of Milwaukee, 67

Jewish cookery, 66-67, 71, 82-84

Jordan, Marynor, 153

Joy of Cooking, The, 72, 106-109, 119

Judson, Helene, 90

K. K. K. Cook Book, 158

Kafka, Barbara, 178

Kander, Mrs. Simon (Lizzie Black), 65-67, 82-84

Kansas State College, 89

Katzen, Mollie, 154, 179-80, 183

Kauffman, Mark, 171

Kedgeree, 167

Kelley, Janette, 110-13, 114, 115

Kellogg, John Harvey, 93

Kentucky: Louisville, 149; Paris, 154

Kentucky Cookbook, The, 56

Kentucky Housewife, The, 47-48

Kimball, Marie, 29

Kirkland, Elizabeth Stansbury, 91

Kitchen Catchup, 47-48

Kramer, Mrs. Bertha F., 57

La Cuisine Creole, 122, 135

Ladies Home Journal, The, 49, 65, 70, 71

Ladies Magazine, 20

Ladies National Magazine, 18

Ladies' New Book of Cookery, 20

Lady (et al.), Cookbooks by a, 4, 18, 26, 30, 37, 56, 69, 79-80, 103

LaFayette Cake, 55-56

Lakeside Cookbook No. 1, The, 48

Lamb Chops Chicago, 133

Lane, Larry and Ruth, 180

Lappé, Frances Moore, 178

Laurel's Kitchen, 178

Lea, Elizabeth Elliott, 27, 32

Leacock, Stephen, 105

Leiter, Joseph, 48

Lemon Butter or French Honey, 32

Lemon Tarts, 154

Leonard, Jonathan Norton, 171, 173

Leone, Gene, 125

Leone's Italian Cookbook, 125

Leslie, Eliza, 16, 17-19, 20, 21, 37, 61, 69, 79, 120

Let's Cook It Right, 177

Life á la Henri, 123

Lillard, Mrs. Reese, 50, 97

Lincoln, Mrs. Mary Johnson (Bailey), 61-64, 70, 76

Lincoln, Waldo, 54

Linzer Torte, 119

Little Acorn: The Story Behind the Joy of Cooking, 109

Loin of Pork Nebraska, 133

Longone, Janice Bluestein and Daniel T., 52, 142

Los Angeles Cookery, 150

Louisiana: New Orleans, 16, 51, 122, 135, 180

Lowenstein, Eleanor, 19, 182

Lüchow's German Cookbook, 125, 126

Lunch Box, The, 91-92

Lyon, Fred, 171

Macaroni au Gratin, 101

Macédoine, or à la Washington, 137

Madison, James, 45

Main Dishes: Amber Soup, 128-29; Beef a la Mode, 28; Beef Soup, 146; Beef Tournedos, 48; Capon, Roast, with Truffles, 85; Cheese Souffle,

168; Chicken Gumbo, 150–51; Chicken (Ohio River), 155; Chicken Tamales, 53; Chicken Turban, 132; Chiles Rellenos de Queso, 53; Clam Pancakes, 26; Club-House Sandwich, 97; Codfish Cakes, 26; Conservation Cutlets, 98; Corn Soup, Cream of, 148; Crab Gumbo, 146–47; Gado-Gado, 183; Ground-Nut Soup, 30; Halibut à la Poulette, 74–75; Ham Baked in Cider, 80–81; Kedgeree, 167; Lamb, Grilled Shoulder, 50; Lamb Chops, 133; Lamb Cutlets, Stuffed, 50; Macaroni au Gratin, 101; Matzos Ball Soup, 82; Meat and Rice Casserole, 83; Meat Pies, 52–53; Omelettes, 52, 137; Oyster Brochettes with Truffles, 127; Oyster Stew, 10; Pompano, Broiled, 86–87; Pork and Apple Pie, 135; Pork Chops, Eggplant, Truffle Sauce, 166–67; Pork Loin, 133; Pot au Feu, 45; Quail, Spanish, 131–32; Sandwiches, Fancy, 85; Seminole Soup, 30; Shad Fillet, with Sorrel Purée, 131; Shireen Polo, 174–75; Shrimp Bouchées, 130–31; Spareribs, Roasted, 47; Stew, Four Hour, 149; Stuffed Peppers, 149–50; Tamale Pie, 116; Tomato Soup, 146; Turkey, Devilled, 149; Turkey, To Stuff and Roast, 6; Venison, 45; Whitefish, Planked, 130

Maine: Salem, 15
Mann, Mrs. Horace, 104
Manuscript cookbooks, 9–14
Maple Sandwiches, 153
Marble Cake, 55
Marguerite Salad, 76
Maria Parloa's Cook Book, 93
Martha Washington's Booke, 12
"Mary Had a Little Lamb," 20
Maryland: Annapolis, 158–59; Baltimore, 15, 27, 32
Maryland's Way, 159
Masons, 20
Massachusetts: Boston, 3, 4, 15, 19, 20, 22, 23, 24, 27, 31, 32, 36, 37, 59, 61–65, 73–79, 104–105, 178, 180; Medford, 21; Northampton,

24; Roxbury, 68; Sturbridge, 33–34; Watertown, 28; Wayland, 22; Worcester, 5, 36
Mastering the Art of French Cooking, 178
McLaren, L. L., 50
McMein, Neysa, 112
Mead, Elizabeth, 11
Meat Pies, 52–53
Meek, Richard, 171, 173
Menus: Breakfast, 86; Breakfast, Dinner and Supper ca. 1910, 148; Breakfast, Dinner and Tea 1825–60, 25; Dinner of Six, Gourmet, 84; Hammond-Harwood House, 159; School Lunch Box, 92; Supper, from manuscript cookbooks, 10; Supper, from the Cataract Hotel, 134; Thanksgiving, from *American Cookery*, 6; Twelve-Course Dinner, from *The Boston Cooking-School Cook Book*, 73–74; Twelve O'Clock Company Breakfast, 78; Vegetarian, 102; Winter Dinner Menu, 81
Mexican cookery (see Spanish cookery)
Michigan: Ann Arbor, 52; Battle Creek, 93, 101; Grand Rapids, 5
Miller, Lewis, 71
Milliers, Gene W., 165
Mills, Marjorie, 100
Milwaukee Public Library, 66
Minnesota: Lake Calhoun, 115; Minneapolis, 46, 65, 93, 109–18
Miss Beecher's Domestic Receipt Book, 42–43, 51
Miss Beecher's Housekeeper and Health-keeper, 42
Miss Corson's Practical American Cookery, 86–87
Miss Farmer's School of Cookery, 64
Miss Parloa's Kitchen Companion, 62, 76
Missouri: Kansas City, 53; St. Louis, 56, 97, 106–109
Mitchell, Leonard Jan, 125
Modern Cookery, 20
Moldavia, 17
Montana: Bozeman, 110
Moosewood Cookbook, The, 179, 183
Morash, Marian, 180, 184

Moses, Anna Mary (Grandma), 22, 113

Mrs. Allen on Cooking, Menus, Service, 88

Mrs. Bliss of Boston, 26

Mrs. Collins' Table Receipts, 45

Mrs. Cornelius, 36

Mrs. Gillette's Cook Book, 123

Mrs. Goodfellow's Cookery, 69–70, 79–80

Mrs. Hale's New Cook Book, 20–21, 28

Mrs. Hale's Receipts, 21

Mrs. Owens' New Cook Book, 50

Mrs. Rorer's New Cook Book, 71

Mrs. Rorer's Philadelphia Cook Book, 70

Mrs. Seely's Cook Book, 67–68, 84–86

Murrey, Thomas J., 124, 126

"My Mother's Recaipts," 10

Nash, Ogden, 160

Native American cause, 22, 41

Native American cookery, 1, 2, 16, 30, 120

Neal, Miss C. A., 103

Nebraska, 133

Neil, Marion Harris, 71, 93, 99

Nero Wolfe Cookbook, The, 163

New Art of Cookery, 4

New Book of Cookery, A, 64

New Butterick Cook Book, The, 90, 92

New Century Club (Guild), 70

New Cookery, The, 101

New England Cook Book, The, 62

New England cookbooks, early, 15–37, 71

New England Economical Housekeeper, The, 36

New Hampshire: Isles of Shoals, 62; Newport, 20; Walpole, 1

New House-Keeper's Manual, The, 42

New Practical Housekeeping, The, 46

New System of Domestic Cookery, 4

New York: Albany, 3, 15, 55; Bath, 15; Brooklyn, 48; Elmira, 44; Johnsbury, 5; Lewiston, 125; Long Island, East Hampton, 39; Long Island, Lynbrook, 123; New York, 4, 5, 15, 19, 23, 37, 39, 41, 42, 45, 51, 59, 65, 67, 68, 69, 71, 84, 85, 86, 87, 88, 89, 90–91, 102–103, 105, 107, 112, 122–26, 127–29, 135, 136, 137, 145, 156, 161, 163, 164, 166, 170–75, 177, 180–82, 184; Troy, 15; Watertown, 15

New York Cooking School, 68–69

New York Times, 164, 180

Nice Indian Pudding, A, 7

Nickles, Harry G., 173, 175

North American Compiler, The, 52

North Carolina: Ft. Bragg, 158

Norton, Caroline Trask, 55

Norwegian Dribble Toast, 156

Novisimo Arte de Cocina, 51–52

Nutrition and diet, teaching of, 69, 70, 93, 96, 101, 102–103

OCLC (see On-Line Computer Library Center)

Ohio: Athens, 155; Cincinnati, 12, 41, 51, 52, 54, 57, 93, 98, 109, 151, 155, 158; Cleveland, 100, 123, 132, 152; Dayton, 46; Kent, 146; Marysville, 46

Ohio River Baked Chicken, 155

Old Sturbridge Village Cookbook, The, 33–34

Olney, Richard, 178

One Hundred Books on California Food & Wine, 131–32

One Hundred Recipes, 93

On-Line Computer Library Center, 5, 107

Orange-Cocoanut Salad, 126

Orange Pudding, 54

Oregon: Portland, 177

Oriental cookery, 17, 18, 108, 121, 172–77, 183

"Over the River and thru the Woods . . . ," 22

Owens, Mrs. Frances E., 50

Oyster Brochettes with Truffles, 127

Paddleford, Clementine, 177

Palmer House Cook Book, The, 133

Parish Pantry, 157

Parker House Rolls, 153

Parloa, Maria, 61, 62, 64, 65, 70, 76–77, 93, 110, 120

Parsnips, 27

Peach Leather, 160–61

Pearl's Kitchen, 166
Peerless Cook-Book, The, 62
Penn Family Recipes, 10, 11
Penn, Gulielma Springett, 10, 11
Pennington, Harper, 45
Pennsylvania: Harrisburgh, 15; Meadville, 86; Philadelphia, 4, 10, 12, 15, 18, 19, 20, 21, 26, 28, 51, 59, 69, 70, 71, 79–82, 93, 103, 169; York, 10
Pepin, Jacques, 178
Pepper and Grape-fruit Salad, 83
Perfection Salad, 88
Perkins family, 64, 75
Petite Cuisinere Habile, La, 51
Philadelphia Cooking School, 18, 70–71
Philadelphia (Practical) School of Cookery, 71, 93
Picayune's Creole Cook Book, The, 180
Pickled Mushrooms, 12
Pillsbury Cook Book, The, 97
Pine, Carol ("Tough Cookie"), 111, 113, 115
Pineapple Upside-Down Cake, 118
Pinedo, Encarnación, 131–32
Planked Whitefish, Rector, 130
Poem, Dedication, 147
Poems for Our Children, 20
Polish cookery, 120, 173
Pompkin Pie, 7
Pork and Apple Pie, 135
Pot au Feu, 45
Potatoes, 29, 51
Practical American Cookery, 69
Practical Cook Book, The, 26
Practical Cooking and Dinner Giving, 128–29
Presidents Cook Book, The, 123
Printers Four Hour Stew, 149
Prunes in Ambush, 56
Publishers: Appleton, D., 124, 131, 137; Applewood Books, 19; Arno, 126; Arnold and Company, 71; Babcock, 30; Barrows, M., 89, 156; Bloch, 57; Bobbs-Merrill, 106–109, 119; Buck Hill, 5; Buckeye Publishing, 46; Burpee, W. Atlee, 71, 81–82; Butterick Publishing Company, 90–92; Carter and Hendee, 27; Charles Tappan, 36; Clarke, Robert, 158; Clarkson & Company, 46; Clayton, A. C., Company, 107; Colburn, 27, 32; Coleman, 135; Congressional Club, The, 29, 167; Consolidated Book Publishers, 90–91; Curtis, 81; Davis and Force, 17, 35; Delineator Home Institute, 90–92; Dodd, Mead, 87; Doubleday, Doran, 88; Doubleday, Page & Company, 124; Dover Press, 5; Eakin-Sunbelt Press, 147; Eerdmans, 5; Estes and Lauriat, 76; Flood and Vincent, 86; Follett, 136; Ford, J. B., 42; Francis, Charles S., 19; General Mills, 65, 93, 109–18, 179; Globe Pequot Press, 34; Grosset & Dunlap, 67; Groves and Ellis, 77; Hansell, 135; Harcourt Brace Jovanovich, 166; Harper & Brothers, 42, 51, 129, 163, 168; Hazard, Willis P., 80; Home Publishing, 46; Housekeeper Publishing, 46; Hotel Monthly Press, 124, 127, 133, 134; Houghton Mifflin, 100; Howland, S. A., 36; Hudson & Goodwin, 1; Hughes, E. C., 131–32; Indiana University, 153; Judy, 166–67; Kansas State College, 89; Knopf, 184; Knowlton & Rice, 28; Lakeside Press, 48; Lane, 153; Levin, Hugh Lauter, Associates, 66; Light & Stearns, 24, 32; Lippincott, Grambo, 26; Little, Brown and Company, 63, 64, 73–75, 78; Macmillan, 67, 85–86, 152; Macrae-Smith, 169; Marsh, Capen & Lyon, 31; Marsh, Capen, Lyon & Webb, 42; McGraw-Hill, 114; McQuiddy, 50; Meredith, 179; Modern Medicine, 101; Morton, 149; Munroe and Francis, 19, 32, 37; Newell, D., 36; Norton, W. W., 135; Nunemacher, 45; Ohio University Press, 155; Owens, 50; Oxford University Press, 5; Oxmoor House, Inc., 68; Parks, William, 3; Passaic, 102–103; Peale, R. S., 136; Peterson, T. B., 28, 80; Pioneer Press, 5; Pool, Isaac A., 56; Price, Stern and Sloan, 164;

Procter & Gamble, 93, 98, 99; Prospect Press, 5; Putnam Sons, G. P., 105; Ramsey, Millett & Hudson, 53; Rector Publishing, 130; Roberts Brothers, 76; Robinson, W. F., 55; Roff, H. B., 54; Russell, 45; Scribner's Sons, C., 49, 67; Shumway, George, 10; Signet, 182; Silverleaf Press, 5; Ten Speed Press, 183; Thomkins, J. H., 56; Ticknor and Fields, 104; Time-Life, 170-73, 175; U. S. Government Printing Office, 99; University of Iowa, 126; University of South Carolina Press, 13, 30; Viking Press, 163-64; Washburn Crosby Company, 65, 93, 110, 111; Weather Bird Press, 132; Webster, 128, 132; Werner, 131; White, Stokes & Allen, 126; Widdifield, S. & M., 26; Women's Co-Operative, 52, 137; World Publishing, 100, 152

Publishing techniques, 16, 93-94, 143-45

Puddings and Dainty Desserts, 126

Pupil of Mrs. Goodfellow, 69-70, 79-80

Quakers, 10, 52, 69

Quaking Plum Pudding with Better Sauce, 33-34

Ralston, Nancy C., 153

Randolph, Mary, 16-17, 30, 35, 120

Ranhofer, Charles, 124, 127-28, 136

Receipt 11, 31

Rector Cookbook, The, 125

Rector, George, 125, 130

Rector's Naughty 90's Cookbook, 125

Revere, Paul, 3

Rhode Island: Providence, 15

Ribbon Cake, 158

Riley, Isaac, 4

Roast Capon with Truffles, 85

Roberts, Robert, 19, 32

Roberts' Guide, 19, 144

Robertson, Laurel, 178

Rocky Mountain Cake, 54

Rocky Mountain Cookbook, The, 54-55

Rolled Chops with Truffle Sauce, 166-67

Rombauer, Irma Louise (von Starkloff), 72, 106-109, 113, 119, 123

Roosevelt, Mrs. Franklin D., 167

Root, Waverley, 171, 173

Rorer, Sarah Tyson (Heston), 61, 70-71, 80-82, 120

Rose, Flora, 90, 92

Rose-water, 36

Rundell, Mrs. Helene or Mrs. Maria Rundle, 4

Russian cooking, 66, 128-29, 133, 173

Ruth Wakefield's Toll House, 64, 89

Rutledge, Anna Wells, 30

Rutledge, Sarah, 13, 30

Rye Drop Cakes, 35-36

St. Augustine Cookery, 161

St. Louis Post Dispatch, 108

Salad á L'Italienne, 128

Salad Portfolio, The, 127

Salads: Marguerite, 76; Orange-Cocoanut, 126; Pepper and Grapefruit, 83; Perfection, 88; Salad á L'Italienne, 128

Sarah Daft Home Cook Book, 160

Saturday Evening Post, 125

Savannah Cook Book, The, 161

Savories, Sauces, Garnishes: Allemande Sauce, 127; Beef Olives, 104; Butter Curls, 88-89; Cabbage Pickle, 154; Catchup, 47-48; Cigarettes á la Russe, 133; Croûtons, 126; Crystallized Flowers, 87; Deviled Chestnuts, 126; Fried Parsley, 85; Lemon Butter or French Honey, 32; Maple Sandwiches, 153; Pickled Mushrooms, 12; Rose-water, 36; Soup Flavor, 82; Swiss Nuts Appetizer, 127; Toast St. Antoine, 135; Vinegars: Chili, Horse-radish, Onion, 81-82

Saybrook Historical Society, Old, 13

Scalloped Onions and Peanuts, 99

Scheissgiesser, Karl, 123

Schlesinger Library, 178

Schoenfeld, Mrs. Henry, 66

Seely, Mrs. Eliza (Campbell), 67-68, 84-86

Seminole Soup, 30

Servants, American, 19, 67-68

Servants and Stars, 165
Serving the Breakfast in Detail, 77–78
Settlement Cook Book, The, 65–67, 83–84, 139
Seven Seas Cake, 159
Seventy-Five Receipts, 18, 37
Shapiro, Laura, 63
Sherman, Mrs. Frederick, 124, 131
Shircliffe, Arnold, 124, 127
Shireen Polo, 174–75
Shore, Dinah, 164–65
Short Process for Bread Making, 97
Shremp, Gerry, 171
Shrimp Bouchées, 130–31
Simmons, Amelia, 1–3, 5, 6–8, 9, 16, 61, 62
Six Little Cooks, 91
Skillful Housewife's Book, The, 36
Sloat, Caroline, 33–34
Smith, Eliza, 3
Smithsonian Institution Collection of Advertising History, 94
Someone's in the Kitchen with Dinah, 164
Sorbet, 75
Soup Flavor, 82
South Carolina: Camden, 33; Charleston, 13, 15, 30
South Dakota: Sioux Falls, 134
Southern Gardener, The, 33
Spanish Cook, The, 131–32
Spanish cookery, 4, 51–52, 53, 71, 120, 131–32, 172–73
Spanish Omelette, 52
Spanish Style Quail, 131–32
Stallworth, Lyn, 171
Stewart, Martha, 172
Stewed Spinach, 30
Stillmeadow Kitchen, 169
Stone, Lucy, 104–105
Story of Crisco, The, 71, 99
Stout, Rex, 163–64
Stowe, Harriet Beecher, 22, 39–41, 62
Streamlined Cooking, 108
Strehl, Dan, 131–32
Stuffed Tomatoes, 130
Suffrage cause, woman's, 44, 96, 104–105
Sugar Cakes, 14
Sultana Roll with Claret Sauce, 75
Sunset All-Western Cookbook, 180

Swan with Reeds and Rushes, 136
Swedish Pepparkakar, 157
Sweet Potato-Chocolate Nut Cake, 184
Swiss Nuts Appetizer, 127
Syllabub, 103
Szmathmary, Louis, 125, 136

Taber, Gladys, 169
Table, The, 124, 128, 132
Table Beer, 100
Table Service by Lucy G. Allen, 78
Table Talk, 71
Taft, William Howard, 166
Talents, 36
Tarbell, Miss Ida M., 169
Taylor, Hilda, 112
Temperance cause, 23, 96, 103
Temperance Cookbook, The, 103
Tennessee: Harriman, 5; Lebanon, 50, 97
Tennessee Cookbook, 50, 97
Terhune, Mrs. Mary Virginia (Hawes), 48–49, 61
Texas: Austin, 147; Denton, 69, 146; El Paso, 53; Galveston, 146; HoneyGrove, 158; Houston, 147
Texas Cook Book, The, 146–47
Texas Woman's University at Denton, 69, 146
Thanksgiving Menu, 6
Thanksgiving, Mother of, 20
Thomas Jefferson Cook Book, The, 29
Thomas, Mrs. Dr. Flavel S., 105
Thornton, P., 33
Time-Life Foods of the World, 170–75
Tipsy Parson, 77
To Boil Cabbage, 7
To Dress Potatoes, 29
To Make A Hen's Nest, 57
To Make Fritters, 12–13
To Pickle One Hundred Pounds of Beef, 28
To Roast a Sparerib of Pork, 47
To Stew Oysters, 11
To Stuff and Roast a Turkey or Fowl, 6
To Stuff Peppers, 149–50
Toast St. Antoine, 135
Toll House Chocolate Crunch Cookies, 89

Tomato Soup, 146
Too Make French Bred, 11
Treasured Recipes From Camargo to Indian Hill, 150–51
Treatise on Bread, A, 23, 31–32
Treatise on Domestic Economy, A, 41–42
Tried and True Recipes, 144, 157
True Economy of Housekeeping, 27
Tschirky, Oscar, 122–23, 130–31
Turban of Chicken á la Cleveland, 132
Turner, Mrs. Bertha L., 147, 148
Twin Cities Reader, 111
Tyree, Marion Cabell, 149

Ude, Louis Eustache, 4
Uncooked Foods and How to Use Them, 102–103
U.S. Department of Agriculture bulletins, 95
Universal Receipt Book, The, 4
Utah: Kaysville, 160
Utrecht-Freidel, Mme., 51

Van Deman, Ruth, 99
Van Rensselaer, Martha, 90
Vegetable Diet, 21, 31
Vegetables: Artichoke Fricassee, 50; Asparagus Biscuit, 49; Cabbage, 7; Corn-on-the-Cob, Roasted, 155; Greens, and Ideas for Serving, 31, 116–17; Onions and Peanuts, Scalloped, 99; Parsnips, 27; Pork and Beans, 46–47; Potatoes, 29, 51; Spinach, 30; Tomatoes, Stuffed, 130, 152–53
Vegetarianism, 23, 102–103, 177–81, 183
Vermont: Bellows Falls, 15; Brattleboro, 15; Burlington, 153; Montpelier, 15; Woodstock, 15
Vermont Maple Recipes, 153
Victory Garden Cookbook, The, 180, 184
Vincent, John Heyl, 71–72
Vinegars: Chili, Horse-radish, Onion, 81–82
Virginia: Amphill, 16; Richmond, 100; Richwood, 17; Williamsburg, 3, 15
Virginia House-wife, The, 16, 17, 29

Wakefield, Ruth Graves, 64, 89
War, the effect on cookbook production, 63, 94–96, 98, 99, 100
Wartime Cooking, 100
War Time Recipes, 98
Washing Dishes, 83–84
Washington Cook Book, The, 123
Washington, D. C., 15, 17, 29, 35, 69, 96, 99, 124, 126
Washington, George, 16, 17, 137
Washington, Martha, 12
Way to a . . . Man's Heart, The, 66–67, 82–84
Webster, Mrs. A. L., 26
Wedding Fruit Cake, 56
What Cookbooks Do Americans Collect?, 185
What Mrs. Fisher Knows, 137
What to Have for Dinner, 64
Whipt Cream, 8
White, Agnes, 110
White House, The, 29, 123
White House Cook Book, The, 123, 136
White, Virginia S., 150–51
Widdefield, Hannah, 26
Widdifield's New Cook Book, 26
Wilcox, Estelle Woods, 46
Williams, Richard L., 170–71
Willis, Mrs. T. F., 53
Wilson, Mary Tolford, 5
Wisconsin: Madison, 149; Milwaukee, 41, 65–67, 83–84, 139; Pardeeville, 149
Woman Suffrage Cook Book, The, 104–105
Woman's Festival and Bazaar, 104–105
Woman's Medical College of Pennsylvania, 70
Woman's National Press Club, 113
World's Fair Souvenir Cook Book, 71
Writer's Digest, 154
Wylie, Josephine, 179

Yankee Pork and Beans, 46
Yeatman, Walker, 99
Young Housekeeper, The, 21
Young Housekeeper's Friend, The, 36
Yum-Yums, 57

Ziemann, Hugo, 123, 136